MY SHAPING-UP YEARS

MY SHAPING-UP YEARS
THE EARLY LIFE OF
LABOR'S GREAT REPORTER

ART SHIELDS

INTERNATIONAL PUBLISHERS, NEW YORK

Illustrations by Peggy Lipschutz

Library of Congress Cataloging in Publication Data
Shields, Art, 1888-
  My shaping up years.

  1. Shields, Art, 1888-   . 2. Journalists—
United States—Biography.   I. Title.
PN4874.S473A35   1983   070.4′49331′0924 [B]   82-21176
ISBN 0-7178-0597-2
ISBN 0-7178-0571-9 (pbk.)

To Esther

---

*My special appreciation to Adelaide Bean for her
constant encouragement, as well as her able and
cheerful assistance in "shaping-up" the manuscript*

Contents

MY SHAPING-UP YEARS

1 · *Amos*

I was born in Barbados, a British Crown Colony, where my father, a preacher, was stationed by the Moravian Church. The Moravian Brethren were the first to preach to the Black slaves in the West Indies. They were threatened with imprisonment by plantation owners when they came to the islands in the eighteenth century.

I was the third of three brothers when I arrived on October 31, 1888. Walter and Teddy came before me. Jim, the fourth, was to follow eight years later.

I have no memories of my birthplace, which I left in my second year. But I have vivid recollections of my playmate on St. Thomas, a Danish colonial island, where we lived next. This was Amos, A Black boy. He was five and I was four.

St. Thomas had a fine harbor, and our favorite hide-'n'-seek place was the German Wharf. It was managed by Mr. Colwood, a young Black man whose mother was my mother's best friend. Walter, Teddy, Amos and I hid behind sugar bags and rum barrels. We burrowed under boats turned upside down on the wharf. And we watched older boys dive for pennies that visitors tossed in.

One of the divers was Amos's brother Joshua, a lad of ten, of whom we were proud. Joshua was not only a champion diver; he was a champion yarn spinner as well. Some boys used to entertain visitors with tales about their adventures with sharks. But none won as many pennies as Joshua's prize story.

And Amos and I listened, breathless, when Joshua told us how a man-eating shark almost got him one day.

Joshua was picking up a penny at the bottom of the harbor—so went his story—when a giant shape, with a wide gaping mouth filled with needlelike teeth—loomed above him. Joshua was protected by a big rock. The monster could not get him until he started upward. A life-and-death waiting contest began. But Joshua held his breath—while his lungs were bursting—until the monster tired and swam away.

I never doubted the story. Joshua's agonized expression as he described those needlelike teeth was too convincing. And I was hurt by Father's skeptical chuckle when I retold the tale.

Amos, my brothers and I also enjoyed catching land crabs with nooses laid around their holes in the ground. We let them wriggle awhile, then let them go. And we often took barefoot rambles to the Danish fort to see the soldiers' pets. One was a fat South American tapir. Another was a long-necked anteater, whom we liked best. No ant could escape him. He licked them up with a tongue a foot long.

The fort had another attraction. That was Amos's mother. She was a cook in the kitchen where the officers' meals were prepared. She never failed to give us tall drinks of brown sugar and water and handfuls of cookies when we arrived.

She was a tall, handsome woman who looked like a moving statue as she walked through the grounds with a big load on her head. I once saw her carrying a tray of rum bottles with no danger of a spill.

I never met my playmate's daddy. Amos said he was a sugarcane cutter on St. Croix, a sister island. His wages were probably twenty cents a day. That was the average pay for ablebodied Black men on this tropical island in the early 1890s.

I've often wondered what happened to my little friend. I never saw him after saying good-by before my fifth birthday. But one thing I know. The Stars and Stripes didn't bring democracy when President

Woodrow Wilson bought the Virgin Islands from Denmark for $25,000,000 in 1917.

I'm glad to say that my birthplace, Barbados, flies its own flag today. But if Amos is living he is a colonial subject. An appointed governor, a follower of the current U.S. President, can veto any law passed by the Virgin Islands' popular assembly. And—worst of all—almost 40 percent of the islands' young Black workers are unemployed.

My father was transferred back to the United States. Our next home was in a farming community in southern Illinois. Our village—West Salem—had seven hundred people and seven churches, including two Moravian churches. Father preached in the English language Moravian Church and grandfather Clement Reinke, my mother's father, was pastor of the German language congregation. The churches were social centers, and farmers' horses were tied to every hitching post on Sunday.

We arrived in 1894, in the depths of the harshest depression this country had yet seen. The freight trains that rumbled through the village were loaded with unemployed men. From time to time hungry men knocked at our door for handouts. I did not understand why anyone was hungry. Life was good to this five-year-old kid. Father was getting only $400 a year, but Mother afterwards said that we had never lived so well.

Mother baked delicious bread. We grew our vegetables and raised our chickens, and we shopped at depression prices in the stores on the village square. Coffee was ten cents a pound at Mr. Hallbeck's grocery. The butcher would often drop an ox liver or calf's heart on his big chopping block and slice it neatly as a present for our dinner when my brothers and I came in. And our diet was supplemented by sausages, hams, berries, nuts and pumpkin pies that parishioners brought in.

Teddy and I often accompanied Father and Mother on horse-and-buggy trips to our members' farmhouses. We kids would catch sunnies and perch in a nearby creek with the farmers' boys. And I still think fondly of the dinners provided for the preacher's family.

The housewife would begin with the usual apology for not having something "better." Mother's compliments would follow and the feast would begin. Chicken, pork, vegetables, hot biscuits with homemade jam and honey in the honeycomb were topped off by luscious fruit pies. Sometimes the main dish was a squirrel chowder. And Teddy and I would chuckle with delight when we bit into a shotgun pellet.

These farm visits won me . I was going to be a farmer when I grew up. I used to tell my hosts about this. They grinned when I said it. And one day an old farmer with a long, grizzled beard told my father

something like this: "Your boy doesn't know how hard a farmer works. I start the day's work before sunup. I'm still working after sundown. I reckon I put in a fifteen-hour day. And what do I get? I get good food. I raise it myself with plenty of sweat. But I get nothing else except debts."

"The brother was right," Father said at supper that night. "Farming is work, not play. I worked very hard on my father's farm in North Carolina. I always had a plow handle or an axe handle in my hand."

Father said that a number of times. But farm economics was not his strong point. He never understood why his church members were in debt. "They're getting good crops," he told us. "I've never seen better corn. But they're always talking about their debts."

Father respected work and hardworking people. But he did not understand why the price of corn went down when the harvests went up.

Nor did I know that Populist speakers were telling farmers to "raise less corn and more hell."

I paid no attention to politics until the exciting presidential campaign of 1896. I did not understand what the excitement was about, but I could not ignore it. Everyone was talking about William Jennings Bryan, the Democratic Party candidate, and his Free Silver plan.

The excitement was on a grass-roots level. Village kids from

Republican families were shouting, "Democrats eat dead rats." And Democratic kids were screaming rhymes against William McKinley, the Republican contender.

Bryan—the Nebraska "boy orator"—was promising farmers a way out of their debts. The farmers had contracted their debts under the bankers' gold standard. Bryan promised them that they could pay off their mortgages with cheap silver money after he got in. He promised to double the official value of silver and to allow "free and unlimited coinage" of the cheaper metal.

This was a one-shot inflation scheme. After the debts were paid, the farmers' troubles would begin again. But Bryan was a powerful campaigner. He spoke to huge outdoor crowds at hundreds of meetings at railroad whistle-stops. He told them that the bankers were "crucifying the country on a cross of gold." And cheering millions rallied to Bryan's side.

Our county was known as a Republican stronghold. Nevertheless Bryan won many of my father's members. But the bankers and industrialists, led by J. P. Morgan, John D. Rockefeller, and Andrew Carnegie, and their agent, Senator Mark Hanna of Ohio, poured gold into the battle. McKinley went into the White House as the choice of the big-money men.

2 · Grandpa

I don't know when I learned to read. I suspect it was when I lay on my belly at Mother's feet with an illustrated book of Mother Goose rhymes before me. I would look at the pictures of Humpty Dumpty and of the barber who shaved a pig, while Mother sang the rhymes.

I was far ahead of the ABC's when I entered West Salem's little red schoolhouse at seven. My teacher was Aunt Alice, one of Mother's younger sisters. I remember her affectionately, but I don't recall what she taught me. I was a mischievous child, and she once told Mother, "Artie always finds new ways to be naughty."

I remember best the tag games we played during recess and the songs we sang. Our school sessions always opened with song. Aunt Alice's favorite was "The Old Oaken Bucket." She led us by singing the first lines: *"How dear to my heart are the scenes of my childhood, when fond recollection recalls them to view."*

"The Old Oaken Bucket" is almost forgotten today. But the scenes of my childhood are fresh in my mind. We lived on one side of the small village square. To the left was the village blacksmith, who shod the farmers' horses. The smith was a family friend, with a dashing teenage son who rode me madly around the square on his high-wheel bicycle.

That bike belonged to a primitive type in which the high front wheel lifted the driver more than four feet off the earth. And I longed for the time when my feet would reach the pedals.

On the opposite side of the square was Jerry Dixon, the harness-maker, who often invited our family to dinner. Jerry had a big black mustache and a warm smile, and owned a treasured possession that Walter, Teddy and I loved. That was *Sea and Land,* an enormous book. It was full of illustrated adventure stories about wild creatures in the mysterious forests of Africa, the tiger-haunted jungles of Asia and the shark-infested seas.

Some of the stories were fabulous. I remember, for instance, the advice a veteran African hunter gave to beginners. If a lion is attacking you and your last bullet is spent, there's just one thing to do: Give him your left arm to chew. Then drive your trusty *poignard* into his heart.

I owe much to this book in spite of its fables. It made me conscious that I was living in a very big world with many brave people—of all shapes, sizes and colors. And it embedded a beautiful poem in my mind. That was Samuel Taylor Coleridge's *The Ancient Mariner,* which filled many center pages, with a page of drawings by a famous French artist for every page of text.

Down the road from our house was my maternal grandparents' home, which I loved to visit. In a well behind the house was the old oaken bucket of our song—

The old oaken bucket,
The iron-bound bucket,
The moss-covered bucket
That hung in the well.

I had many cool drinks from this iron-bound, moss-covered bucket. It hung in the well in a little grove where I played with my brothers and the neighbors' children. Our biggest playground, however, was the German Woods that stretched beyond Grandpa's yard. There we played hide-'n'-seek under the big trees. We hunted hickory nuts and walnuts. We dammed and undammed a little rivulet. And we enjoyed the summer picnics organized by Grandpa's Sunday School.

The Sunday services in Grandpa's church were very solemn. But the German Sunday School picnics were jolly affairs, with feasting and play. I still grin when I think of a smearcase contest between two youngsters of four or five years.

The two kids were blindfolded and mounted on a high table for all to enjoy the match. A big bowl of smearcase—a sticky, semiliquid homemade cheese—was placed between them. Each kid was supposed to feed the other with a long wooden spoon. A prize was promised to the one who made the most hits. But the fun was in the misses. White smearcase was soon plastered over both chubby faces. Fifty youngsters around the table were howling with delight. And none seemed happier than the plastered kids themselves.

I also spent many happy hours in Grandma Carolina Reinke's kitchen. Grandma was very indulgent. She fed me cookies in the shapes of elephants, lions and other wild animals. She never seemed to mind when I got in her way. And I read my first book through as I lay on my belly on her kitchen floor.

That first book was John Bunyan's *Pilgrim's Progress,* which was found in many American homes at that time. I also read Bunyan's *The Holy War.* I still think Bunyan was a great writer. His stories are more than religious allegories. They are tales of struggle by the poor against the rich, and they left their mark upon me.

At home I delighted in *Gulliver's Travels* by Jonathan Swift. I dreamed at night about Gulliver's adventures with the six-inch Lilliputians and the sixty-foot Brobdingnagians. I've never tired of Gulliver. I've read the *Travels* half a dozen times since. And today I enjoy Swift's satires against the powers that be, as well as the adventures that charmed me as a child.

There was also a Civil War novella, *Winning His Way,* with a boy hero, which I read over and over. It was permeated with hatred of slavery.

But another book distressed me. That was the Grimm brothers' *Fairy Tales,* with its cruel stepmothers and witches in the Black Forest.

The Bible was the book I knew best. Father read a chapter to us before breakfast, while our cornmeal mush was cooling on the table. And Grandpa gave me an illustrated Bible. "Every word comes from heaven," he said. My Bible was a bulky copy of the King James version, which had the finest prose of the seventeenth century. Its melodious sentences tuned my ear to the musical qualities of the English language. Its dramatic stories are told with the simplicity and brevity that I admire as a newspaper writer. I can't forget the comment of my first newspaper editor after his eye ran down an overwritten story I had turned in. "Have you read the story of David and Goliath?" he inquired. "That's a bigger story than this one. Just be as brief."

There was another side to the Bible, however, and it troubled this child. That was its contradictions. I found that what was said on one page was sometimes reversed on another.

I also found—to my sorrow—that some of the Bible's heroes were very cruel men. I turned against the Prophet Elisha when he sent a savage bear to kill children who annoyed him. And I didn't like King David after he cut up prisoners of war. But when I took my troubles to Grandpa he shook his head sadly. I had no right to criticize David. He was a "man after God's own heart." That's what the Bible said.

Grandpa grew up with the Bible in his hand. His father, grandfather and great-grandfather had been Moravian preachers before him. He often talked about them as I sat on a furry polar bearskin in front of his rocking chair. The bearskin was a present from a friend, Reverend Kilbuck, a Native American Indian who was a missionary to the Eskimos on the Kuskokwim River in Alaska.

Some things Grandpa said went over my head. But he held my attention. He loved me. I loved him. He was a good storyteller. And I remember the pride with which he spoke of his great-grandfather, Abraham Reinke, who was my great-great-great-grandfather.

Abraham Reinke, a Swede, the son of a rich Stockholm merchant, broke with the established state church, the Lutherans, and joined the Moravian Church while a student at the university in Jena. In doing this he sacrificed a fortune. Under Swedish law, he could not inherit his father's wealth after leaving the state church.

By joining the Moravians, my ancestor was uniting with an organization that had advanced ideas for its time. The Moravian Brethren were followers of John Huss, the Czech religious reformer and patriot who opposed state churches and feudal tyranny. Huss was burned at the stake on heresy charges. But his followers took up arms against the Austrian feudal lords who oppressed them. They were led by a one-eyed general "who never lost a battle." I felt Grandpa's pride as he said this. The Hussites gained a measure of freedom by their heroic struggles. And their ideas spread over Europe.

When the Hussite message reached Abraham Reinke, he quit the German university and became a full-time worker for the Moravian Brethren.

My great-great-great-grandfather's first assignment was to St. Petersburg, as a Hussite missionary to czarist Russia. He stayed only a year, however. Grandpa doesn't know why he left so quickly, but my guess is that the czarist officials objected to the youth's progressive ideas and told him to go.

A romance with a young Norwegian woman—a Hussite convert— came next. The wedded couple spent three years in England in a Hussite community, then sailed to colonial Pennsylvania. There they became founders of the Moravian Brethren's settlement at Bethlehem. This was in 1744. That was one hundred and eleven years before smoke began coming from Bethlehem's first iron mill on the Lehigh River.

In Bethlehem, my ancestors and their brethren and sisters toiled together in workshops and fields and shared the products equally.

As I listened to Grandpa, I did not know that I was getting my first lessons in communism, although communism of a primitive kind. Nor did Grandpa know it. He said that Abraham Reinke and his wife were following the principles of the Christian Economy. That's how the church fathers described their collective system.

I learned more about the Moravian Brethren's collective ways when Grandpa loaned me his copy of Benjamin Franklin's *Autobiography*. All the Bethlehem people "worked for a common stock," said Franklin, who had visited the communal colony in 1755. All dined together at big tables. All children were in school, in a period when free education was almost unknown. And Franklin was delighted with Bethlehem's musicians.

The Moravian colony had more than twenty workshops that made a wide variety of useful things. Grandpa didn't know what kind of work his great-grandfather did. But he knew that Abraham Reinke didn't work with his hands very long. His knowledge of languages made him useful as a Hussite propagandist. He became a preacher and spread the Brethren's message in German, English and Swedish in Philadelphia, New York, Lancaster and other towns until he died.

Abraham Reinke's son, Grandpa's grandpa, became a worker. He learned the tanning trade in the Moravian Brethren's communal tannery in Nazareth, a Christian Economy town near Bethlehem. He liked the work, Grandpa said. Grandpa had read the tanner's diary. But the church elders "called" him to the ministry. He became a high church official. And he had the good fortune to be in Bethlehem when General George Washington rode into town during the Revolutionary War.

There's a letter from Washington in Bethlehem's church files. He thanked the elders warmly for entertaining him. And he expressed his deep appreciation to the Moravian Sisters for their tender care of many wounded Revolutionary soldiers in the church's nursing homes.

I liked that story. My brothers and I used to play Revolutionary War games. And we always wanted to be on Washington's side.

The Christian Economy did well for fifty years. But the tide of capitalist enterprise was rising in Pennsylvania as the eighteenth century was going out. Moravian artisans were setting up their own shops. Independent merchants were selling goods in private stores. Abraham Reinke, Jr., tried to stop this ungodly competition, but he was voted down in the Council of Elders.

I got that part of the story from Bethlehem sources later.

I often think of what Grandpa told me. The fact that my ancestors were members of a collective community, where men and women worked together, has never left my mind. The stories I was listening to brought me closer to Grandpa himself. I can still see him leaning forward in his big rocking chair, with his white beard covering his lean neck and affection shining in his eyes.

Grandpa lived until his eighty-ninth year. He is buried in the Moravian Brethren's cemetery in Gnadenhutten—which means Tents of Grace in the German language—in Ohio. This village was built by Native Americans of the Delaware tribe. They had united with the Moravian Brethren and become farmers. They were doing well when a huge mob of white racists descended upon them in 1782. Ninety—mostly women, children and old men—were clubbed to death and their scalps were taken to Pittsburgh and hung up in the village square.

Grandpa told that story with tears in his eyes.

3 · Hell

Sunday was the dullest day of the week in our little farming village with its seven church steeples. No kids had much fun on the Sabbath, except those naughty boys who played tag or flung a baseball around. I loved the outdoors, but had little time to enjoy it on Sunday. After breakfast came Sunday School. After Sunday School came preaching. After dinner came the Junior Christian Endeavor service. I was the preacher's son, who had to attend. And supper was followed by more preaching.

There were some delightful distractions, however, which stay in my mind. I remember one spring morning when a little brown owl took over the service.

The little owl had been sleeping on a rafter under the ceiling. It woke up when the singing began and flew wildly back and forth over the heads of the congregation. The sexton—a worn-out old farmer—opened a window, but the frightened bird couldn't find its way out. It hooted and hooted, to the joy of us children. It finally settled on a kerosene lamp overhead, but the hooting didn't stop. And I doubt if any of the bearded adults down below knew what the preacher was saying.

A snake was the attraction at another Sunday service. This wasn't a deadly rattler. It was a harmless little garter snake without a sting.

My brother Teddy, who was two years older than I was, had picked up the little serpent on our lawn, just before the service. Teddy was a lover of wildlife. He wanted the garter as a pet. It was in his pocket as he sat between Mother and me in a front pew. But the snake became tired of confinement. It crawled out quietly and was slithering down the aisle when a little girl saw it and shrieked.

Several men tried to grab it, but the garter was finally caught by Teddy himself. No one blamed him at first. Suspicion fell on another youngster, who had been accused of putting a snake on the teacher's desk a few days before. The truth finally came out, but Teddy escaped with a mild parental rebuke.

One of our hymns was "The Old-Time Religion." The chorus ran something like this: *That old-time religion! That old-time religion. It was good for John and Peter and it's good enough for me.*

But my father's sermons did not follow the "old-time religion" strictly. The "old-time religion" of my childhood was chock-full of hellfire. The sinners of our village—the drunkards, gamblers, whoremasters and blasphemers—were beaten into repentance by other preachers with a red-hot weapon—the threat of eternal torture.

The touring evangelists, who lived off village collections, made the fires still hotter. And my Sunday School teacher—a tall, skinny lad of seventeen—told us that bad boys would be thrown into fires that would never go out. The Second Coming of Christ might take place at any moment, he said. If we were naughty when He arrived, we might be sent to hell.

Each weekly Sunday School lesson was illustrated by a poster about three feet long, which came from a religious publishing house in Chicago. The poster week depicted Jesus on his way down from heaven to judge the world. His face was stern, and my teacher pointed to it as he threatened naughty boys.

My father never gave any encouragement to these cruel and pre-posterous beliefs. He did not defy them openly. That would have been dangerous eighty years ago. He simply avoided this difficult subject. He based his sermons on the love of God and the brotherhood of man. He liked to quote the saying of Jesus that one should love one's neighbor like oneself.

I was scared, nevertheless, by the thought of hellfire. I had once burned my hand on a hot kitchen stove and cried half the night. I was too healthy to think about hell much of the time, but I shivered with fear when I did. And I'm thinking now of a scare I got from a hell-roaring evangelist, just after my eighth birthday.

We were on our way to our new home in the Indian Territory—now Oklahoma. Father had gone on ahead of us. He had been assigned to the Moravian Brethren's mission to the Native Americans of the Cherokee tribe. The ties between the Moravian Brethren and the Cherokees went back a hundred and forty years. Moravian preachers had accompanied the Cherokees on the Trail of Tears from North Carolina, when nearly five thousand men, women and children of the fifteen thousand deportees died.

Mother, Teddy and I were traveling together, and our train had stopped at Fort Smith, Arkansas, when the evangelist came aboard with a bag full of paperback books.

The books were all copies of *Ten Nights in a Barroom,* a best seller in the 1890s. The villain of the story was an Irish bartender. The victims were a mother and two starving children. This was written in the time of vicious anti-Irish propaganda—the time when some factory doors carried the warning: "No Irish need apply."

The evangelist gave us the book's story and showed us its lurid pictures as he made his rounds, selling copies for ten cents apiece. We saw the drunken husband squandering his wages on whiskey. We watched the bartender throwing the mother out when she tried to bring her helpless man home. And we saw the villain getting his punishment when a bottle, flung by another drunk, shattered his head.

"That bartender is burning in hell," the evangelist shouted. "He will never get out. And every other sinner will burn with him," the hell-roarer continued, "if he doesn't come to Jesus."

This hellfire talk went on until the train was about to start, and the evangelist roared his way out with a pocket full of dimes.

I was distressed; Mother was angry and she spoke out against hell for the first time. She told Teddy and me that she didn't believe anyone was going into a fiery furnace after death. God was too merciful, she said.

I never worried about hell after that.

Our new home was a tiny cottage in Braggs, a village of a hundred and fifty people in the Cherokee tribal lands. My father was often away on long horseback trips to distant Cherokee centers. And Mother read aloud to Teddy and me at night.

Mother had progressive ideas for that time. She was much better read than Father. She loved novels, poetry and popular science. And I vividly remember two popular science books she read to us after she tucked us into bed. These books were written from a religious point of view, but they broke with some of the cruel myths of my former Sunday School teacher. And they gave me the beginnings of a scientific attitude toward life.

One book—*Sun, Moon and Stars*—showed the immensity of the universe. The sun was not just the big light that God put in the sky in the story of creation in *Genesis,* the first book of the Bible. It was only one of billions and billions of suns, separated from each other by many light-years.

Another book—*The Earth's Foundations*—told us that the making of our world took much longer than the six days described in *Genesis.* It taught me that the rocks, the seas and the fertile soil developed very slowly. I learned that billions of years passed while life was evolving from microscopic creatures into dinosaurs, mammoths, horses, elephants and thousands of other creatures.

It excepted only man from the evolutionary process. Man, it said, was handmade by God.

In spite of this exception, my thinking was now on its way. And I can't thank my mother enough for giving me this start.

4 · Cherokees

I spent the most interesting years of my childhood in the Indian Territory. That was more than eighty years ago. But the people and the countryside are still alive in my mind.

I can never forget the Native Americans of the Cherokee tribe whom I lived with, and the tales of their grandparents, who had tramped across half the continent on the terrible Trail of Tears.

I'm setting down the pictures as they unreel inside me. How precious is childhood! I still see the flowers sparkling on the prairie in early spring. The prairies were a carpet of color until the sun burned them brown. I still imagine myself pulling catties, sunnies and perch from Little Greenleaf Creek. I've never enjoyed such fishing since. The prairie was full of rabbits, which my brother Teddy and I would catch in our homemade figure-4 trap in the tall grass behind our home.

That grass was knee-high. It was the primeval grass that mighty herds of buffalo used to crop. The earth beneath it had never been torn by a plowshare. The *Grapes of Wrath* dust storms were far ahead, and no oil drills were boring into the earth. The only oil we knew was coal oil (kerosene) for our lamps. It cost ten cents a gallon at the Madden and Patrick stores.

My father was an old-style circuit-riding preacher, with Cherokee congregations. His longest ride was to Spring Place, fifty miles away. He also stopped in Muskogee, Fort Gibson and Tahlequah, the Cherokee capital, before we saw him again. He was gone for a week or more.

Father rode Pat, a powerful young horse. He straddled a big Western saddle, equipped with big saddlebags filled with sandwiches, shirt, writing paper, razor, toothbrush, Bible, hymnbook and a cup for drinking water from streams along the road. He carried nothing else except a mackintosh—an old-fashioned raincoat—rolled up behind the saddle.

Our other mount was Jewel, an ancient mare, a descendant of the Spanish horses the conquistadores brought to Mexico hundreds of years ago. Jewel had no saddle, but Teddy and I would tie a blanket around her and gallop over the prairie, pretending we were Cherokee warriors.

Our horses lived in a stable that Father helped to build—log-cabin style. His skill with an axe came back as he fitted the end of each log into a notch cut into the one beneath it.

Teddy and I attended the Cherokee school in a little one-room building. Our Cherokee teacher, Miss Hattie Gore, was a tall, beautiful young woman with black hair and bronzed skin. She was very proud of her people and liked to talk about the heroic chapters in their history. Her grandfather, Chief Bluejacket, had been a friend of "The Prophet," the brother and adviser of Tecumseh, the famous Native American leader. The Prophet was a brilliant organizer and agitator. He helped his brother bring rival tribes together against the white invaders who were seizing their land.

Miss Gore became a warm family friend. She often stayed with Mother when Father was away. Mother felt safer when she was with us, because drunken horsemen sometimes rode by. We lived on a crossroads on the outskirts of town.

Miss Gore gave Christmas presents to kids for perfect attendance. Mine was a little book that introduced me to Robin Hood and his merry men. I prize it dearly.

My teacher had five classes for five age groups. Her pupils wore two garments—a shirt and overalls—and came in bare feet, as I did until the late autumn cold. My seatmate was little Warrior Saunders. His father was white, but his mother—a Cherokee—named the kids. I used to swap pecans with Warrior for buckshot. Our soldiers were little clay men, which we did in with slingshots.

The buckshot was only supplementary ammunition. We depended mostly on little lead car seals, which sealed the doors of railroad freight cars. We picked them up on the tracks, divided them into quarters with hammer and chisel, then rounded them into bullets with hammer taps.

Much of the kids' talk was about snakes. The countryside was alive with rattlesnakes. Ponds and creeks swarmed with deadly water mocassins. And everyone agreed there was only one remedy for snakebite. My father shared this widely accepted opinion, with which medical science differs today. And though he was a teetotaler, he kept a bottle of brandy in the house for a snakebite emergency.

Roggie, another Cherokee boy, sat near me. His real name was Rogers, but he was Roggie to us kids. Roggie was very proud of his big brother Levi, who was a dozen years older. Levi was recovering from severe bullet wounds. "He's all shot to pieces," said Roggie, "but they can't kill him."

The shooting had taken place soon after we came to Braggs. We lived in a cabin on the other side of the railroad tracks from the dirt road that served as business street. Teddy and I had just eaten lunch when we heard furious *bang-bang*ing nearby. We dashed across the tracks and saw two Cherokees helping Levi away. Blood poured from his head and body, leaving red puddles on the white December sleet that covered the road.

A bearded white man was sitting on the road and yelling while blood ran from his leg. "I shot him in the head. I shot him in the head," he cried again and again. He was a patent-medicine faker named Johnson, one of the cure-all quacks who preyed on the people. The story was that a Cherokee woman fell sick after drinking one of Johnson's bottles. Levi met the quack on the street and told him to give the woman's money back. The argument got hot; Johnson was drunk and began shooting.

Levi was taken by surprise. The first shot struck between his nose and right eye, coming out behind his ear. It knocked Levi flat and blinded him, but he emptied his six-shooter from the ground while more bullets hit him. I can still tell where each bullet entered and where it came out. The kids talked about the battle for many days.

"He's a brave man, Levi is," said our friend Dr. Maxwell, the Cherokee physician. "Levi never winced when I was probing for bullets." The probing was done without anesthetics. This was in 1896 and far from any medical center.

But Johnson, the white quack, "howled like a dog," the doctor said with disgust.

Everyone agreed that Levi would have won in a fair fight.

Almost every man in the Indian Territory carried a gun for protection. The Territory had many outlaws or desperadoes. Both words were used for men who tried to live by the gun. But the bandits led a precarious life. They wandered over the prairie on horseback, stopping overnight with Cherokees or poor white farmers, who furnished hospitality whether they wanted to or not.

Most of the outlaws were landless whites. Many were wanted men from across the Territory's border. One day, not long before our arrival, three white strangers armed with Winchester repeaters rode into Braggs and shouted, "Hands up!" at a crowd of twenty or more men in front of the Patrick store.

A sixteen-year-old youth started running and fell dead with a bullet in his heart. He was the son of Mr. Morris, the railroad station agent, a Civil War veteran whom we liked well. He lived in a two-room home on a bridge over the tracks. His wife tutored Teddy and me for a while.

The three bandits left with only a few dollars after this bloody raid. Sometimes bandits got nothing, because their victims *had* nothing.

I'm thinking, for instance, of the story that Reverend Thomas, a Methodist preacher, told us while he was tying up his horse in our yard. He said that he was riding through a small bit of woodland on the prairie that day when two men stepped out of the bushes shouting, "Hands up!" Thomas pleaded, "I'm a preacher. I got only two cents." The Winchester barrels lowered and one bandit cried, "Ride on, preacher."

I think Reverend Thomas told the truth about his two cents. He lived by collections and a little farming, and the collections were slim.

The bandits usually let preachers alone. They never bothered Father. But one of his friends worried because Father had no gun. "A gun's no good when someone has the drop on you," Father replied. "Yes, Preacher," his friend said, "but you could get the drop on him, another time."

There were more killings than I mentioned. Mr. Madden, our landlady's husband, the owner of the Madden store, had been shot dead on the street a year before we arrived. But shooting was often only an outlet for suppressed emotions. Teddy and I saw an example of this one day. We were standing in front of our cabin when a six-shooter began roaring alongside us. A drunken man was yelling madly as he emptied his pistol into the ground, while his mules were running away.

Teddy and I dug up the slugs as mules, wagon and drunken driver vanished in the distance. The slugs had been flattened like buttons in the hard ground. Father guessed that they were fired by an impoverished sharecropper, who was venting his frustrations in this explosive way.

Gunfire never bothered the kids I played with. They knew that no one would hurt them. They were used to the gunpowder concerts on Saturday nights, when men rode into town to shop or celebrate. The bullets had no special target. The weapons were pointed at the sky. The road that ran past the general stores was littered with empty Winchester shells and six-shooter cartridges on Sunday mornings.

There was plenty of liquor for these celebrations. The Indian Territory was supposed to be bone dry. All liquor was officially banned by federal prohibition. But Mr. Morris told us that mysterious packages kept coming in by railroad freight. The names of the addressees meant nothing, but the men who came for the packages carried their own kind of credentials. "I never argue with a Winchester," the railroad agent told Father.

The Winchester was the favorite weapon of the old West. It was a short, sixteen-shot repeating rifle that could be slung from a saddle. The cartridges were snapped into place and fired by a three-finger lever. Some of the boys I knew looked forward to the time when they would own their own Winchester. And my eleven-year-old playmate McKay, put a spent Winchester cartridge to a novel use.

The lad's father and mother, Mr. and Mrs. McKay, belonged to a team of six evangelists, called "the Crusaders," who held nightly meetings in the schoolhouse. While they were beating drums and sounding tambourines and calling on sinners to repent, their eleven-year-old son was manufacturing a pistol.

The pistol's barrel was made from a Winchester cartridge's metal casing. Young McKay fitted this brass tube to a stock that he whittled from a piece of wood. He then punched a hole in the barrel near the base, inserted a fuse, filled the barrel with powder and buckshot—and was ready to pick his target.

His target was the neighbor's ram. The homemade pistol, however, was effective only at three or four feet. McKay had to lure his target into range. So he climbed the split-rail fence between the two yards, tossed stones at the ram, dangled his bare legs to tempt him to attack, then lit the fuse and pulled up his legs just before the ram hit the fence with a bang.

The birdshot didn't penetrate the ram's hide, but it stung. And I saw the angry beast charge at the legs and bang his head again and again, while young McKay giggled with glee.

The ram got revenge, but not on the guilty party. McKay dared me to climb over the fence and walk up to the ram. "He has nothing against you," my wily friend said. I never refused a dare; I fell into the trap and was met by a woolly projectile. It knocked this nine-year-old kid head over heels, and I rolled down a steep bank into a muddy rivulet, while my playmate howled with delight.

My overalls were a muddy mess for my mother to wash when I came home. But I hope that my readers won't judge my playmate any more harshly than the creator of Tom Sawyer and Huckleberry Finn would have judged him. Young McKay was simply looking for fun in a town that had no organized entertainment for children and adults except revival services.

5 · *The West*

I used to wonder why few Western films came out of the Cherokee lands in the Indian Territory. They had much that Hollywood wants. There were wide-open spaces, galloping ponies and plenty of guns. There was also much killing—and killing is what Hollywood loves. But the romantic glamour that screen writers delight in was missing.

I lived in a poor man's West, where there were no rich ranchers' daughters for cowboys to wed. The tick-bitten cattle that cropped the brown prairie grass were owned by poor farmers, red and white. I never saw any big cattle drives in the Cherokee lands. Few farmers had more than two or three head of cattle, which they sold to a cattle buyer who visited our town every month or two.

Tom Morgan, the cattle buyer, planted himself by a cattle car on a railroad siding near our home. He had three features that a cartoonist would love to depict. One was an enormous belly that puffed out like a balloon below a thin chest. Another was a bulging cheek, filled with a giant tobacco chew. The third was his eye. He had only one eye. It was very cold. And I remember the freezing glance he gave a steer that an old Cherokee farmer was bringing in. "Thirteen dollars," was all he said.

Thirteen dollars! This was robbery! The old Cherokee told my father that he had expected $20 at least. But $13 was all he got for a main item in his annual cash crop. He took it, because he had no one else to sell to. Tom Morgan was the only cattle buyer.

No one ate fresh beef in Braggs. There was no ice to preserve it. In the Patrick and Madden stores you could buy lean ham from razor-back hogs that had fended for themselves on the prairie, slabs of bacon and fatback, and cans of corned beef, potted ham and potted tongue from Armour, the big Chicago meatpacker.

I've hated the name of Armour ever since. His product made me sick. This was the time of the poisoned meat scandal during the Spanish-American War. Many American soldiers were stricken with acute gut pains after eating the packers' chemically preserved meat, and some died. There was a congressional investigation that roused the public but brought no indictments. Joe Hill wrote about the poisoners in his anti-war song, "Stung Right," in which he said, *Most of those who died were killed by Armour's pork and beans.*

And I remember how my brother Teddy and I rolled on the floor in pain after a dish of Armour's corned beef.

Many white farmers were poorer than the Cherokees. The Cherokees still had some of the land allotted to them after they had been expelled from North Carolina by the army. But most of the white newcomers had nothing.

I remember one family of sharecroppers especially. They were as poor as the Okies of John Steinbeck's *Grapes of Wrath* and the dustbowl refugees of Woody Guthrie's songs. They came to our cabin in a little wagon with a high canvas cover. The father and mother sat on the driver's seat together. Inside, a boy and a girl of about my age were piled up among a plow, a hoe, some blankets, flour sacks, pots and pans and a whining dog. Everyone looked hungry. The father only asked for water, but my mother put a hot meal on the table and got their story. They had come from Arkansas to sharecrop Indian land.

I saw the father, mother and kids a year later. The kids looked thinner than before. The mother's cheeks had fallen in. They had come, the mother said, to say good-by. The land wasn't good. The rain didn't fall. They couldn't make a living and were going on to Texas, where the mother had some cousins.

The visitors' story went on as we ate dinner together. My mother was much moved. While Teddy and I played in the yard with the two kids, Mother decided to give them a treat from the cookie box, her precious storage place for goodies, which was only opened on Sundays. But when Mother began taking it from the cupboard, the visitor begged her to put it back.

"Please don't give them anything like that," she pleaded. "They only like cold 'taters."

Mother learned what was behind this remark as the conversation continued. The sharecropping family had been living on a hungry diet of potatoes and cornbread all year. The kids never tasted meat or anything sweet. My mother guessed that their mother didn't want them to acquire a taste for what they couldn't get.

Our home was brightened that year by the arrival of Mother's younger sister, Emily. She came from West Salem, Illinois, to help Mother while a new member of the family—my brother Jim—was on the way. We loved Aunt Emily. She was very patient with us kids and very complimentary when we came home with a string of fish from the neighboring ponds and creeks. And we weren't jealous when a young man won her heart.

This was Clarence Hackendorf, a friend of our family. He managed the farm of his brother-in-law, Dr. Maxwell, who depended on crops rather than fees, which seldom came in. Teddy and I liked him well. He used to take us fishing to his favorite fishing spot. This was a deep stretch of water in the Little Greenleaf Creek, where the gaping mouth of a catfish, two or three feet long, sometimes broke the surface.

I didn't land one of those big ones. But many catties a foot long grabbed my hook during our visits to the deep hole. And lots of fat perch and sunnies were added to my string.

Clarence, Teddy and I also harvested peanuts together. We picked them off the roots when Clarence turned them up with a hoe, and we divided the harvest with him on a share-and-share basis.

Clarence and Dr. Maxwell were also generous with watermelons, which were juicy and big. The melons remind me of another suitor, who made his bid a bit late. Aunt Emily had already left us for Illinois after Jim was born.

This suitor lumbered to our house on a creaky old wagon one blazing August day, while Father was away on a long circuit-riding trip. He was a middle-aged sharecropper with deep lines of care on his face, and he told Mother what he wanted at once, without any preliminary talk about the temperature, which probably registered 100° Fahrenheit or more.

I'm giving the conversation as I got it from Mother, who often repeated the story.

"I hear you have a nice sister, ma'am," he began. "Everyone's talkin' about her. I want to marry her, ma'am. My wife died. I got no one to look after my children. I got four. They need a mother mighty bad."

"She isn't here," Mother replied. "She went home to her family." But the suitor wasn't listening. He was overwhelmed with his loneliness and thoughts of his motherless children. He pleaded again that he "needed her mighty bad" and would "take good care of her."

"But she isn't here, she's in Illinois," Mother insisted.

Illinois made no impression. All the suitor understood was that Emily wasn't home at that time. He asked Mother to excuse him, then came back with two little watermelons. At the Patrick store, watermelons were sold at two prices: big ones for ten cents; little ones, five cents. These were barely in the five-cent class.

As he handed the melons to Mother he said, "They're for her." Then he told Mother where we could find him, at a crossroads some miles from Braggs. "I want her. I want her badly," he said.

"I guess that's all he could give," Mother used to say. "I felt sorry for the poor man. I thought he ought to be remembered so I sent Emily a jar of preserves that I made from the watermelon rind."

Aunt Emily and Clarence had a happy marriage. I visited them twenty-three years later. They had moved to a farm in northern Oklahoma, just below the Kansas border, and raised many fine children, some of whom live in Tulsa today.

6 · *Evangelists*

My mother cut my hair in early childhood. I sat in a barber's chair only twice before my eleventh year. Once was in West Salem, the little farming hamlet, where the village barber charged ten cents. The next time was in Braggs, when an itinerant barber came to town.

This barber, a tall, lean man with a drooping red mustache, was sadly handicapped by lack of equipment. He apparently had no scissors and depended solely on a pair of dull clippers, which he could carry in his pocket. The clippers worked by hand. There wasn't any electric power in the Cherokee lands. When he squeezed the cutting edges together, they didn't cut through all the hairs. He had to jerk to get the half-severed hairs out. This was painful. I yelled with every jerk, and my hair was in patches when the job was done. The kids on the street laughed at me when I came out. And Mother almost cried when she looked at my head.

This barber didn't last long. He was succeeded by a jolly Black man with sharp scissors. The Black barber was well-liked by the villagers, both Cherokees and whites. He welcomed every visitor as a friend. He had a fund of amusing stories, and the pineboard bench for customers was usually crowded.

But most visitors only came to chew tobacco together and to listen to his stories. They were very poor people, who could hardly afford the fifteen cents the barber asked for a haircut. So our Black neighbor had to leave us before long.

There were more Black people in the Creek tribal lands—not far away. There the blood of Native Americans and African Americans often flowed in the same veins. The blending began when runaway slaves joined the Creeks in Georgia, before the cruel deportations. And one day a Black evangelist came to Braggs from the Creek lands.

Almost any evangelist could draw a crowd. That was because he had no competition. Our village had no church and no organized entertainment of any kind. But this Black preacher outdid all the rest. The little Cherokee schoolhouse—the only preaching place in town— was always full when he appeared. His preaching had a dramatic quality. He talked of the golden pavements in paradise as if he had been there. He gave such a vivid picture of the Prophet Elijah galloping to heaven in a chariot of fire that I could almost see the sparks flying from the steed's nostrils. And when he spoke of the love of Jesus, one felt that he knew him like a neighbor.

The Black preacher was a fine singer, with a deep, resonant voice. Sometimes he began singing in the midst of a sermon. That happened when he was telling Jesus' story of a sinful, runaway son who came home from a faraway land where he had nothing better to do than feeding the swine. The repentant sinner was welcomed home with a feast. And the Black preacher began singing:

> *Glory to God, he's come home;*
> *Glory to God, he's come home*
> *From sin and from crime and from feeding the swine,*
> *Glory to God, he's come home.*

I'm guessing that the singer composed that song himself.
This Black preacher never threatened sinners with hellfire. Other

evangelists made our little schoolhouse sizzle with sulfurous fury as they warned sinners to repent before it was too late. But this man preached brotherhood instead of hate. He told us to do unto others as we would be done by. And I realize now that he was fighting against racism in his own way.

Some evangelists had organization and money behind them. But many were free lancers, who tried to live off collections. They were often the poorest of the poor in the poverty-stricken Cherokee lands. Native Americans—with few exceptions—put nothing in the hat when they came to hear white preachers. White sharecroppers and other poor farmers had almost nothing to give. And I remember the hardships of the band of six evangelists who called themselves the Crusaders. They belonged, they said, to a sect that had split off from the Salvation Army.

The Crusaders included two married couples, a single young man and a single young woman. They put on their show every night, with drums, tambourines, singing and hellfire preaching. They won a few converts, but I wonder how they survived.

My father, a good storyteller, often talked in later years about one of the Crusaders' collections. Only three coins were in the hat—a quarter, a dime and a penny—when it came back from the benches. That was thirty-six cents for six adults and two hungry children.

Father had given a quarter, Dr. Maxwell a dime. But there was a mystery about that collection that Father and the doctor discussed.

The mystery was: Who gave the penny?

Dr. Maxwell and Father knew everyone at the meeting. They were Cherokees, poor whites and several Black men and women from a small Black settlement near Braggs. Fifty or sixty people were crowding the benches together. None had ever been known to drop a cent in a preacher's hat. But this penny was a fact. And Dr. Maxwell remarked with a smile that the penny must have fallen from heaven like the manna, the heavenly food that the Israelites ate in the wilderness when they were fleeing from Egypt.

Another visiting evangelist had a second source of income. This was a tall, lanky Texan, who stepped on the platform with a handbag in his fist. The Texan would lash sin and sinners for an hour or more. Then he would take a brightly colored pill from his bag and say something like this in a drawling voice:

"Dear brothers and sisters, I came to save your souls from hell. But I can save your bodies, too. I want you to look at this medicine. It's a powerful medicine. It can drive out all your misery and cure all chronic diseases."

"How he loves that word 'chronic,'" my father once said.

The cure had a price, however. And my father noted that the contents of the bag brought in more coins than the hat that passed around.

The evangelist's claims amused Dr. Reece, the only white doctor in town, whose office served as the village drugstore. Dr. Reece was our nearest neighbor. He lived on the other side of our pasture, at the edge of the prairie. He never attended religious services, but he liked Father. And he told him that he wished the pills were as good as the Texan asserted. "If they were, I'd be the best healer in the Indian Territory," he said.

"Those were my pills," Dr. Reece continued. "The preacher got them from me. He begged me to sell him some powerful 'thartic pills.' He meant cathartic. I sold him what he asked for. They were only good for moving bowels."

Father often told this story.

One of Father's favorite stories was about a white teenager who was driven to the mourner's bench by a gun.

The gun belonged to Choot Star, a handsome young Cherokee with an odd sense of humor. Choot (I'm spelling phonetically) had killed a white man in the Patrick store not long before we arrived. I'm not sure why he shot him. Some said the white man had wronged him. Anyhow, the Cherokee police didn't bother him, perhaps because he belonged to a well-known Cherokee family.

Choot had a circle of young men around him. His closest follower, however, was the white teenager, the son of the poorest of the three merchants in town. Choot was his hero. He ran errands for Choot; he smiled when Choot smiled and frowned when Choot frowned. And one day Father saw Choot at a revival service, with the teenager beside him.

The hero and his follower were sitting in the far rear with their backs to the wall, while the evangelist, a big, chunky Methodist named Pitkin, was making his final appeal. "I want every sinner who hopes to meet me in heaven to come and take me by the hand," the preacher was crying.

There was a moment of silence; then Father heard Choot whisper, "Go up to the preacher."

The lad was embarrassed. "Naw, Choot; naw," he pleaded.

Choot was becoming irritated. "Go up there," he snapped sharply.

"Naw, Choot, naw," the lad pleaded again.

Then Father saw Choot's hand drop to his hip pocket. And Choot was no longer whispering as he growled, "Git!"

The trembling youth shambled forward to be grabbed in a bearhug by the preacher, who threw him down on the bench between two converts and began praising the Lord for bringing another soul to the altar.

When the service was over, Father could not resist asking the evangelist if he knew how he got his last convert. Reverend Pitkin laughed heartily when he heard the story.

Now comes a postscript. I was sitting in the schoolhouse several Sundays later when two shots cracked outside. I ran out and saw Choot lying in the road with blood gushing from two wounds in his body. The shots had come from a clump of bushes and knocked him off his horse. I never learned who ambushed him and why. He recovered to become a policeman in another town after the Indian Territory became the state of Oklahoma.

As for the white teenager, his conversion didn't last long. He joined a band of hijacking outlaws shortly before we left the Cherokee lands.

7 · Fighting

My father enjoyed a good fight. And he liked to talk about the battlers in his native countryside, where there was lots of fist-fighting in his youth.

One of his heroes was his cousin "Lishe"(for Elisha), pronounced with a long *i*. Lishe never lost a fight. One day Father and Lishe were standing in front of a country store with a number of young friends when a stranger rode up.

The stranger, a big man, gave a contemptuous glance at the youths, who ranged from eighteen to twenty-two years of age. Then he shouted, "I can whip any man in this crowd." Lishe didn't say anything. He just grabbed the bragger by the cheek, pulled him off his horse, and beat him until he said, "Enough!"

Another one of Father's heroes was "Old Man" Stafford, a relative who might have been in his forties. Old Man Stafford had become a countryside legend. People were filled with wonder at the enormous loads he pulled up from wells he was digging. In house-building he easily lifted logs that two men could hardly handle. As a fighter, he was unbeatable. And one day, said Father, Old Man Stafford was standing in front of his distillery—a small one that he kept for himself and his friends on his farm—when a strange horseman trotted up.

The stranger wasted no words. "I hear," he said, "that you are the best man in this county. I'm the best man in mine. Take off your coat. Get ready."

"I'm ready now as I ever will be," said Old Man Stafford, without removing his coat. The old man swung as the challenger rushed in. The blow grazed the challenger's skull, "spinning him around like a top," said Father, until he fell down with the old man upon him. Then Old Man Stafford began "cracking hickory nuts," as Father put it, until the beaten man cried, "Enough!"

Father said he remembered this story so well because it was told and retold in the countryside again and again.

But Old Man Stafford faced another challenge in his own household when his eldest son was twenty-one. The son was a physical marvel, with big, rippling muscles on a two-hundred-pound frame. He thought he was stronger than the old man himself. On his birthday he told his father, "Pap, I'm a better man than you are."

The old man smiled at the audacious challenger and said, "Son, I can tie you the best day you ever had."

The struggle nearly tore the farmhouse porch to pieces. A table was knocked over, a rocking chair was wrecked and flower pots were smashed. And when the contest was over, the herculean youngster was hog-tied—his hands lashed behind his back and a rope running from his wrists to his tied-up feet and pulled tight.

Father never hit back when he boxed with his little sons. And we were never able to hit him. We never got past the fists that whirled up and down in front of his belly. He called that his "windmill defense."

Those fists had a size that a prizefighter would envy. They were molded by the axe handles and plow handles that he gripped in his childhood and youth.

Father never spoke of himself as a battler and I only saw him fight once. That was in our pasture in Braggs, when he gave a ram the thrashing of his life. That ram was my enemy. He had butted me into a mud puddle some months before. Since then he had begun bringing his ewes into our pasture from the open prairie. There they cropped the grass, which belonged to our horses, and they cropped it very clean. Sheep crop much closer to the roots than horses. And there wasn't much left for Jewel and Pat.

Father used to cry "Drive 'em out, Artie!" The ram would run when I threw stones at him from the safe side of the fence. I soon lost all fear of the runaway and one day dashed right at him without any ammunition. That was a mistake. The ram waited until I was a yard away, then leaped at me, plunging his huge rounded horns into my belly and knocking me flat.

My fingers instinctively locked themselves in the ram's wool while I yelled for help. In moments Father was with me. The ram backed up for a belly plunge at Father, dragging me with him, but he hadn't a chance. His horns were wrapped in a pair of great fists. I stood there while my hero swung my enemy off his feet and whipped the ground with him again and again. Then he dragged the ram to the fence and shoved him under the barbed wire .

The battle was witnessed by two teenage boys—the sons of our neighbor, Dr. Reece. Father became a village hero. The loungers, who sat on the flour barrels and ammunition boxes in the village stores, could talk of little else for a week. "The preacher could pick up one of us and knock six men down with him," said Mr. Patrick, our leading merchant.

Our little prairie village had no newspaper, and radio and television were many years ahead. But we subscribed to the *Kansas City Star*. Father had a good reading voice. He always broadcast the news to the family when the paper came in. The first story I remember is very fresh in my mind. That was the heavyweight fight in Carson City, Nevada, between Bob Fitzsimmons, the Cornish blacksmith, and Jim Corbett, the California bank clerk, who had won the championship by defeating John L. Sullivan, the famous "Irish Strong Boy" in 1892.

Father once told us that he had eagerly read the press stories of the Corbett-Sullivan fight when he was stationed in St. Thomas.

Father's attitude to fighting was not always consistent, however. When we lived in Illinois, he once spanked me for exchanging slaps with another child. But he delivered his broadcast of the Corbett-Fitz battle with much pleasure. We kids gathered around his chair to enjoy the illustrations. They were done by a staff artist while the telegraphed story was coming in. And I can still see Fitz's glove buried in the soft spot between Jim's lower ribs. That was the blow that won the championship. The paper called it "the terrible heart blow."

We soon began getting fight broadcasts of a different kind. Cuba was aflame with revolution. The sugar island's colonial rebels were winning dramatic victories against their Spanish oppressors. My heroes now were the "insurrectoes." That's what the Kansas City *Star* called Cuba's revolutionary patriots. They became my people. I felt that I was with them as they ambushed Spanish troops and cut them down with machetes, which Father called "macheets."

I was now taking sides with a national liberation movement for the first time. And these liberation battles gave a new quality to our war games.

Our soldiers—the little clay men that we lined up in opposing formations—now became Cubans and Spaniards. When Teddy and I peppered each other's men with our slingshots, we were fighting for or against the Cuban revolution.

The side that won became the Cuban side in the next battle.

We told our playmates in the Cherokee school about Father's broadcasts. And Warrior Saunders and his brother Squirrel joined our listening circle. Sometimes their mother, a fullblooded Cherokee, came with them; the boys were much closer in outlook to her than to their white father.

Warrior and Squirrel taught us a new war game—with two on each side. Each boy had his own weapon—an eighteen-inch length of cornstalk. We cut one end off diagonally, took out some pith, inserted a mud ball, and then snapped the sticky thing at our foe. The mud left a mark on his overalls, which showed whether the wound was deadlly or not.

The two Native American boys always insisted on being Cubans. Teddy and I didn't like to represent the defeated aggressors. We had a good time nevertheless. But my mother wasn't happy when we came home with muddy clothes to be washed.

We often played this war game in the woods near the Saunders' home, where we ambushed each other from behind bushes and trees. And sometimes Teddy and I lunched at our friends' home at a table full of children. The main dishes were cornbread, potatoes and fat pork. And once we enjoyed the mother's specialty, a delicious squirrel chowder.

Our game was interrupted one day by frenzied squealing. It came from a razorback hog that was caught under the Saunders' house. The little frame building stood off the ground on very short posts. The clearance was only about a dozen inches—and in some places less. Rooting razorbacks often cooled off in this deep shade. And this one was caught between the earth and the bottom of the building.

The pig's squeals brought a crowd of men and boys to the scene. I was wedged in alongside a white neighbor who was inching forward to reach the pig. The six-shooter in his hip pocket was scraping against the bottom of the house. He was afraid it would go off and handed the weapon to me. I was overwhelmed with pride. I had never held a pistol before. We kids talked about guns every day. Now I had a real six-shooter in my own hand. I was sorry when the pig was released and the gun was taken back. But my pride in holding it stayed with me for a long time.

Then the battleship *Maine* blew up in Havana Harbor, killing two hundred and sixty men. The Spaniards were blamed, although there was never the slightest evidence against them. The United States went to war against the Spanish monarchy, with soldiers and sailors crying "Remember the *Maine!*" The "insurrectoes" were forgotten by the Kansas City *Star*. And our family was carried away by a tidal wave of war propaganda.

Warrior and Squirrel dropped out of our war games. They wouldn't take the part of Spain or the United States. They didn't explain why. I'm guessing now that it was because two dominantly white countries were fighting each other.

We did not know then that the United States was fighting for sugarcane fields and strategic positions. Nor did we know that the age of imperialism was beginning. We thought that our soldiers and sailors were bringing freedom to Cuba, Puerto Rico and the Philippines.

We were being swindled. But our disillusionment was to come a few years later.

8 · *Trail of tears*

Some childhood memories never fade. I'm thinking as I write of a daylong ride over the Cherokee land in my tenth year. Teddy and I had long begged Father to take us along on his trips to the Cherokee villages. And one July day he rolled out our old buggy, hitched up Pat and Jewel and started with Mother, Teddy and me for Tahlequah, the Cherokee capital.

We traveled all day along a dusty dirt road. Our wheels fitted into two parallel ruts in the crumbling earth. The sun beat down fiercely, and the tall, rusty grass looked as if fire had scorched it. But we boys were happy. Frightened rabbits were always bounding away. Turkey buzzards were always circling overhead. A big catfish rose to the surface when we forded a creek. And when we entered one of the little forests that dotted the prairie, we looked for the wolf that Father had seen on an earlier trip.

Oklahoma weather is tricky. The sky turned black in late afternoon. The rain came down like a flood as we neared another forest. But Father knew where to go. He pulled up at a little log cabin. An old Cherokee and his wife welcomed him as a friend. Wood was heaped on the fireplace. Our dripping clothes soon dried. Our supper was cooking in an open pot on the embers. I was soon stuffing myself with rabbit stew and sweet potatoes. And Teddy and I fell asleep on a deerskin rug while munching pecans.

I woke to the murmur of voices. Our aged hostess was telling my mother about her childhood in the green North Carolina hills. I cannot give her words now. She spoke a broken English with some Cherokee mixed in. But her gestures were eloquent. I remember the story, which my mother often retold. And my mind is alive with pictures of a child's life in those beloved green hills, where her people had lived for hundreds of years.

It sounded like a very good life to this boy, who loved the outdoors. Her father and brothers did the hunting. It was good hunting. They brought in plenty of fresh meat. Her mother and sisters raised the crops, cooked the food, looked after the cabin. She lived on luscious deer meat, wild turkey, fish, corn, vegetables, berries, honey and other good things. The children had plenty of playtime. They were happy, very happy, she said.

I interrupted to ask a question—a typical boy's question. What kind of weapons did her brothers use in hunting? Our hostess didn't hear me. Her mind was back in her childhood, sixty years ago. But her husband took up the story with a kindly smile at the boys on the floor. He told me about the bows and arrows he used as a child. He learned how to chip flint arrowheads into shape. And he described the blowgun, a Cherokee invention. It was a long, hollow tube with a feathered dart inside. You put it in your mouth, aimed at a rabbit and blew. And the rabbit rolled over with a dart through its middle.

Our hostess, meanwhile, was going on with the story. I was not listening closely at this point, however, because that blowgun was on my mind. I imagined I was shooting that rabbit. And I was wondering how I could make my own blowgun when I heard her mention soldiers. That got my attention again. And I listened intently as she said that she was happy, very happy, until one terrible day when white soldiers broke into her home.

A mob of white civilians broke in with the uniformed men. They were very bad people, she said. The looted the tepee. They stole bows and arrows, tools, hoes, spades, pots, pans, fur garments and her mother's spinning wheel. They stole everything, she said, while the soldiers were pushing the family outside. They drove this family of Native Americans down the narrow mountain trail "like cattle." Then they shut the little girl, her father, mother, brothers and sisters inside a filthy stockade. It was fenced with long poles driven into the earth, and soldiers stood on guard, with fingers on triggers, to prevent escapes.

She told us that she slept on the naked earth under the open sky with hundreds of other Cherokees. The rain came down upon her. The lightning flashed overhead. The people fell sick, and she saw one of her sisters die.

Two thousand Cherokees perished in those death camps just below the hills, said Dr. Elizur Butler, a medical missionary, who lived with his dying patients and lost his daughter there. Many died from dysentery, he said, because the Cherokees were denied decent sanitary facilities.

My mother was much moved by this tragic story. We kids on the deerskin suffered, too. Our lives had been sheltered. We had never been close to mass cruelty before.

The little girl spent two months in this hellyard. But the worst was yet to come. It came when the stockade gates were opened. The Cherokee captives were driven out in a column, with soldiers on horseback beside them. And the twelve-hundred-mile Trail of Tears began, the little girl toddling at her mother's right hand.

Our hostess said the column stretched out for miles as prisoners from other stockades joined in. There were 15,000 Cherokees of all ages in line. Many were sick. It soon became a trail of death as well as tears. Old men, women and children began dying as the column went over the North Carolina hills into Tennessee. The deaths continued as the route led through Kentucky, with a dozen or more Cherokees dying every day.

I've heard people say that Native Americans never shed tears. That isn't true. Our hostess's eyes were wet as she described her mother's death. My mother began crying, too. Our hostess said that her mother became sick while she was tramping, barefoot, with a mounted soldier urging her on. Her moccasins were worn out. Her strength was gone. She had been sharing her rations with her children. Winter was coming on. She slept without blankets on frigid nights when the dew was turning to frost. She never stopped coughing. But the cruel soldier wouldn't let her rest. He was prodding her with his bayonet and cursing her when her heart stopped.

Another sister was stricken with fever as the column reached the banks of the Mississippi in southern Illinois. The dew had turned to frost. Great cakes of ice were floating down the Father of Waters. The sister's fever grew worse as the column waited until a ferry could cross.

Days went by as the sister wasted away. No medicine was given her. No doctor attended her. All the soldiers did for her was to lay her in a hay wagon. The ten-year-old child lay there until she died.

This story had nothing in common with romantic tales about Native Americans such as Cooper's *Last of the Mohicans,* which Teddy and I read together. But fact—deadly fact—was more gripping than fiction. And Teddy and I listened intently as our hostess continued with the story of the death march.

The column sometimes had to break new trails through dense forests. Sometimes the route led through swamps full of deadly water moccasins. The little girl's feet would sink to the slimy bottom as soldiers pushed the Cherokee deportees on. And once she almost drowned while fording a rapid river.

That was in Arkansas. The swirling waters carried her off her feet, washed her far down the river and cast her on the opposite bank, where she lay unconscious until her father found her.

The motherless child tramped along this cruel trail for half a year. The forced march from North Carolina began in July 1838. That was six decades before I heard the story. It ended in January 1839, when winter sleet covered the prairie. And little was left of the little girl's body but skin and bones when she reached the new Cherokee land.

My mother was saddened by this savage story, which she retold to friends after returning to Braggs. This retelling fixed the tale still deeper in my mind. My father gave me more details. He had gotten the story from our hostess's husband during earlier visits.

The new land was hard to get used to, the old Cherokee told Father. It was much drier than the green hills of North Carolina, which had more rainfall than the national average. But the old man said that his people didn't go hungry in the early years. His father once caught a catfish as long as a man in the Arkansas River. The prairie was alive with antelope and deer, and immense herds of buffalo turned the high grass into red flesh every year. The bulls were "this big," he said, as he held his hand above his head.

But the abundance of wildlife lasted only one generation. He hadn't seen a buffalo for twenty years, the old man said. The buffalo were slaughtered by hide hunters and by racists who wanted to destroy the food supplies of the Native American people. The extermination reached its peak in the 1870s. In those years he often saw the hideless carcasses of buffalo rotting in the sun.

The old Cherokee said he had one big consolation after the buffalo

were gone. The land was now theirs. They were free of white inter-
ference at last. The U.S. government had promised in a solemn treaty
that the Cherokees would own the new land and govern the new land
"as long as grass grows and water runs."

Father said that old Cherokees often reminded him of that pledge.

But that treaty went the way of all U.S. treaties with Native
Americans. When we reached Tahlequah, Father was told that a
representative of President McKinley's administration had just visited
the tribal council. He told the Cherokee elders that government
surveyors were coming to cut down their holdings.

The promise that the tribe would own all the Cherokee land "as long
as grass grows and water runs" was made when the Washington
government was not much interested in western prairies. But this
country's population doubled during the next half century. The
frontier pushed westward. White men wanted Cherokee soil—and
they got it.

Until the late 1890s the land was controlled by the tribal council in
Tahlequah. A Cherokee farmer would cultivate the good bottom land
by the rivers and creeks, and graze his cattle on the dry prairie, which
was common tribal land. But control was taken away from the tribal
council in 1898. And each Cherokee family was to get only 160 acres of
land—mostly poor land.

This was robbery and betrayal. The Cherokee soil was robbed, too.
The high prairie grass was plowed under to grow cotton. The thin soil
lost its protective cover. And later, dust storms would begin lashing
Oklahoma.

The Cherokee tribal council also lost control of the police. A few
days before we left the Indian Territory, I saw six U.S. marshals riding
into Braggs. They wore blue jackets with brass buttons. A sixteen-shot
Winchester was slung from each back. A heavy .44 caliber revolver
hung from each hip. Cherokee autonomy had ended.

I haven't been back since, but I've visited the old Cherokee land in
the high North Carolina hills. There I talked to the great-great-
grandsons of the Cherokees, who eluded the U.S. Army in 1838. They
led General Winfield Scott on a wild-goose chase through brush and
brier until he gave up. There were less than a thousand who escaped
the Trail of Tears. There are 5,000 to 6,000 in the tribe's old hills today.
They elect their own chiefs, who sit in their capital, the lovely town of
Cherokee. And they have official title to 50,000 acres—in place of the
50,000 square miles or more that the tribe once had.

9 · *My first strike*

I said good-by to horseback-riding and good fishing when we left the wide-open spaces of the Cherokee lands. And I missed my Native American playmates sadly when in 1900 we moved to Lebanon, a small industrial city in southeastern Pennsylvania.

Teddy and I were not entirely deprived of outdoor life in our new home, however. The automobile had not yet spoiled the countryside. I never saw a single car until my middle teens. A short walk took us to wooded hills, where we dug up sassafras roots for delicious sassafras tea, and knocked down bagfuls of chestnuts. We caught an occasional google–eyed rock bass in a big pond at the edge of the town. Teddy became a good batter on a sandlot ball field. And one of my favorite sports was chasing the fire engine when the siren sounded. The engine was pulled by two big black horses who clattered madly over the cobblestones, with kids howling behind.

Father was pastor of a small working-class congregation of the

Moravian Church. Its members included only one capitalist. This was Mr. Rebstock, a plump man with a heavy mustache, whose big family lived in a wide, three-story house on the main street. His money came from a hot steam laundry, where Teddy put in ten-hour days during the summer vacation.

Mrs. Rebstock—a woman of enormous size—ran the children's Loyal Christian Temperance Union, to which I belonged. She taught us that wine-bibbers, and beer and whiskey-drinkers were sinners who killed both body and soul. We closed every meeting by singing our temperance pledge, which ended with these lines:

> *From all tobacco I'll abstain*
> *And never take God's name in vain.*

The rest of Father's members were wage earners, or skilled workers who sold their own homemade wares in their own shops. There were many such independent craftsmen at the turn of the century. One of our people, Mr. Lowry, made candy. I can still taste the chocolate drops, lozenges and delicious caramels I enjoyed in his shop. Another was a jolly independent trucker, who took me on rides behind his big grays and gave me a few pennies to hold the horses while he was loading or unloading.

I remember another of these worker-businessmen with still more affection. This was Mr. Granillo, an old watchmaker, my Sunday School teacher. I often visited the little cottage where he lived alone after his wife died. It was surrounded by roses, dahlias and other beautiful flowers that he spent hours tending. And inside were precious books.

Among them was a complete set of James Fenimore Cooper's Indian tales and sea stories, more than thirty novels altogether. He loaned them to me, one by one. They were illustrated with old-fashioned woodcut drawings that showed tomahawks flying, rifles blazing and men in hand-to-hand combat. We talked about the stories in Sunday School, sometimes to the neglect of the Bible lesson.

Mr. Evans, a retired carpenter, the treasurer of our congregation, used to visit our home every Monday morning. He was a kindly old man with a streak of rich tobacco brown running down his long white beard. He carried a little wooden box, which rattled as he set it down. It contained Sunday's collections. When he counted out Father's pay,

I could see why the quarters I brought in Saturday night from an after-school job were welcomed.

I got seventy-five cents a week. I was one of fifteen boys delivering Lebanon's daily afternoon paper to subscribers. My pay was considered normal for boys of eleven and twelve years. And I didn't grumble until I was put on overtime, at a cut rate, several months later.

"I want you to come in at five-thirty tomorrow morning,' said Mr. Sowers, the newspaper's owner, one afternoon as we were starting out on our delivery routes. He had gotten a contract, he said, to deliver the Philadelphia *Times* (a paper that since has died) to Lebanon readers. We would get fifty cents a week for this early-morning work.

The boss talked as if he were doing us a favor. We would now make $1.25 a week, he told us. "That's good money for a boy," he added with a smile.

Mother almost vetoed this overtime deal when I came home for supper. They were already buying my clothes with what I brought in, with something left over, she told Father. "And this child needs sleep," she argued.

Father agreed. I could quit both jobs. "Sowers is too stingy," he said. But this was summertime. I had no classes to worry about. I would get part of the fifty cents for spending money. And I wanted to hear what the other boys would do. So I set the alarm.

There was a lot of grumbling when the kids came together next morning. One boy said his father was angry because the alarm woke him up half an hour before he had to get up for his foundry job.

But we didn't rebel until we found a leader. This was Polly Gorman, a scrappy Irish boy, who was two years older than I was. Polly talked the wage cut over with his father, a mechanic in a nut and bolt shop that was later taken over by Bethlehem Steel. And one morning Polly came in with a sheet of paper that he called a petition. On top was a request for seventy-five cents, in Polly's handwriting. Polly's name was underneath. Our signatures were promptly scrawled down below. And we waited by our newspaper bundles for Mr. Sowers to come.

We were on strike, but didn't know it. We waited three hours until Mr. Sowers stormed in. The publisher was a skinny man of about thirty-five, with a scraggly red beard that bobbed up and down as he shouted at us in a high-pitched voice.

"You boys did a lot of damage this morning," the boss yelled as he stamped up and down between the bundles. "Nobody got his paper before breakfast. Some people will cancel their subscriptions. I've had enough of you little fools. I can get plenty of other boys. You'd better have some sense and pick up your papers before it's too late."

The boss's fuming went on for an hour or more. But Polly, our leader, was firm. We were scared, but we stuck together. The bundles weren't moving. At last the boss went into an inner office to telephone someone. And Polly whispered, "I think we got him."

I thought so, too. But a different Mr. Sowers came out a half hour later. This man was quiet and smiling. He settled down in an easy chair, began puffing a long cigar, and said, "All right, boys, you can have it."

The boss let us enjoy our moment of triumph. Then he began again: "But I want to tell you something for your own good." And he was no longer smiling as he said that if he gave us the seventy-five cents, we would have to "walk the chalk line" from then on. He would fire us one by one, whenever there was a complaint. We could take our choice. "It's up to you, boys," he said.

That shook us. Some subscriber was always complaining that his paper was dirty, torn, wet from rain or missing. No explanations were accepted. The boy was always to blame. Once a subscriber's son threw mud in my face. I jumped on him and we rolled in the mud together. His mother wrote an angry letter to the paper and I was almost fired, although justice was on my side. But it was the boss's new manner that weakened us most. He made us feel that power was on his side.

Our front began weakening. Polly pleaded with us to stick together. But the break came when one boy picked up his bundle. And we were all on our routes by ten o'clock.

This was the inglorious end of my first strike. We gave in because we were not used to rebelling against grown-ups in authority. We were inexperienced kids, with no one to advise us. None of us—except perhaps Polly—knew any union men or union women. Lebanon was an open-shop town eighty years ago. But the experience was not wasted on me. I often thought of what Polly said after the defeat: "We had him, if youse had stuck with me."

My first labor battle was fought and lost that summer of the year the new century came in. It had come with flashing lights at our church's annual Watch Night service. The pews then were filled with men, women and children drinking coffee and eating *fast-nachts* (sweet cakes) as they waited for the New Year. I drank my first coffee—

forbidden until then—and enjoyed the cakes, made from a recipe brought from Germany in colonial times.

Men and women were rising to make good resolutions for the coming year. I remember one young man holding up a pack of cigarettes and promising not to smoke "this sinful stuff" again. The organ was playing softly. And all eyes were on a six-foot grandfather's clock that someone had loaned to the church for the night.

As the clock began striking midnight, the words "Twentieth Century" flashed on the wall in electric lights. Sight and sound came on together. The dazzling climax took everyone by surprise, except the magician behind it. That was Mr. Lichtenthaler, the organist, a piano tuner by trade and a versatile mechanic. None of the rest of us had any practical knowledge of the new scientific wonder—electricity!

10 · York

Father was transferred to York, Pennsylvania, a bigger industrial town, after my fifteenth birthday.I liked it better than Lebanon. A broad creek—the Codorus—ran through the town, with swimming holes at the outskirts. I found good fishing in the mile-wide Susquehanna River, not far away. And we had a big backyard, with apple trees to climb, a henhouse and plenty of play space. There I spent many hours acting out animal stories for my little brother Jim.

I quickly made friends with the boys on our block and shared their enthusiasm for York's professional baseball team and its home-run king, Bill Clay. Bill was our hero and personal friend. He spent the winter in a fish store a few doors from our house, and we kids used to crowd into the store and get Bill talking about his home runs until the boss chased us away.

I was also awakening to world affairs. America's conquest of the Philippines, its new colony, was still being resisted by the Filipinos.

Father subscribed to a Philadelphia paper, and he read the news to us at the breakfast table. The U.S. Army's atrocities were shocking. Discharged soldiers were telling a Senate committee how independence leaders were interrogated. Water was poured into the mouths of captured patriots as they lay on the ground. The victims' noses were held shut to compel them to swallow. The pouring continued until bellies were almost bursting. Then army boots stamped on swollen bellies, inflicting frightful pain, and questioning started again.

This torture was called "the water cure." It was used wherever the army had control in the islands. It had been introduced by General Arthur MacArthur, the father of General Douglas MacArthur, for the purpose of getting the names of "insurrectoes," the patriotic guerrilla fighters. When MacArthur captured an insurrecto he hanged him. There are official records of seventy-nine such hangings.

I was getting my first lessons in the cruelties of imperialism.

I was also learning about the robbery of the poor by the rich. I was delivering the York *Dispatch,* an afternoon paper, to subscribers for the sum of one dollar a week—sixteen and two-third cents a day. After finishing my route, I often visited the YMCA reading room on the way home. There I became an avid reader of the anti-monopoly "muckraking" magazines.

These muckraking magazines reached millions of Americans in the early years of the century, before the bankers cut off their credit. That was a golden time for investigative reporters. Lincoln Steffens, Ida Tarbell, David Graham Phillips and other fearless writers were digging into the dirty records of big business and its political puppets. They taught me that John D. Rockefeller, the sanctimonious oil king, was a hypocrite and crook who bribed politicians in both major parties. I learned that J. P. Morgan, the banker and trust builder, was a swindler; that the U.S. Senate was a millionaires' club; and that this country, in the main, was run by enemies of the people.

These truths about the ruling class impressed some of my classmates as well as myself, and they were sometimes reflected in a little paper I edited in my second high-school year.

This paper was my first attempt at journalism. It was called the *Scuta Weekly.* Scuta was my high school nickname. It means shields, in Latin—the plural form of *scutum*—shield. My classmates got it from Julius Caesar's book on the conquest of Gaul, which we were translating.

The *Scuta Weekly* was a mini journal, handwritten on two sides of a long sheet of yellow paper, and it was passed from seat to seat in the classroom. It consisted mostly of jokes on fellow students by the wits in the class. But it also ran verses sometimes. And a song about J. P. Morgan, the lord of Wall Street, filled the back page of the final number.

This song had been written by Ralph, a short, curly headed chap who was usually grinning. It said the devils were dancing in glee when

they heard that Morgan was shut out of heaven by Saint Peter and was flying down to hell. The lines I remember best begin when Morgan comes through the brimstone door and Satan himself is singing:

> *Oh, Welcome Mr. Morgan,*
> *I'm happy as can be*
> *They're waiting for you*
> *In furnace number three.*

Some literary critics may not be impressed. But Ralph told me that his father, an iron molder, invited shopmates to his home to hear his son sing it.

The devil song also made a hit with my classmates. Boys and girls were grinning as it went around. And one plump girl with flaxen ringlets giggled so much that Professor Porter, our mathematics teacher was interrupted while he was explaining a problem in algebra. He picked up the paper, read it and smiled. He was our favorite teacher. Then he told us that the *Scuta Weekly* must not come out again. "Mr. Pennypacker won't like it if he hears about it," he said.

Mr. Pennypacker was our high school principal. He was an active member of the Republican Party and a very solemn man, without an ounce of humor, who presided over our morning assembly sessions in a formal black suit.

I was very sorry when Ralph left school a few months later to become a machinist's apprentice in a big farm-equipment plant. There were many dropouts. The average boy or girl pupil was at work by the middle teens. Only fifty-four members of my class remained until graduation day. That was a small percentage of the teenagers in this industrial city of forty thousand people.

York education was run on class lines. Families with higher incomes sent their children to private schools that charged fees. But most of my classmates came from working-class families. Exceptions were the sons of three preachers, of several small businessmen and of one lawyer, who was not high in his profession. He picked up low-paying clients, such as prostitutes and petty thieves, in the courtroom. So his son said.

Most of my fellow students had summer jobs, where they toiled under hard nonunion conditions. I remember how tired my friend Gottwald—we called him "Guttie"—looked when I met him one July morning. He had just finished an all-night shift in a hot, steaming paper mill. His shifts, he said, alternated from night to day. The night shift lasted thirteen hours, the day shift eleven. And there was no weekend rest.

Guttie was paid $28 every two weeks, after working 168 hours. He went back to the mill after graduation in the hope of saving money for college. If he stayed in the mill, I hope his strength survived until the new industrial unions won the eight-hour day in the 1930s.

I was becoming, meanwhile, an ardent lover of poetry. I owe this to my mother, to my oldest brother, Walter—a poet himself—who had been away from home during most of my boyhood, and to my high school English teacher. She was Miss Holland, an attractive young woman, who won the hearts of the boys in her class.

I would tell my parents at night what Miss Holland said about Shakespeare, and they responded in a beautiful way. Father had seen the famous Edwin Booth play Macbeth and Julius Caesar many years before. And when I woke on my sixteenth birthday I found a complete set of Shakespeare in individual volumes by my bed. This was more than my parents could afford. I lived with the plays and sonnets all the next year, though I enjoyed *A Midsummer Night's Dream* and *Henry IV's* Jack Falstaff most at that time. Shakespeare has enriched my life ever since.

Miss Holland never mentioned Walt Whitman, who is now my favorite poet. The great bard of Brooklyn Ferry was sadly neglected for twenty years after his death. But I was enamored with the organlike music of Milton's *Paradise Lost,* and with the passion of Byron and the beauty of Keats and Shelley. And I enjoyed reading them to a number of poetry lovers among my classmates.

I didn't understand the class struggle then. But I was a rebel against oppression. And Shelley's call to the masses to rise after the massacre of strikers at Peterloo in 1819 was engraved in my heart. His wonderful lines follow:

> *Rise like lions after slumber*
> *In unvanquishable number!*
> *Shake your chains to earth like dew*
> *That in sleep has fallen on you;*
> *Ye are many; they are few.*

I did not know then that Russian workers were rising "like lions" while I was reading Shelley's call to battle. The 1905 revolution was shaking the throne of the hated Czar, but Father had dropped his subscription to the Philadelphia paper—so I was missing the most important event in the century's first decade.

11 · Grandpa Andy

I have vivid memories of my first visit to the U.S. Southland as a boy of sixteen. I had given up my newspaper route for a full-time job in a clothing store when the school year ended. It was a long-hours job. I was pedaling a bicycle as a delivery boy or standing at the haberdashery counter until late at night. And I was glad to get away when Father took Mother, my eight-year-old brother Jim and myself to visit his people in the North Carolina countryside.

Forty years had gone by since General Lee's army gave up the fight. But time had not dimmed the memory of America's bloodiest conflict. The Civil War was still a common topic of conversation when Southerners got together. And I began hearing war stories as our train was leaving Washington.

The stories came from a tall man with a white goatee and a long cigar, who had lounged into the seat beside me. His white Panama hat and gray summer suit looked like money. He told us that his family had a tobacco plantation with a hundred slaves before the war. And his talk quickly turned to the war.

"You're talking, sir, to one of General Moseby's captains," he told Father. "I reckon you heard about Moseby. There warn't no one like him. He had the best horses and the best men in the whole Confederate Army. We cut up them Yankee lines in northern Virginia. We sure did. We even captured a Yankee general." And he boasted that the Confederates would have won the war but for one thing: "There was just too many Yankees."

This relic of the slave-owning aristocracy told us that he never accepted President Lincoln's proclamation of emancipation. "No, sir," he repeated, "I never did. Them slaves belonged to us." He fled to England when Black men won the vote and did not return to Virginia until President Rutherford B. Hayes took federal troops out of the South and all-white rule returned in 1877.

The captain left us in Lynchburg, Virginia, a tobacco-marketing town. As the train rolled in to Lynchburg, my father began singing a song he heard as a boy:

> *I'm goin' along down town;*
> *I'm goin' along down town;*
> *I'm goin' along to Lynchburg town*
> *To carry my tobakker down t' town.*

Father had heard Black drivers singing this song as their tobacco wagons left North Carolina for Lynchburg before the war.

My father, Tom Shields, came from Scotch-Irish stock. He belonged to the fourth Shields generation in North Carolina. He was born in 1850 in a log cabin that his father, Andrew Shields, had built in a woodland about twelve miles from Salem—now Winston-Salem, North Carolina.

This cabin with its thick oak walls was still standing when we drove up, although its hand-shingled roof had fallen in. It had two rooms on the ground floor—a combination living room and bedroom, and a kitchen. There was a tiny loft overhead, where the little ones huddled together on straw mattresses.

My grandma, Betsy Ann Shields, gave birth to fourteen children in that log cabin, without any medical attention, but nine died in infancy or early childhood. The families of the survivors and other close relatives were spread over three counties. We spent a month traveling from farmhouse to farmhouse by horse and wagon, and we slept in ten or more homes altogether.

Our relatives grew almost all their own food except coffee. They saw little money, but had plenty of cornbread, sorghum molasses, fruit and vegetables. Their hogs rooted up food for themselves in the woods near every home. Their chickens fattened on grasshoppers and worms in summer. The broilers were ripe for the table in August. And we enjoyed the first of many chicken dinners at the home of Aunt Sarah Jane, Father's oldest sister. The chickens were cooked in heavy iron frying pans on the hot ashes of the open fireplace.

My aunt's husband tilled his farm with the help of a twenty-two year old son. Several older children had married and left. Father and son got good crops, my father remarked. "That's right," replied my uncle, "but hardly anyone wants to buy them." He took us through pear and apple orchards heavy with fruit that it didn't pay to pick. Thousands of bees were making honey in a long row of hives, and the corn in the corn fields stood over my head.

"But there's one crop I'll never plant again," my uncle said. "That's tobacco. I swear that every year, because tobacco work is never done. That little tobacco field keeps me working thirteen months a year." I was to hear that wry joke from other tobacco growers as our trip continued.

My cousin, who was going with a girl, said he got some courting money with the help of his whittling knife. The farm had fine hardwood timber. He carved it into axe handles in the winter months and sold them to a country storekeeper for ten cents each.

My aunt had had only one railroad ride in her life. But she made a long horse-and-wagon trip at six. Her father—my grandfather Andrew Shields—sold his farm and took the family to Indiana in 1852. This was part of a big migration. Six Shields brothers and many neighbors left North Carolina to get cheap government land.

That was a rough trip, Aunt Sarah Jane said. Children, plow, harrow, hoes, spades, axes, pots, pans, blankets and the family shotgun were piled into a covered wagon. The journey went on for six weeks. "We bumped over mountain roads and got stuck in swamps," she said. "And little Tom, your father, was almost drowned when he was washed away while the wagon was fording a swollen stream."

Indiana was "God's promised land" to some of her uncles, Aunt Sarah Jane said. The rich virgin soil brought bountiful harvests. And her favorite uncle, Sam Shields, prospered in politics as county treasurer, though that proved his undoing. Uncle Sam never drank until he went into politics, my aunt said. Then he began doing what other Indiana politicians did. He carried a demijohn of whiskey in his wagon when he visited farmers seeking votes. He drank drink for drink with the men he talked to. He got the whiskey habit and whiskey killed him.

But the new land almost killed Grandpa and Grandma in a different way. The undrained swamps gave them "chills and fever," as malaria was called. They fought it for three years, but the chill and fever got worse, until finally Grandpa loaded the covered wagon for North Carolina.

Those were hard times. Grandpa lost all he had in Indiana and started life again as a tenant in the old log house. "But your grandpa was smart," my aunt said. "He began doing some horse-trading. He could make an old horse look like a young colt. That helped us when crops were bad."

Worse times came with the Civil War. The Confederate Army took part of Grandpa's crops. Aunt Sarah Jane said the family had to live on what it raised. "We made 'coffee' out of burned sweet potatoes and Grandma began spinning yarn for the family clothes again." Then the army took my father's oldest brother, Elisha—the family's best worker—at seventeen. Aunt Sarah Jane, Grandma and young Tom—my father—worked in the fields like men. And finally the recruiting sergeant took Grandpa himself.

Grandpa was forty-four and he was suffering from a bad hernia. Aunt Sarah Jane called it a rupture. It came when he lifted a log for a neighbor's log house. But the Confederacy was scraping the manpower bottom in 1864. No poor farmer or fifteen-year-old boy could escape. Grandpa was taken to a distant military camp, where no one knew him. And a roomful of guests from neighboring farms laughed with my aunt when she told what Grandpa did to get out of the army. And none objected when she said that he didn't like slavery, war or secession.

"Uncle Andy—my grandpa—always said it was a 'rich man's war and a poor man's fight,'" said Harry, a one-armed man of about sixty. He lost his arm in the fighting below Richmond shortly before peace was signed. I was to hear the same remark from other Confederate veterans later.

Grandpa had to find his own way out of the army, said Aunt Sarah Jane. And he took the blind man's way. He wasn't entirely blind. He could see just a little, he told his sergeant. But he couldn't see the sights of his gun and he stumbled into everyone while doing camp chores.

The captain was furious. He cursed Grandpa up and down. He cursed the recruiting sergeant who had sent him a blind man. Finally the captain had enough. He put Grandpa out of the camp and said, "Never come back."

My great-aunt Amanda, Grandpa's sister, now took up the story. Aunt Amanda, a widowed woman in her eighties, lived with Aunt Sarah Jane, and she was sitting in a rocking chair by the fireplace. Her voice was very weak and I could hardly hear her when she said, "Andy did right."

I moved up beside her. I was sitting on the floor, and she put her arm around me and said, "I want you to know, Arthur, that Andy wasn't afraid to fight. He'd have done like his pa and his grandpa if it had been a good war." Her father, William Shields—my great-grandfather—fought against the British in the War of 1812; and his father—my great-great-grandfather Shields—served under General Nathanael Greene in the Carolina campaign in the Revolutionary War.

Aunt Sarah Jane then told me a story that Father had often told before. Grandpa Andy took the family by surprise when he walked into the house. Grandma hugged him and kissed him, then said, "You must be hungry, Andy."

"I sure am," Grandpa replied.

"I'll make a big chowder," said Grandma. "Tom, get me some squirrels. The woods are full of them."

And Tom had his hand on the shotgun that hung from the wall when his father jumped out of his chair and said, "I'll get those squirrels, Tom."

"You can't, Pap. The army sent you home because you're blind."

"I'm only blind in the Army," his father replied with a grin. In two hours he was back with a bag full of squirrels. And the chowder that day was one of Grandma's best, Aunt Sarah Jane said.

More war stories followed as the coffee cups were refilled and the Sunday afternoon went on. The conversation finally turned to the deserters from the Confederate Army. "They were hiding everywhere," the one-armed veteran said. And Father remarked that he knew one deserter very well. This was Jack, the seventeen-year-old son of a neighboring farmer.

"Most of the boys I knew were doing all they could to keep out of the army," Father said. "But not Jack. He was a red-hot rebel. Jack told us that he was going to Washington first thing. 'I'm goin' there to

take Abe Lincoln's skull in my two hands and use it for a soap scoop.'"
(The farmers' homemade soap was very soft. It was made from lard
and wood ashes.)

But Jack's martial enthusiasm didn't last. He disappeared into the
deep woods after the first battle. "We all knew where Jack was," said
Father, "but no one betrayed him." He was hiding in a little bark hut
beside a creek and living on trapped rabbits and the food his little
sister brought him.

This young deserter became known as "Bushwhacker Jack." The
name stuck to him after the war. But Jack had nothing in common
with the real bushwhackers in the southern mountains. They fought as
guerrillas against the Confederate armies. "Jack whacked nothing but
rabbits." Father said.

Aunt Sarah Jane told me more about my grandparents the next
day. "Your grandpa, Arthur, was a very good man, although he liked
his morning dram and never went to church. We got our religion from
our mother. We said our prayers to her every night.

"Your grandma was a very strong woman," my aunt continued.
"She was the strongest woman I ever saw. When we harvested our
fields together with our neighbors, she could lift heavier loads than
any of the men. But her strength wore out during the war."

Grandma died the year the war ended. "I think she worked herself
to death," my aunt said. "She never had any rest. Her death hit your
grandpa very hard. He didn't marry again until he was almost sixty,
although many women wanted him."

Grandpa's last years seemed to have been contented ones. He had
two lovely children by his second wife and he finally got title to his
farm again. That gave him "a lot of satisfaction," my aunt said.

"He was a very sociable man," added Harry, the veteran, who
visited us again. "He always liked to be with young people and they
liked to be with him. He was the life of the evening at the meetings of
the rural debating society and always got the laugh on the other
fellow.

"We all miss Uncle Andy. We sure do."

12 · Cousin Gene

An evangelistic revival was going on in Yadkinville, N.C., our next stop. Yadkinville was a village of five hundred people near the rapid Yadkin River. It was ten miles from a railroad. There were no automobiles in the community in 1905, and the town seemed very isolated at first. But I soon found that Yadkinville was the busy shopping center for a big farming community extending around it. And the town was the county seat of Yadkin County, with a judge, a courthouse, a jailhouse and a high sheriff.

But all other business took second place while the evangelist was packing people into the biggest church in town.

The evangelist, a lean, wrinkled man in a baggy, black suit, was threatening sinners with damnation in a thundering voice when I took my seat. I no longer believed in hell, but this man's visions of eternal torture chambers were more vivid than any I had seen before. Hellfire flamed into the eyes of the people as he thundered. It was a terrifying performance, which disturbed me, and sent a stream of frightened sinners to the mourners' bench.

Some of the evangelist's "sinners" were "wicked old men," who shaved off white beards to "catch" innocent young women. He shouted against those "smooth-chinned hypocrites" for several minutes. My father, who sat on the platform, was amused and embarrassed at the same time. He had shaved off his own russet beard when the first gray strands appeared a few months before. My mother teased him after the service.

One of the sins the evangelist was damning was tobacco-smoking. This was a bold line to take in a state where tobacco was the farmers' biggest cash crop and the richest men were tobacco manufacturers. The evangelist's eloquence was overwhelming, however. And sinners, repenting at the mourners' bench, were promising to quit the "vile weed," as the evangelist called it, and the "wicked bottle."

The evangelist was taking the Yadkinville community by storm. Farmers' horses were tied to every hitching post in town. There was one jolly holdout, however. That was my cousin Gene, a big, athletic young man who strolled outside the church smoking a defiant cigar while the smokers inside were repenting. His smokes came in packs labeled "Old Virginia Cheroots, Three for a Nickel."

"They all like me," Gene told me, "though they think I'm going to burn in hell. And I tell them that they will soon be sinning again. It's always that way. The whole town becomes very holy for a week or two when an evangelist comes. Then it's back in its old ways again."

Gene also took pleasure in defying the community's political traditions. Almost all Yadkinville voters cast their ballots for the Democratic Party. But Gene proudly boasted that he was a Republican. He told me that his father and grandfather had been Republicans since the time of Abraham Lincoln. I don't know, however, whether Gene was aware of what had happened to his party since its early revolutionary years.

Gene's spirit of independence was encouraged by his physical strength. When we went swimming in the Yadkin, he swam against the powerful current, which carried me downstream. When we left the water, he put his hand under my shoulder and lifted me over his head with ease. His father, who was watching, remarked that Gene could whip any man in town if he wanted to do so.

My cousin was a successful, self-employed mechanic. He owned a water-wheel mill, which he designed, built and operated by himself, without hired help. It was a combined sawmill and grain mill. Water from a small creek spilled on a wooden power wheel twelve feet wide.

That was an unusual width. I've only seen one to equal it out of scores I observed during several southern trips.

While I was visiting the mill, a farmer drove up with a wagonload of corn, which Gene ground into meal for corn bread and animal feed. I noticed that no money passed in the transaction. Gene's payment was a share of the meal, which he packaged neatly for sale in Yadkinville stores.

Gene—then thirty—was the oldest son of Father's younger sister Elizabeth, who had died several years earlier. Gene had two brothers—Charley, a Winston-Salem lawyer, whom I was soon to meet, and Edgar, a fine amateur baseball pitcher and a preacher. My father taught Edgar the A B C's of chess and he became the North Carolina state champion later.

A five-hour wagon ride behind a pair of mules took us to a tobacco farm owned by Father's cousin Dave, a son of my great-aunt Amanda. Dave's family of five lived in an old roomy farmhouse on the banks of a deep creek. Father and Dave had been playmates in childhood. They laughed about old times as we enjoyed a big chicken dinner. And one schoolboy tale sticks in my mind.

"Do you remember when our teacher climbed a tree?" asked Dave.

"Indeed I do, he was afraid for his life," replied Father.

This teacher, a farmer's son, had defied a time-honored community custom. If the teacher was a man, he was expected to bring a present to every pupil on Christmas Eve. But this young teacher resisted. He couldn't afford to do so, he explained. He was only getting a few dollars a month.

The big boys were angry. "Let's throw him in the creek," cried one boy, who was a big as the teacher himself. As the boys were advancing, the teacher fled. A hot race began. And the boys were catching up with their prey when the teacher climbed a tree. "Let's get an axe," one boy suggested. The teacher then gave up. And he was allowed to come down safely on the promise that he would give every pupil a big slice of his mother's Christmas cakes when school reopened after the holidays.

Dave spoke affectionately of the old schoolhouse that Father and he attended. It was built of logs laid crosswise in notches that Dave's father helped to chip out. Attendance was voluntary. All classes met in one room. School opened in November, after the harvests, and closed in February, when spring sowing was about to begin.

My father was the teacher, in his nineteenth and twentieth years.

After that he taught in the Moravian Brethren's boarding school for boys in Nazareth, Pennsylvania, before entering the ministry.

The next Sunday I sat through the longest sermon of the hundreds I listened to in childhood and youth. Dave belonged to the Primitive Baptists, who were better known as the Hardshell Baptists. The Hardshells had very rigid ideas. In Europe they would probably be called Calvinists. They believed that everything that happened was ordained by God. Nothing could change unless the change was decreed by God. That's why, said Dave, his church didn't believe in sending missionaries to China, India and other foreign lands. "When the Lord gets ready to convert those heathens, he'll do it himself," he told Father.

Dave discussed this at Sunday breakfast, when I wanted to think of nothing more than the crispy hot biscuits with honey, and the bacon and sausages and other succulent foods on the table.

The Hardshell church service had little in common with the Yadkinville revival meeting. The preacher began talking about the baptism of Jesus by John the Baptist. His text came from God, he said. He had not prepared what he was going to say. He believed that when he opened his mouth, "the Lord would fill it." If he tried to prepare his remarks from one day to the next, "they would stink." That's what happened, he said, to the heavenly manna that God dropped on the Children of Israel in the wilderness during their flight from Egypt. When they hoarded it from one day to the next, "it stank," the Bible said.

The preacher went on to tell of the "heavenly joy" that filled him when he came out of the creek in which he was totally immersed during baptism. His talk went on for three hours. The church was filled with farm families to the end.

I felt better after a big rabbit soup and chicken dinner, topped off with blackberry pie, and still better after a swim with Dave's two sons—one twelve, the other fourteen. They were jolly playmates and nimble athletes. I admired them very much. They easily outswam me and they did dazzling aerial flipflops as they dove into the creek from a tree overhead.

The younger boy was a fine rural folksinger. As we shared a watermelon after the swim, he sang the "Watermelon Song" that his father learned as a boy. And I'm sorry that I only remember the following lines:

Oh see that watermillion a-smiling on the vine,
How I wish that watermillion it was mine.
You may talk about the peaches, the apples and the pears,
The 'simmons growing on the 'simmons tree;
But bless your heart, my honey
That truck it ain't no wheres
For the watermillion am the fruit for me.

Dave was sitting with Father in a big double swing seat under a spreading oak tree when we came back. They were talking in low tones. I could not hear them. But Dave looked very unhappy, and Father later told Mother and me that Dave was afraid that the bank in Winston-Salem would seize his farm.

The bank was controlled by the R. J. Reynolds Tobacco Company, a giant firm that dominated the tobacco market.

Dave was behind in his mortgage payments. "I put a lot of sweat into this land," he told Father. There was nothing except trees, bushes and swamps when he came, he said. "Everything here is my work," he went on. "The bank never did anything for the land, and now it wants it.

"I'm getting good crops," he continued, "but my debts are eating me up." How could he meet his mortgage payments, he asked Father, when the tobacco buyers paid him less than the cost of production. The price was fixed by Reynolds, the biggest buyer.

This company had humble beginnings in the last century. It now has several billion dollars in assets, and owns the biggest container line in the U.S. merchant marine.

My least happy trip was to High Point, a company-ruled industrial town that was the center of North Carolina's furniture industry. One of Aunt Sarah Jane's sons was living in a small pineboard house with his wife and two small children. His home stood in a row of houses that were exactly alike. They were owned by the company that built the new furniture factory nearby.

My cousin took a day off to show us around, but there wasn't much for a boy to see. No one was playing in the ballfield and the swimming hole was too far away.

My cousin ran a planing machine that smoothed hardwood boards. He worked ten hours a day, six days a week. He said the pay wasn't much, but he could get along if he didn't fall sick. There wasn't any union, and a man working alongside him lost his job when he was sick. This shopmate had three kids and left town.

We didn't stay overnight, because my mother wouldn't let my cousin and his wife give up their bed and sleep in a neighbor's house.

13 · Black captives

Our longest ride took us to the foothills of the Blue Ridge Mountains, where Father's youngest sister, Maggie, lived on a small farm. Aunt Maggie was the child of Grandpa's second marriage and was still in her twenties. Her beauty had attracted several young men, who wanted to marry her, when she had visited us in Lebanon five years earlier. But she was already betrothed to Mott Guy, a young farmer and sawmill worker.

My aunt lived with her husband, children and mother in a frame house that Uncle Mott built. Her two children—a boy and a girl—were full of life and laughter. Her mother, my step-grandmother, who was to live thirty years longer, was active in her mid-sixties. She spun the family yarn on an old spinning wheel. My aunt used the yarn for making the family clothes.

"We never need a doctor," Uncle Mott said. "We eat nothing but fresh food we grow ourselves."

Uncle Mott was cultivating the kind of farm one seldom sees today. It produced for the family rather than the market. A well-kept garden and orchard supplied the vegetables and fruit that Aunt Maggie preserved for winter. "We seldom buy sugar," my uncle said. "We use sorghum molasses, made from homegrown cane instead." I watched his gray mare going around in a circle as she pushed a pole attached to the cane grinder.

Uncle Mott showed me the wheat field that gave the family its bread. He patted the grunting sow that gave birth to the pigs that provided the family's meat. I listened to the cackling hens that were laying the family's eggs. And I picked cotton on the little cotton field that paid the taxes.

Uncle Mott never hired labor, but he got good volunteer help. His nearest neighbors were members of a Black farming family. "They are our best neighbors," he said. "The wife helps Maggie when she needs help. Maggie helps her. And we men work together at harvesttime. I thank God for such neighbors."

I met the Black neighbor next day, when he drove to Aunt Maggie's door in a small wagon. He was a smiling young man of about Uncle Mott's age. A chubby little girl of three years was with him. She ran to Aunt Maggie and hugged her. "I heard your brother was visiting," the young man said. "I thought he might like my melons." And he carried three oversized watermelons into the kitchen.

My uncle said his family often drove several miles on Sunday to attend the Black church services. "They have a good preacher and the best church music I ever heard," he told me. "They always give us a good welcome. I like to be with them. We're all God's children, the Bible says."

Uncle Mott talked about Black people for some time. The best congressman his district ever had, he said, was a Black man named George White. He had represented Uncle Mott's district in Washington for many years, until the Black people were disfranchised in North Carolina at the turn of the century. George White was the last Black congressman in the South to survive the racists' attacks.

I heard more good things in later years about this Black congressman, from an elderly educator who grew up in Uncle Mott's district and came north. This was Charles Hendley, who was the president of the New York Teachers Union in the 1930s. He told me that the Black congressman got the votes of most of the white farmers as well as the votes of the Black people.

Racism never took deep root in this upland country, which had few slaves before the Civil War. But I was learning about the oppression of the Black people as our travels continued. The story of a lynching in the plantation lands of eastern North Carolina shocked me profoundly. I met few Black landowners. When we returned to Winston-Salem, I found that Black workers were shut out of the textile mills except for a few labor jobs. They were getting the lowest-paid work in the big R. J. Reynolds Tobacco Co. plant that I visited. The only white men I saw in the tobacco-leaf stripping rooms, where conditions were very bad, were foremen. And we were constantly passing Black chain gangs on our travels as our wagons rumbled over the narrow dirt roads.

Those chain-gang scenes are with me still. I would see six to a dozen Black men bending over shovels, pickaxes or crowbars in the blazing August sun. They were dressed in convict stripes. A white captain with a heavy revolver was barking directions. Another white man with a rifle was standing near by. And sometimes a Black lad was bringing a bucket of water to the sweating men.

I was told that the road slaves were bound together at night by a long chain running from one pair of ankles to the next. Their food consisted mainly of beans and cornmeal mush.

Always, one, two or three Black men were dragging heavy iron balls behind them. These balls were about the size of small bowling balls. They were chained to the Black captives' right ankles. They left a scar behind, and I was told that a man who dragged a ball and chain for a year had a limping gait for the rest of his life.

I remember one cruel scene most of all. We were rounding a steep hill with a cliff on one side and a precipice on the other. A tumbling creek lay below us, with a forested hillside beyond. It was a magnificent panorama. But the beauty was blotted out of my mind by the sight of a chain gang. The gang was widening the narrow road. A big Black man with a ball and chain was working with a long iron crowbar. The captain yelled at him to pry a rock out of the embankment on the inside of the road. The prisoner had to drag the heavy ball upgrade to do this. He was wincing with pain. But when he stopped to rub the sore spot, the captain gave him an angry push in the back and screamed angry words into his ear.

This cruelty disturbed my father. "We had no chain gangs when I was a boy," he told me. "And there weren't many slaves in the county where I grew up. The farmers got together and repaired the roads themselves. My brother, my father and I did our share of the work."

Father once asked a chain gang captain why his men were arrested. But the captain didn't know or didn't care. "They're here because they're bad n----rs," he replied. "I wouldn't go near that man if I didn't have a gun," he said as he looked at a big prisoner with a ball and chain.

Guilt or innocence meant little in North Carolina courts when sheriffs were recruiting Blacks for the county roads. I saw this myself in Winston-Salem's temple of justice. My cousin Charley, Gene's brother, the young lawyer from Yadkinville, took me inside the courtroom railing as a trial was about to begin.

The prisoner was a small Black youth. His age was given as sixteen—the same as mine—although he looked younger. The charge was theft. He was accused of stealing a pair of shoes from an older

man. They were wretched, worn-out, patched shoes of no commercial value and much too big for the boy, as the judge could see for himself when a deputy sheriff laid them before him.

The Black boy was a lamb led to slaughter. The judge didn't look at him when the deputy, a bloated red-faced man, brought the boy in. He had no lawyer, and the judge didn't ask any of the attorneys who were present to represent him. Nor did the judge ask if he had any defense. I listened carefully. The shoes were not found in the prisoner's possession and no evidence of guilt was presented.

Only two witnesses were called. One was a middle-aged Black man, who identified the shoes as his property but did not implicate the defendant in any way. The other witness was the deputy who had brought the prisoner in. When the judge asked, "What kind of a boy is he?" the deputy replied, "He's a bad boy." Only that and nothing more.

"Six months on the county roads," the judge said without looking up.

This may sound like an incredible story. It was an everyday fact in North Carolina, however.

I was shocked at this monstrous scene. I couldn't explain the guilty verdict. But when I asked Cousin Charley about it, he merely said, "They wouldn't have convicted him if he had been white." Charley said this in a matter-of-fact way. He had seen such things happen often before. He didn't like it, however; he told me so that night. And I pondered on the first of the many frame-ups I was to see in my life.

14 · *Jack London*

I thought of little but football for three months after returning from the South. I played right guard on York High School's team. Those were the days of heavy line plunges. My job was to knock a hole in the opposing line for one of our backs to plunge through. Every game was a physical battle in which I was outweighed. But I learned to fight against odds. I came out of the season with a cracked rib and broken hand. But I felt amply repaid when our coach patted me on the back at a school meeting and said, "Good old Shields."

Our coach, Eddie Williamson, was a twenty-two-year-old reporter for the York *Dispatch.*

Time passed quietly until January, 1906 when I heard my first revolutionary talk. It came from Jack London, the famous writer, who spoke in our high school auditorium. He told a tale of cruel exploitation, which destroyed most of the capitalist illusions I still had.

Jack London had been my favorite storywriter since I was fourteen. Buck, the most magnificent dog in U.S. literature, won me for life when *The Call of the Wild* appeared in five installments in the *Saturday Evening Post.* I followed the stormy voyage of *The Sea Wolf,* and the fate of Wolf Larsen, its brutal and almost superhuman captain, with passionate interest in the *Century* magazine. And I devoured every tale of the Arctic trail I could get.

They were stories of struggle against hostile natural forces that encouraged me to fight without quitting. But Jack's Socialist writings and his labor battle stories were excluded from the magazines I saw in York. And I did not meet the revolutionary side of Jack until that January.

Jack, then at the height of his popularity, was making a national propaganda tour for the Intercollegiate Socialist Society, of which he was president. He had spoken to big audiences at Harvard and Yale and other universities and colleges. One of his last stops was at our high school auditorium, which was used as a public lecture hall. His Socialist talks had not been publicized in York. My father took the family to hear him, and Miss Holland, our English teacher, urged her students to meet the great writer.

Jack charmed us from the beginning. He didn't wear a black swallowtail coat like the professional lecturers of that time. He was clad in a jacket that opened on his broad chest. And best of all was his smile, which he beamed at the high school boys and girls most of the time. I felt at home with him as he talked about his life at my age. His story sparkled with more dramatic details about that period of his life than he put into his autobiographical writings later. And it is still deeply etched in my mind.

Jack was a skillful propagandist and began his talk with adventure stories that won us at the start. He had shipped out of San Francisco in 1893, at seventeen, as an able seaman on the *Sophie Sutherland,* a fast little schooner that was raiding the fur seal herds off the Asian coast. This seven-month voyage was full of battles. First came battles with older seamen, who tried to use the youngster as a servant until he won the argument with his fists. Some of Jack's best stories—such as *The Mexican* and *A Piece of Steak*—are tales of the boxing ring. And Jack was at his best as he described his battles on the tossing deck of the *Sophie Sutherland.*

Then came battles with a typhoon, and other storms that almost sank the ship. And ever present was the peril of capture by Russian and Japanese patrols, with imprisonment in the mines to follow.

Jack was a compelling speaker. He kept his audience with him. I lived with the boy sailor as I had lived with the sealing pirates in *The Sea Wolf.*

The sea adventures were appetizers that made us hungry for more. The political meat came when he spoke about what followed ashore. Jack—by then eighteen—expected to begin making his fortune when he signed off the ship in San Francisco. His mind, he said, was filled with the capitalist success stories he had been reading for years. These novels were in my Sunday School library. In them, the typical hero won success by working hard for his boss and by finally marrying the boss's daughter.

"But no boss wanted me for weeks," Jack told us. The docks in San Francisco and Oakland were filled with hungry men seeking a few hours of casual labor. Long lines of jobless workers stood in front of every factory in 1894. Jack finally got a job at ten cents an hour in a jute factory, with lots of overtime. His illusions survived nevertheless, even after he'd been breathing jute dust for months. He believed that he could still win success by learning a trade in a growing industry.

"Electricity is the hope of the future," Jack said to himself. He took his dreams to the chief executive of Oakland's small electric power plant. And his education in capitalist trickery began.

"The great man was very sympathetic," Jack told us with a wry smile. "He was happy to meet ambitious boys like myself, and he assured me that I might become superintendent some day." But that would take time, the big boss cautioned Jack and he listed the steps on the ladder to success. Jack must be a good engineer before he became a superintendent. But that was not the first step. Before he became an engineer, he must fire a furnace under the boiler. But neither would he begin as a fireman. He would begin by passing coal to the fireman.

"I accepted the challenge," said Jack, "and it almost killed me." The "sympathetic" boss gave him $30 a month, with one day off every thirty days. "I suppose that was for the development of my mind," Jack remarked with another wry smile.

The boss gave Jack no time for lunch. That was the cruelest feature of this savage job to a boy like myself, who was always hungry. Jack said that he just grabbed mouthfuls of sandwich while he was shoveling frantically to keep the furnace hot.

Nor did the boss let Jack rest at the end of his official twelve-hour shift. Jack had to continue piling up coal alongside the furnace for two more hours, until the night fireman had enough fuel to last until morning.

"My muscles were so stiff at night," Jack told us, "that I staggered like a drunk in the trolley car on the way home." Passengers looked at

him with sorrow or disgust, and Jack heard one motherly woman say, "That poor boy is terribly dissipated."

"I was dissipated," said Jack. "I was dissipated with work." And he fell asleep at his mother's table before the first spoonful of soup reached his lips.

But Jack stuck to this monstrous job, fixing his hopes on the future. He stuck until he learned that his "sympathetic" boss was a liar and robber. He learned this when the day fireman made a confession, after first swearing Jack to secrecy. "You are doing the work of two men," he told Jack. The boss had fired two $40-a-month coal passers to replace them with a $30 boy. The boss was saving $50 a month by his dirty deal, but it cost a human life. One of the discharged men shot himself because he couldn't feed his kids.

York, a conservative, nonunion town, had never heard a capitalist get such a dressing down. But everyone listened, especially the youngsters, as Jack London went on. He told us that the powerhouse boss destroyed all his "success" illusions. He never dreamed of marrying a boss's daughter anymore. He vowed to himself that he would never work with his muscles for an exploiter again. He became a hobo, riding the rods and tops of freight cars, dodging railroad bulls and begging handouts from housewives in many states.

More illusions vanished when Jack was arrested in Niagara Falls, New York, because he had no money or job. He was sent to a filthy prison for thirty days, without any trial. It was a court without justice, like the one I had visited in Winston-Salem, where an innocent Black lad of my age had been sent to the barbarous chain gang.

But Jack London said that his lost illusions were replaced by understanding as the hobo trip continued. Older men told him that they had once been as strong and ambitious as he was, but the bosses threw them on the scrap heap when their muscles wore out. But some men Jack met on the freight trains were not discouraged. They knew that a wonderful future was coming. The workers would take the world for themselves when they were united. There is nothing so strong as the working class, they said, when workers are united.

I don't remember whether Jack mentioned Socialism. He probably did, because he joined the party when he returned to Oakland after the hobo year, and he was proud of his membership. But he may not have used the word "socialism" much, because he was tempering his remarks to the understanding of the boys and girls in front of him. In any case, the word would not have meant a lot to me at that time. What meant a lot was Jack London's promise of a splendid future for the people who did the work of the world when they were united. This promise came from a man I admired immensely. I got a consciousness of the role of working people that I never forgot.

15 · Socialism

I heard a little about Socialism the next summer from a friend named Ray, the son of a Lutheran preacher. We were working in the plant of the York Bridge Company at the edge of town. I was running a machine that cut threads in iron bolts, while Ray had an office job. Ray's oldest brother, Earl, was a member of the Socialist Party in South Dakota.

Ray showed me Earl's letters, which said his party expected to win a state election in a few years. When it did, South Dakota would get clean government and own electric power plants and big grain elevators. Eventually the Socialists would win a national election. Then the country's business would be run from Washington—"like the Post Office," Earl said.

I wasn't impressed. At seventeen, I was blindly prejudiced against politics and politicians. I thought all politicians were crooks like our alderman, a well-known grafter, and our constable, who tried to buy Father's vote with the promise of a Thanksgiving turkey. And I didn't see how my job fitted into Earl's post-office system. Earl said nothing about workers. And I wanted to know how I could do better than ten cents an hour on a sixty-hour-a-week schedule.

I left the job in September, when Father got a scholarship for me at a small church college in Bethlehem. It was an old-fashioned school with about fifty students. We started the day with compulsory religious services, then attended classes taught by preacher-professors. And I didn't hear Socialism mentioned until I developed acute eye trouble the next spring and returned to York to work in a big metal fabricating plant.

There I heard about working-class Socialism—the real thing.

This shop was owned by a portly old millionaire, who started as a preacher in York. He left the pulpit after marrying a rich farmer's daughter and acquiring a plant to make electric power equipment. He remained a church leader, however. He was chairman of the joint board of trustees and elders in the Moravian Brethren's Church. And he was serving communion when I first saw him, in 1901, after arriving in York.

The old man looked very venerable. His white beard and white surplice blended together as he went from pew to pew with a tray of grape-juice glasses. I did not know then—I was under thirteen—that he had broken a strike of machinists in his plant that same year. I learned that when I was working in the plant six years later.

"He starved us back to work," an old machinist told me.

That was a craft union strike. Only machinists went out. "We thought we could win by ourselves," another machinist said. "We might have won, if our helpers and the foundrymen had come out."

The plant was expanding with the growth of the electric power industry. It had nearly five hundred men when we arrived. The old man was hiring more workers from the farmlands around York. They were mostly of German-American stock. The community had few foreign-born workers and still fewer Black men and women.

My father was filling the pulpit where the old man had preached before he became rich. The old man died two or three years after we came to York. His place was taken by his eldest son, a tall, cold man who inherited his father's plant and his anti-labor policies.

The son also inherited his father's position as head of the church board of trustees and elders. This board had two functions. As a trustee, the chairman was supervising church finances. As an elder, he was supposed to be a spiritual shepherd of the church flock, which included some of his underpaid employees.

The chairman's family sat in a front pew across the aisle from my mother, my brothers and me. The chairman himself usually arrived twenty minutes late. His entry was an impressive event. He stood in the aisle with his back to the pulpit while he slowly, very slowly, removed his heavy winter coat. His eyes were sweeping coldly over the parishioners in the rear as he did this. Many were poor people. Among them were his own employees, who were getting less pay than men doing the same kind of work in other York plants.

I entered the plant in 1907 as a machinist's helper. This paid thirteen and a half cents an hour, or $8.10 for a sixty-hour week. This was 10 percent below the ordinary York scale. There was no vacation time and no sick leave. I lost three days without pay when my machinist, Fatty Firestone, accidently crushed my finger with his hammer.

The time-study man had not yet come to York, and the beltline, which sets the worker's pace, was still years away. One could talk to one's fellow workers and I had many good chats with the men around me.

There was Ed, a former navy boxer in the light heavyweight class, who was supporting a widowed mother. I liked him very much. Ed didn't intend to remain a machinist's helper. He had started to learn the trade in his own way, without becoming an apprentice. "I can't afford to work for fifty cents a day like that boy," he said, as he looked at a lad who was beginning a four-year apprenticeship. Ed was learning what he could as a helper. He would shift to another shop later and learn more. Then he would hire out as a machinist in another town. If he was fired, he would be hired out as a machinist again. "In two years I'll be a damn good mechanic," he said.

This was called "stealing the trade."

My job often took me to the toolroom, where old Tom was in charge. Tom was an atheist and his favorite topic was the contradictions in the Bible. He got them from the pamphlets of Robert Ingersoll, the famous agnostic lecturer.

Sam and Henry, two old timers, talked about the 1901 strike. It was the biggest thing in their lives. "I wish that machinist organizer would come to York again," Henry once said.

I sometimes lunched with John, a skilled iron molder in the

foundry. John was a warm, hospitable man. Our family had dined at his house and I had gone fishing with him. But one day John's work ended suddenly. A traveling crane cable snapped and a chunk of iron crushed his right hand flat.

My father was much distressed. John was an active member of his congregation and a family friend. John's wife and four children would be hungry. Father begged John's employer, as his "brother in Christ" and the chairman of our board of trustees and elders, to help him. And Father was comforted when John remained on the payroll.

What John didn't tell Father, at first, was that his pay was cut in half. He was carrying blueprints back and forth in the shop, on errand boy's wages. He was getting no disability allowance to help him in those days. Nor did he have a union to aid him. The AFL molders' union had been crushed in York several years before. So John fought back as well as he could by bringing a suit for damages against his company.

John's lawyer had a clear case. The company's attorney could not take refuge in old court decisions that absolved employers from responsibility if another employee could be blamed for an injury. This was called "fellow servant's neglect" in the law books. In this case, the testimony showed that *no* employee was to blame. The traveling crane cable was defective, and John won a verdict of $3,000, but his lawyer got almost half of the award.

This cost John his job. He was called into the office and abruptly fired when the verdict came in.

When my father pleaded with our chairman to treat his fellow church member with brotherly kindness, he got this cold reply: "Why didn't he come to me for help, instead of suing? I would have given him a thousand dollars."

John was on the industrial scrap heap for life. No employer would have him. His oldest son quit school at fourteen for a factory job at boy's pay. There was anger among the poor workers in our congregation. And my own bitterness is with me still.

Big factory layoffs began in 1907. A severe depression—they called it a "panic" then—had begun. Our plant's jobs were temporarily saved by orders from a hydroelectric project in North Carolina. But these orders were filled by the next spring. Fatty Firestone and I had little to do except look busy when the boss was around. And I remember well how excited Fatty was one day as he whispered, "Gimme my file!" The superintendent and the big boss, our church chairman, were coming our way. Fatty was feverishly filing at a turbine generator as they passed by. They were pointing out the men to go. Thirty percent of our jobs perished that day.

New orders came at last, and I was put to work smoothing the rough, air-chipped runners of turbines with a file. "Don't let that file get cold," the superintendent would say. I didn't, but I was doomed to ten hours of boredom. And I welcomed men who talked to me as they passed by.

I liked Bob, a young machinist, best. Bob was an enthusiastic Socialist, but I didn't pay much attention to his Socialist talk at first.

We had much in common on other things. He had a fund of good fish stories and made the baseball games he had seen live again. And he knew how to mimic our bosses in a very entertaining way.

Bob always returned to the subject of Socialism, however, in our one-minute chats. When he did, he never envisioned an America "like the Post Office," as Ray's brother Earl did. And I began listening more closely.

This was 1908, a presidential year. The merits and demerits of William Howard Taft, the three-hundred-pound Ohio Republican, and William Jennings Bryan, the Democrat, were bawled into my ears at streetcorner meetings. But Bob could see no candidate except Eugene Debs, the Socialist. "He's one of us. He used to be a railroad fireman, and he went to jail for the working class," Bob said.

This didn't win me at first, however, because of my prejudice against politics and politicians. Then one day Bob asked, "Do you like the ten-hour day?"

Do I like ten hours? What a silly question, I thought. "Well," continued Bob, "the eight-hour day comes after a Socialist is elected. "We'll be working for ourselves then, not for our big boss."

But eight hours, Bob said, will be only a start. Six hours will come next. And someday the workday will be shorter than that.

This won me. I thought of all I could do with those extra hours. Bob had given me no literature, only an idea, but I was a Socialist sympathizer after that.

A POSTSCRIPT: Three months after this, our board of trustees and elders asked Father to resign. The board—made up of small businessmen—was taking orders from the millionaire chairman. Father might have kept the job by taking the case to the congregation, where the members loved him. To my regret, he quit without a fight. His next pastorate was in Dover, Ohio, a steel town.

16 · Black veterans

I worked with Black men for the first time in 1908 on a dam in southeastern Ohio. I had heard about the job in a letter from my aunt Alice, a rural schoolteacher, while I was in the electrical equipment plant. The dam was going up on the Tuscarawas River, a tributary of the Ohio, not far from my grandparents' home. "You will like it," Aunt Alice said. "Mr. Joe Daly, the boss, is a nice man—a very nice man. I met him at a friend's home."

Aunt Alice's "nice man" was thundering damnations from the other side of the river when I reached the dam. Something was wrong with the steam engine of his pile driver, which was driving two parallel rows of piles across the river. The pile driving—an essential preliminary operation—had been interrupted. The boss was venting his frustrations in picturesque profanity. The Tuscarawas at that point was a hundred yards wide, but I heard every word as though he were ten feet away. His cursing came to a climax as he shouted, "Great jumping Jehoshaphat! I feel like a Christ on the cross."

This was one of Joe Daly's favorite expressions. I heard it often in the following months. He varied it sometimes by saying, "It's enough to aggravate a Christ on the cross."

Joe's gang was building a rock dam with a timber framework. It was intended to divert water into an abandoned canal, which the State of Ohio promised to revive. I waited until the boss waded to my side in his hip-length boots. Joe Daly was a big, overweight man, sunburned, blue-eyed and six feet two. He looked me over, nodded and growled, "You're hired—to work like hell."

Next morning at six I was digging into blue gumbo clay by the river. This is heavy, sticky stuff. Bob Edwards, an old Black man, was spading the muck out with me. We were digging the foundation of a retaining wall to save the bank from washing away during spring floods. Bob was over seventy, but his body was muscled like a wrestler's and he swung back and forth with effortless ease. He came to the dam after thirty-five years of toil as a teamster and laborer in a half-dozen states. His home was in Pittsburgh, where he had a wife and three grandchildren. I didn't have Bob's rhythm. I was tired out at the end of the ten-hour day and I barely lasted until Saturday night.

A Sunday rest refreshed me. I spent the day with my grandparents in Gnadenhutten, a village six miles down the river, where they had retired. The next week went better. I studied Bob's rhythm and took his advice. "Let your legs do the work," he said. The next week went still better. And I began enjoying daily swims in the deep water below the dam, after the five-o'clock whistle.

Joe Daly's gang had twelve workers when I arrived, in addition to the white pile-driving engineer and his white fireman, a lad of eighteen. Six of the twelve were white, six Black. The workforce later swelled to eighteen men, but the ratio of white to Black didn't change. I learned why when I heard Joe talking to the Ohio state engineer, who was inspecting the job. "I keep 'em divided evenly so they won't combine against me," the boss said.

Most of the whites came from farms around us. "I'm getting a little hard money for my debts," a young farmer told me. The Blacks' background was very different. They were professional workers from the Deep South, with lots of job knowhow. They were not intimidated by the hell-roaring boss. They stood by each other on the job. And they lived together in an old barn near the dam, where Bob's daughter, Mary, did most of the cooking.

Joe Daly's ideas about sanitation were primitive. Our drinking water was seepage from the river. We pumped it out of a shallow well a few feet from the water. Our restroom was a clump of bushes behind the levee bank. The trouble with the restroom was that Joe didn't like us to use it. I can still hear his bellow when I came out of the bushes the first time. "I ain't payin' you $1.65 a day to ——— on my time," he said.

"Don't mind Joe," Bob said. "His mouth is bigger than his fist."

I boarded with Fred, the carpenter, at first, but this only lasted a week. Fred—a long, lean man of forty or more—was a good craftsman and a conservative Republican Party man. At dinner he always sounded the praises of William Howard Taft, the fat Cincinnati millionaire who was soon to win the presidential election of 1908. I let this go on for several days; then I said, "I like Eugene Debs, the Socialist, better." Fred didn't reply. He just sulked through the rest of the meal.

But politics didn't bring the break. It came when Fred's wife told me she couldn't afford to keep me. I was eating too much. She didn't understand why a nineteen-year old cleans his plate, and then fills it up again—after ten hours of heavy labor.

I was taken in then by Captain Cunning, a white-bearded friend of my father. Mother Cunning was very hospitable. She heaped my plate high while I listened to the captain's Civil War stories. The captain had won his commission by recruiting a company of volunteers. Almost all were farmers' boys. "They were the best men Ohio sent to the front," the captain said.

He had been at Gettysburg, but he talked more about the Battle of the Wilderness, where he lost a quarter of his men. I heard this story several times. It ended like this: "The battle was won by Ohio men." The captain was very positive about this. "Abe Lincoln couldn't have won without the Ohio men. They were the best men he had."

I used to tell the captain's war stories to Bob, at the noontime breaks. We sat together on the high levee bank while Bob enjoyed an after-lunch smoke. The old man listened quietly while I rambled on, and never made any comments—until one day I said, "The captain tells me that Ohio won the war."

This was too much for my Black fellowworker. He took his corncob pipe from his mouth, shook his head and said, "Your old captain

forgot one thing, Arthur. He forgot us Black soldiers." Then he
paused, and said, "We know who won the war."

That's when I learned that Bob was a Civil War veteran. I was
enormously interested. A closed page of history was opening before
me. I had grown up with Civil War stories, but I had never heard that
Black men turned the tide of battle against the slaveowners in the most
critical year of the war. I didn't even know that any Black men had
fought on freedom's side. My history teacher never mentioned them.
My Civil War novels ignored them. And the role of the Black soldiers
was utterly neglected at the flag-waving meetings of the Grand Army
of the Republic, the Civil War veterans' organization, in York.

I wanted to hear much more, but the pile driver's whistle was calling
us back to the ditch. And Bob didn't feel like talking during the noon
break the next day. The ditch was now below water level. We were
working in mud and water. The boots Joe promised hadn't arrived.
"My rheumatiz is givin' me the misery again," Bob said.

By the following week, Bob wasn't working with me anymore. He
was hauling supplies from the railroad in Joe's freight wagon. His
power came from two big gray horses. "I always liked horses, Arthur,"
he said one day when I was helping him unload a couple of tons of
cement. "I was in the Black Cavalry after the war."

The Black Cavalry! Dramatic pictures of flashing sabers went
through my mind, and my questions were spilling out. But Joe was
yelling, "Get a move on, men. We ain't got all day!" I didn't have a
good talk with Bob for another month.

We met again on a gravel bank some distance up the river. We were
loading gravel for the concrete mixer. Gravel is much easier to handle
than gumbo clay. Joe couldn't see us. And I began getting the first
chapters of Bob's life story as he talked of his boyhood while we
lunched on the gravel bank.

My old Black fellowworker grew up on a slave plantation in the
Deep South. His plantation straddled the border of southeastern
Georgia and northern Florida. That was a lonely, swampy land. No
railroad came near it. Deep forests of oak and cypress surrounded it.
And one side was bounded by the biggest lake in Georgia.

"That lake was full of alligators," Bob said. "They was mighty big.
They could eat a man like I'm eatin' this pie. They was snakes, too.
Water mocassins was swimmin' all around. They kill you when they
bite you. And sometimes," added Bob, "Black people was hidin' in
that lake."

Bob's older brother, Tom, was one of the hideaways. The "old master" never caught him. The lake was full of swampy islands where no dogs could track him. And no slave would lead the catchers the right way. "They whipped me many times to find out where Tom was hidin'," said Bob. "I told 'em nothin'."

Bob visited Tom one night. He was living on fish and snapping turtles. Tom told Bob he was going to follow the North Star to freedom. He was gone when Bob went to see him a second time. His family never heard from Tom again.

Bob's father was stolen from Africa when he was a boy by white men with guns, and then was sold in Savannah by the ship's captain. Bob's "Mammy's Mammy," whom he loved, came from Africa, too. She cared for Bob as a baby in a tiny log cabin. It stood in a row with other slave cabins and Bob slept on a straw pile.

When I asked Bob about the slaves' food, he replied, "Corn bread and fatback. That's all the old master give us." But that wasn't all Bob's family ate. "Us boys," said Bob, "set out catfish lines at night. Sometimes we got big ones like this," and Bob spread his arms wide. Sometimes, too, the boys trapped a rabbit. And once in a while they caught a possum. That was dangerous. The overseer tied boys to a post and whipped them for catching possums. All possums, he said, belonged to the big house.

"I was workin' when I was this big," said Bob, holding his hand out less than waist-high. The plantation gong woke him before sunrise, and he worked until dark—hoeing corn, chopping cotton, picking cotton, husking corn and caring for horses. And he was cutting timber and hauling it, when he was big enough to do it.

"You think Joe is a driver," Bob once remarked. "Well Joe ain't nothin' to the overseer on my plantation. I wish you had seen him." Bob described the long leather whip that hung from the overseer's saddle as he rode among the men in the field. "He watched us like a hawk," said Bob. "That whip was across your ass if you stood up to straighten your back."

Bob was talking of his plantation sweetheart one day. "Her name was Rosy. She was the sweetest gal you ever did see."

Bob planned to escape to a free state, and to work and buy Rosy's freedom. His plans were good. After the harvest the Black men cut timber in the cypress swamps. Bob hauled the logs to a river that ran to the Atlantic not far away. At the coast, a small Yankee schooner with Black seamen was waiting. "They was free men," said Bob. "They was goin' to hide me in the ship and carry me to Philadelphia."

But Bob's hopes were blighted. The sheriff always searched the ship from stem to stern before it sailed.

The overseer had his eye on Rosy. She saved herself by hiding in the bushes when he was drunk at night. That's when he attacked slave women. But Rosy was in constant danger. The lecherous brute was also attacking other women. So Bob and his young friends planned to kill him. One of Bob's friends was the son of a slave preacher, who gave this advice: "He's a devil from hell. It's no sin to kill a devil, but you must not do it. The old master will whip some of you to death, even if he doesn't know who did it."

But the boys didn't give up. They hoped to catch the devil alone when he was drunk. They would kill him with his bowie knife and throw his body in a swamp. But the drunken enemy was never alone. The old master always kept a house slave with him when the overseer was drunk.

Bob was giving me a side to the Black slave's character that I had not found in *Uncle Tom's Cabin,* which my mother had read aloud to the family at night. It must be said, of course, that Harriet Beecher Stowe's Uncle Tom was not an "Uncle Tom" in the sense that term signifies today. He refused to inform on two women slaves who were running away. This cost him his life. He died a hero. But he was not a liberation fighter. He didn't hate his oppressors. He prayed for his cruel master, Simon Legree, while he was being beaten to death.

Uncle Tom, however, was a novelist's invention. Bob and his friends were real people. They hated the enemy enough to kill him.

The slaves were better informed about current events than Southern whites realized. And one day, Bob said, big news came from the big house. It came from house slaves who knew everything the white folks were saying or doing. Two cousins of the old master rode to the plantation. They were old men themselves, from Atlanta. They were sitting with the old master on the wide front porch. The brown jug was going around. Voices were rising. The house slaves heard one cousin say that Georgia had broken with the government in Washington. The Yankees had nothing to do with Georgia anymore.

The old master was happy. "We'll get slaves from Africa," he said. They won't cost a thousand dollars no more." And the brown jug went round again.

"This will make life worse for us," the old preacher said.

Then came bigger news. The slave states joined together and formed the Confederate States of America. Their president was one of the South's biggest slaveowners. They were going to fight the Yankees, the old master said.

This was followed by the biggest news. The war began. The old master bragged that the Yankees would be whipped by winter. The overseer got "drunk as a fool," Bob said. He was "firin' his pistol and whoopin' and hollerin'" that he was going to kill Abe Lincoln.

But the old preacher said the "year of Jubilee was coming."

Bob told his tales very slowly. He would often stop and smoke for a while as his youthful memories overwhelmed him. That day the whistle called us back to our shovels before he could go on with the war story. And we had barely started to fill the wagon again when Joe burst into the gravel bank. With him was the Ohio state engineer, a thin-mustached man, who was on a visit of inspection.

"This is dirty gravel, Joe," the engineer said, as he thrust a long hand into my last shovelful. Joe's face flushed with anger. "That's damn good gravel," he retorted. "I know gravel. I've worked with gravel for twenty years."

"And I know dirt," the engineer replied. "It's dirty. It won't make good concrete. We won't pay for any concrete made from this gravel bank."

This hit my boss hard. Joe was a member of the firm that had the state contract. He was speechless with rage for a moment. Then the "goddamns" bellowed out. But he was licked.

Bob and I went back to the dam, where a mountain of dirty gravel stood. That mountain was a monument to days of useless labor. It was piled up near a pit that was about thirty feet long, six feet wide and six feet deep. When the pit was filled with concrete it would become the enduring base of the retaining wall.

But concreting was delayed. The engineer was watching. The concrete mixer would not begin revolving until Joe got clean gravel. Meanwhile the boss was faced with another serious problem. River water was seeping into the pit from underground. Sand and water were rising. I shoved my feet into rubber boots and joined a gang of men who were tossing out the mess with long-handled shovels. Bob was hauling supplies from the railroad again, and his life stories did not resume for another two or three weeks.

Shoveling quicksand was an agonizing job. Half the contents of each shovelful dripped back into the pit as I slung the stuff out. Sometimes another man's drippings went down my back, for many shovelers were packed in together. Meanwhile the mess continued to leak, in spite of the sheath piling along the sides of the pit. The sheath piling was made up of heavy wide boards fitted snugly side by side. The bottom ends were sharpened by the carpenter so they would sink deeper under the blows of a sledgehammer. Sometimes I took my turn with the heavy sledge. This was the hardest work of all for one not used to a sixteen-pound hammer.

Meanwhile I was missing Bob very much. The ten-hour day passed faster when he was by my side. My old Black fellowworker was my best friend on the job. He had taught me how to save my body while doing heavy work. He entertained me with his caustic remarks about our blustering boss. And I was eager to hear his life stories again. So I skipped my usual Sunday rest with my grandparents and visited Bob in his stable instead.

Bob was currying his big grays when I arrived. "I never whip 'em, Arthur," he said. "A horse is good to you if you're good to him." He told a story to illustrate this and was starting another when I interrupted. "Tell me about the war, Bob," I begged. I asked him to begin with what happened on his plantation when the Black people heard that the war was underway.

Bob grinned in delight as his memories came back like a flood. "None of us did much work after the war began," he said. "We was thinkin' of nothin' but freedom, and we was singin' songs at night."

"The white folks in the big house was helpless as babies," Bob continued. "They knew nothin' about work." The overseer and his whip were far away. The old master was too weak to go out in the field and boss the men. His son came back from Atlanta, where he had been living, and tried to take the overseer's place. "He hollered and hollered at us," said Bob. But nothing was done right. Weeds sprang up in the cotton fields and the vegetable garden. Fences were not repaired. Hogs ate the sweet potatoes. The tobacco wasn't cured. And the house slaves said the old master was "hollerin" at the cook that she "didn't know nothin' no more."

Then one day the hated overseer rode into the plantation. He wore a gray Confederate uniform, with a sword at his side. He called the Black people together. He was "drunk as a fool again." He "hollered" that he was a captain in the army and he was going to "whip the ass off" the Yankees.

"The Yankees will be whipped before cornhusking time," the overseer shouted, as he waved his sword again and again. And he growled that the people had better work hard. He would whip the lazy ones after the war.

Months passed. The cotton was finally picked. "Worst crop we ever had," said Bob. The corn was finally husked, leaving many ears on the stalks. The Black men were cutting timber in the swamps by the big lake. This was dangerous work. The big cypress trees, which were several feet thick, stood on enormous roots that rose like curving pillars out of mud and water. In the dark, cavelike space between the roots there was often a nest of deadly water mocassins. Bob worked barefooted in mud and water up to his knees, sometimes up to his hips, while he watched out for gigantic alligators that might drag him away. So he was glad when the old master took him out of the jungle and put him in charge of the plantation's horses.

The horses no longer hauled logs to the river that ran to the Atlantic coast. The South's big timber exports had been stopped by the North's naval blockade. The old master's main buyer now was the Confederate Army, which needed lots of food for its hungry men. And Bob had just returned from a three-day trip to an army camp when a squad of six men in Confederate gray rode into the plantation.

The squad sat on the big porch with the old master. The brown jug was passing from mouth to mouth, and the slaves could hear what the sergeant was saying. He was talking in a loud, bellowing voice, as if he were giving orders to his army platoon. His general had told him to "git five 'boys' from this plantation to drive army mules."

The sergeant added that the general only needed the boys until Spring. "The Yankees can't fight. Abe Lincoln will be whipped by Spring."

Talk and drinking went on. The old master was grumbling, but the slaves heard him say, "I reckon you kin have them boys till spring. They ain't no use to me now. No good cuttin' timber this winter. The damn Yankees is stoppin' the ships."

Bob was one of the Confederate conscripts. His new master was an arrogant young captain, the son of a big cotton planter. His outfit was bound for the North. The rains were coming down. The wagon wheels sunk deep in the red Georgia clay. Bob's mules were tired out. The more the sergeant beat them the less they did.

The mules' hardest time came when a small cannon was loaded on Bob's wagon at a railroad station in central Georgia. The rain was still falling. The wagon barely moved, and suddenly it stopped. The mules were looking at a waterlogged hole in the middle of the road.

The sergeant began beating the mules with the butt of his gun. But the mules wouldn't move. "They knowed what would happen if they stepped into that hole," Bob said.

The captain rode back in a fury. "You're holdin' up the army, Boy," he yelled at Bob. "I told him," said Bob, "we need more mules." He cursed Bob as a Black so-and-so and stuck the point of his sword into the rump of a mule. The mules sprang forward. The front wheels were buried in the mudhole. The captain beat the mules with the flat of his sword, but they wouldn't move. They stuck there until two more mules were hitched to the wagon, as Bob had advised.

"A mule's got a heap more sense than a fool man," said Bob. He had many wise sayings like that.

I was with Bob again the following Sunday. The company was now in the mountains of northern Georgia, where its battles began. "The mountain people hated slavery," said Bob. "They was fightin' on the Yankees' side. The captain called 'em 'bushwhackers.'" He was going to kill every one, he told the company. He captured two men with guns in their hands. "They was a father and son," said Bob. "They was brave men. They talked back to the captain when he cussed 'em and told 'em he was shootin' 'em at sunrise."

But someone untied the captives at night. Bob thought it was one of the white soldiers. The Black muledrivers couldn't do it. "We was chained under our wagons at night since we got into the mountains," said Bob. "And we was happy when we heard the captain cussin' in the mornin' because he had no one to shoot."

The bushwhackers were dead shots, Bob said. Their marksmen sniped at the company from hills overlooking the roads. The captain's foraging parties ran into bullets when they went out for food supplies. The soldiers were hungry and angry, and the captain had to pull back with some badly wounded men.

I don't know how Bob's company reached Virginia, nor did he tell me when it arrived. We were often interrupted that Sunday. Bob's story came out in fragments. But his mule team must have been with the army of General Robert E. Lee for more than a year, because he saw two springs come and go while he was a slave teamster. But Bob told me little about that final period of Confederate servitude, because just one thing filled the rebel slave's mind. "I was goin' to join Lincoln's army," he said. "I was thinkin' of nothin' else."

Bob's thinking was shared by Jack, a slave teamster from Tennessee, who was about Bob's age. They helped each other load their wagons and drove in the same supply trains. "We was like brothers together," said Bob," and we watched for every chance to escape." But a soldier sat on every supply wagon. And a sergeant gave the two friends a grim warning when he saw them talking together. "If you try to run away, we'll kill you," he said.

This wasn't an idle threat. Another Black camp worker, who did chores for the officers, was shot when a sentry caught him behind the lines. "I knowed that man well," said Bob. "He was always talkin' about his family. He had five children."

The freedom fighters' liberation came suddenly, one stormy day.

Bob and Jack were driving back from a distant commissary center. Their mule teams were part of a long supply train. Their wagons were heaped with pig meat, flour, cornmeal, hominy grits, potatoes and other stuff for army rations, as well as a lot of demijohns filled with whiskey for the officers. The road was very rough. Mules and drivers were tired out. Night was falling, and Bob said he was half asleep when a volley of shots rang out. A squadron of Yankee cavalry was attacking. Rebel soldiers were dropping from their horses. Rain began coming down and lightning was flashing. Bob's mules were running away. He saw his chance and rolled off the wagon as if he had been hit.

Bob didn't know how this battle ended. He dove into a woodland alongside the road and ran a long way without stopping. This was a woody, bushy land. Bob lay undercover by day and traveled at night.

"I was mighty hungry when I come to the Yankee army," he told me. "I had had nothin' to eat for three days, except a crayfish and a minnow I caught in a little creek with my hands."

A Black sentry took him to a white officer, who got his story. He slept that night on the floor of a tent, with other Black escapees. He met Jack coming out of another tent the next morning. The two friends had a very happy reunion and they were sworn into the army a few days later.

"That was the best day of my life," Bob said.

Next day Bob was drilling with a Black company. In two weeks he was firing a gun. He could soon hit a tree a stone's throw away. "I was twice as good before my first battle," Bob said. "I was fear'd of nothin' with a gun in my hand."

Bob wished his overseer was in front of him when bayonet practice began. "How I wished that!" he said.

"The officers was white," Bob said, "but we had a Black sergeant. He was one of the best men I every knowed. He hated slavery like I did. His wife and children had been sold away from him. He told us we had to kill or be killed; the slaveowners' side was killin' Black prisoners." He told the men about the murder of hundreds of Black prisoners after a battle on the banks of the Mississippi River. That was the Fort Pillow massacre. It was directed by General Nathan Bedford Forrest, a rich, professional slave trader who later founded the Ku Klux Klan.

Bob's company was part of a small Black division. His general was a bald-headed man, who had confidence in Black volunteers. "We called him 'Old Baldy' when we was talkin' among ourselves," said Bob. And Old Baldy didn't let the Black troops wait long for action.

The campaign against Petersburg, the Confederate stronghold below Richmond, was beginning. The defenses were powerful. Bob had vivid memories of the fortified earthworks. "They was high as three men," he said. "Guns was shootin' us down as we went up."

The air was full of black-powder smoke. Bayonets were ripping through bellies. Gun butts were knocking men down. Bob was rolling down the other side with his arms around a Confederate. When he got up, the enemy was retreating all along the line. "We took many prisoners and artillery pieces," said Bob.

But Bob didn't enjoy the victory. Jack was dead with a bullet in his head. "Best friend I ever had," said Bob. My day with Bob ended on this sad note. And I never got the rest of his Civil War story, though he had fought in more battles in that last climactic year of the war.

My toughest job on the Tuscarawas River dam came when fall was edging into winter. I was wheeling rocks out of the shallow riverbed to pile against the dam. Icy water was leaking into the shoddy boots that Boss Joe gave me. But I had not yet taken my first drink. I could not warm myself from the rotgut whiskey bottle that Joe passed among the men in the water. So I was happy one day when Joe took me out of the water and sent me to the railroad to help Bob load supplies on his freight wagon.

I was doubly happy because I would be with Bob again for a while.

We had not enjoyed a get-together for a month, because my fond grandparents insisted I spend my Sundays with them. Just being with Bob was a pleasure. And I was hoping for more war stories while we were driving back to the dam.

But Bob's mind wasn't on the war when he took the reins in his hand. He began on one of his favorite topics—horses. The grays he was driving were mighty good horses, he said. "But nary one of 'em is good as Buck. Buck was the best horse I ever had. He could go like the wind and he never got tired. I rode that big brown horse five years when I was in the Black Cavalry. That was down in Arkansas. I could guide Buck with my knees when I had a gun or saber in my hand."

Bob said he had joined the Black Cavalry after the war. The army was about to discharge his company when the captain asked if any men could ride a horse. Bob volunteered. They tried him out, he said. He galloped very fast, holding the reins with one hand. A colonel who was watching said, "I'm taking this man for the Black Cavalry."

The colonel asked how he learned to ride so well. "I told him," Bob said, "I learned as a small boy. My old owner used to send me with messages to his brother's plantation many miles away. They was always in a hurry, so I galloped much of the way."

The Black Cavalry regiment was sent to Arkansas to help the Black people, Bob said. "My people wasn't free when the Ku Klux Klan was around. The KKK was killing 'em, whipping 'em, burning down their schoolhouses and stopping 'em from votin'. They wanted to buy and sell my people again." This was new to me. The Ku Klux Klan had passed out long before I was born and didn't revive until just prior to World War I. I didn't know its terroristic history. My high school history book had dismissed the Klan as a bunch of comic nightriders who pranced around in nightshirts. I asked Bob about this, and he smiled. "They didn't do no nightridin' when the Black Cavalry was 'round. They were deathly afraid of the Black Cavalry." And Bob told how the Kluxers ran like rabbits when they saw Black troopers coming.

"They was raidin' a village of Black cotton-farm tenants when we come upon 'em," said Bob. "When the cowards heard us comin', they jumped on their horses and run for their lives. But we had better horses. I was ridin' Buck and caught up with one of the devils. And I was goin' to cut him down with my saber when the white lieutenant stopped me.

"They all should have been killed," Bob continued. "They burned down some cabins. They shot holes in the church door. They stole a lot of cornmeal, and they whipped the Black preacher near to death. He was lyin' in his bed with a bloody back when I saw him. He had led the men in his village to the votin' place in the last election. He was a mighty brave man. I feel very proud of my people when I see men like that."

But the killers didn't all come from the Klan. There were other murder gangs. And Bob began talking about Captain Bill Erwin, who had hundreds of men. Erwin did much of his killing in the rich cotton-growing delta between the Arkansas and Mississippi rivers. He was backed by the big cotton planters.

"We was sent to Osceola against Erwin," said Bob. "That's a big delta town. I saw the ashes of a school he burned down. That's the first school the Black people of Osceola ever had. And I talked to women whose husbands he killed. But he run as fast as he could from the Black Cavalry."

I asked Bob if the Black people joined the struggle. "They sure did," my old friend replied. "Young Black men was fightin' up and down the delta while we was in Osceola. They run Erwin out of the whole delta country with the help of the army." And at last Erwin got out of the state.

Bob was proud of the army's Arkansas record. His regiment was stationed at Black Rock, near the northern Arkansas border, though some of its companies camped at other places from time to time. There were other army outfits in Arkansas as well. Under their protection, the Black people built schools and elected Blacks and democratic whites to office.

The breath of democracy was blowing through Arkansas for the first time since white invaders took the land away from the Native American people.

But one big thing was missing. The Black people didn't get the land that politicians had promised. The soil they tilled was still owned by the former slaveowners. They paid much of their crops back to men who didn't work. "The people was always complainin' about that," said Bob.

Nevertheless, Bob had reason to be proud of what the Black Cavalry men and their military comrades did. "We could have done a lot more if our white officers had let us," said Bob. "We could have run all the Ku Klux Dragons and Kleagles out of the state."

"The Black people was with us," Bob continued. "They took us into their homes. The girls was very friendly. I'd have married my girl if they hadn't taken us out."

The withdrawal of the armed forces from the former slave states was a shameful surrender to the racist planters. All democracy was wiped out when the army left. Black freemen became peons. Black voters were disfranchised. The Black people lost all rights in the courts. And lynch gangs hanged militant Blacks or burned them to death.

Nevertheless, what Bob and his comrades had done was not in vain. The memory of those liberation years was not lost. That memory gives a promise that a bigger liberation is coming. And I'm happy I had the privilege of working with this Black liberation fighter. He broadened my outlook very much.

17 · Slim Jackson

I was back in the water with my other Black and white friends after Bob and I unloaded his wagon. I had gained much respect for most of my fellow workers after toiling by their sides for three months. They had the rugged strength that comes from lives of struggle. And I learned many things about life as they talked about their hardships and pleasures.

I seldom heard any references to religion from my Black fellow workers, although Bob once spoke of God when we were talking about the weather. A cool, wet wind was blowing down the river, and I wished aloud that it would stop. But Bob smiled as he replied, "That Old Man up above knows what kind of weather to send us." He pointed to the sky as he said this.

The Black men used little profanity, though men cursed in anger sometimes. I remember the bitter answer I got from Randolph, a short, powerful Virginian, when I asked how he liked Norfolk, his native town. "God damn that country!," he exploded. "God damn it to hell!"

Randolph told me that he had loaded cargo for years on the Hampton Roads waterfront. The longshoremen had no union. The top bosses were hardboiled contractors for the shipowners, and men were hired under the vicious shape-up system. The hiring boss pointed out the men he wanted for each shift as they circled around him with steel cargo hooks in their belts.

White men got all the best jobs on the docks, Randolph said. "A Black man wasn't hired unless he kicked back much of his pay to the bosses. I owed them plenty Saturday night."

I had never heard about such things before. I had grown up in communities where almost no Black people lived. I was learning bitter truths about U.S. racial discrimination.

"God damn that country!" Randolph said again. "I couldn't get anythin' when I left the docks. Jobs was closed to my people. I got tired of ridin' in back seats all the time and not bein' allowed to vote. I don't want to see that country again."

Randolph was probably the strongest man in our muscular crew. And he was so handy with tools that Joe, the boss, sometimes used him as a carpenter's helper—at laborer's pay. He had a wife and three children in Cleveland. "I miss them," he told me.

I liked to work with Harris, a tall, broad-shouldered Black man who was prying rocks out of the river bed beside me. He was always good-humored. Harris was unmarried. He, too, lived in Cleveland, where he sometimes fought in the ring.

"I get little training," he said. "I need it, but my bouts don't pay enough to buy it." The promoters, he said, usually put a white man against him. "That gets the crowd excited. They yell for blood, but I don't get hurt much. When I fight a better man, I cover up and make him come to me."

Harris came from southern Alabama and walked with a slight limp. "That's from draggin' a ball and chain two years," he said. "I was eighteen when I went on the chain gang. I hit a white boy who called me a 'Black son of a b———.' The white boy was a storekeeper's son. There wasn't any trial. The judge was the brother of the biggest landowner in the county. He wouldn't listen to me, said he'd have give me ten years if I was twenty-one.

"The chain gang was hell," Harris went on. "The guards kicked us and hit us when they felt like it. Once they threatened to kill me. And they cussed us all the time."

My most entertaining companion was "Slim" Jackson, a long, lean Black man in his late thirties, who came from the South Carolina uplands. He had a rich sense of fun, and I wondered how he kept it, because he had led a hard life. He had a good little farm, he once told me. "But," said Slim, "I had no chance." The sheriff's brother wanted to buy the farm at a "give-away price." When Slim wouldn't sell, the county doubled his taxes. Then someone poisoned his dogs, and someone broke his windows and yelled that his house would be burned down.

That's why Slim accepted the "give-away price" and moved his family to Cincinnati, where they had folks.

Slim was a talented mimic, with a witty tongue. His humor was at its best when he imitated the hurry-up cries of our blustering boss. Joe Daly must have sensed that Slim was behind the smiles with which we sometimes greeted his outbursts. For Joe began scowling when he looked at Slim, though Slim was an excellent worker.

The utmost care was needed in our riverbed operation. The rocks had to be loaded on wheelbarrows and wheeled to the dam for unloading. And the wheeling was done over a treacherous roadway. It consisted of a network of heavy, single planks that rested on rocks projecting from the river.

These foundation rocks were of different shapes and sizes. They jutted out of the water at crazy angles. It was impossible to balance planks securely upon them. The slightest deviation by the wheelbarrow meant disaster. My own buggy twice went into the river. But Slim's record was unbroken until one November day when Joe came upon us.

Joe was roaring from the rocks on top of the dam, five feet above us. "Get a move on, men, we ain't got all day." This was one of his usual hurry-up cries.

Joe had picked a wrong time to provoke us. The water had turned colder, and our feet were wet in the worn-out boots Joe gave us. I could sense Slim's anger. But he kept control of himself as his buggy reached a danger spot almost under the dam. The plank was quivering under him and he was slowing down for safety when Joe yelled, "God damn you, Slim! Get the hell out of here if you don't want to work."

We were used to Joe's swearing. But I had never heard him curse anyone to his face before. He knew the men wouldn't take it. I once heard Joe "damn" someone's "ignorant heart to hell" when the object of his wrath couldn't hear him. But face-to-face cursing was another thing—until Joe's hatred of Slim overcame him. And Slim replied like a lightning bolt. Turning his buggy into the river, he leaped on the dam and rushed at Joe. Then followed a sight that delights me still: Joe bounding from rock to rock in headlong flight.

Harris, the boxer, was especially happy. "I'm bettin' on the welterweight, not the heavyweight," he said. Joe was a plump 210- or 220-pounder.

But the battle never took place. Slim's fury turned to laughter as Joe disappeared over the levee bank. Slim's job was ended, but Joe wasn't finished with him. Slim was sitting on the levee bank next morning in a neat blue serge suit when the whistle blew. "Good mornin' Joe," he cried in a clear tenor voice that carried across the river. "I hope you got rested after your run."

Joe pretended not to hear, but I could see that he was boiling inside.

Joe's tormenter had a strategic position. The concrete mixer was churning gravel, sand and concrete together on a platform above the unfinished retaining wall a few yards away. Joe was supervising the job of feeding the mixer. I had been transferred to the concreting gang. This gave me a ringside seat for Slim's show.

Slim's timing was perfect. His stinging blows fell when they hurt most. And I'm giving two samples from his show.

That morning I was wheeling cement to the base of the mixer. Our standard load was three bagfuls, weighing a total of three hundred pounds. But once Joe piled a fourth bag on my buggy, grabbed the handles, ran it to the ramp that led up to the mixer, and panted, "That's the way to work, men." The boss was still puffing while Slim was saying, "I'm worried about you, Joe. I thought you was one white boy who had a chance to beat this big Black man Jack Johnson (who soon became world heavyweight champion). But you're fat as a pig, Joe. Jack Johnson will kill you if you don't get into better condition."

Joe's sunburned face became still redder. But Slim had no mercy. He deflated the boss whenever Joe tried to impress us. When Joe was puffing again, after rushing up the ramp with a hundred-pound bag on each shoulder (the standard load was one bag), Slim said, "I'm sorry for you, Joe. You're in terrible condition. It must be drinkin' that bad whiskey you give us in the water. I want to help you. Let's have a friendly round before you meet Jack Johnson."

Slim's show entertained us workers all day. It played havoc with the boss's work schedule. Next morning a big deputy sheriff was standing beside Joe when the whistle blew. But Slim was on his way.

I left the job in late November for my parents' new home in Dover, an Ohio steel town a few miles up the Tuscarawas River. But I look back on those months on the dam as the most valuable time of my youth—the time when I learned most.

18 · Miners

I owe much to America's miners—both coal diggers and hard-rock miners. They gave me unforgettable lessons in working-class solidarity that bound me to the workers' side in the class struggle. These lessons began at the age of nineteen, when I was a guest at a local union meeting of the United Mine Workers of America. They continued ten years later, when I did my first labor reporting in Alaska during a gold miners' strike for the eight–hour day. After leaving the Arctic, I was inspired by the fighting unity I found among the strikers in the coal mines of West Virginia, Kansas and Pennsylvania.

These lessons were driven still deeper into me by the coalfield struggles I witnessed during five later decades. But my memory is occupied now by that first miners' meeting in Ohio, which introduced me to the world of organized labor.

I had never been inside a union hall before. I was taken in by two miners I met when I was working on the Tuscarawas River dam two miles from my friends' coalpit. Ed and Jim, the two miners, were enthusiastic fishermen. They angled for bigmouth bass in the deep water ten yards below the dam. When they pulled in a big one, they held it up for the dam workers to admire. I remember how we applauded when a fighting four-pounder was hauled in after a hard struggle.

We were wheeling rocks out of the shallow water behind the dam when the big fellow was landed. Our wheelbarrows stopped rolling while the glistening monster was wriggling in the sunshine at the end of a line.

This infuriated Joe Daly, our hell-roaring boss. "Get back to work, men, or get your time," he bellowed. "I can get plenty more men in Ohio, God damn it, if you don't want to work."

Jim, the older miner, was grinning during Joe's outburst. And when Joe went to the other end of the dam Jim gave us this friendly advice: "You need a union, men," he said.

None of us—Blacks or whites—had any union experience. The United Mine Workers was a lonely outpost of organized labor in American basic industry in 1908. But I learned how union miners fought for their fellow workers when I talked to the fishermen after an after-work swim.

"Why aren't you working?" I asked them. "Our mine is shut down. We're on strike," replied Jim. "The foreman fired a man who refused to work in a dangerous place—a hell of a dangerous place, where the slate roof was likely to fall and kill him. We poured out our coffee and walked out. We'll stay out until our brother is back, with pay for the time he has lost."

That strike was won in four days. But Jim and Ed were fishing again in two or three weeks. "The foreman cursed a man," Jim said. The mine was closed for two days until the foreman apologized at an open-air meeting in front of the pit.

My two friends were casting for bass again after the mine foreman assigned a boy to a man's job—at boy's pay. But this experiment in wage-cutting didn't work. Another short strike brought the miners to the river for a fourth time when the company failed to supply enough mine props to keep the slate roof from collapsing.

Jim walked me to the miners' meeting after that last strike. The Tuscarawas Valley local, he proudly said, was one of the founders of the United Mine Workers. Its members met in a long, low hall that they built with union funds in the 1890s. About a hundred and fifty miners were gathered together, out of the two hundred or more men in the pit. There was a jolly, clublike atmosphere as they waited for the call to order. "We're all buddies," said Jim as he introduced me around. "That's right, Jim," said a young man I met. "We're all fighting against death together when we go underground." And he pulled a heavily bearded man of about forty-five towards me and said, "This brother saved my life."

Jim afterwards told me the story. The young man was buried out of sight by a cave-in. The older man rushed in to save him. Slate was falling upon the rescuer as he shoveled at frantic speed. And this brave man was badly battered and bloody before his buddy was pulled out.

I was much impressed by the democracy of the meeting that followed and by the good fellowship. The miners were "brothers" to each other, and the Black recording secretary was given full respect.

The first business was the discussion of a resolution to give the local union's safety committee the right to inspect all workplaces on company time while getting company pay. This was a life-saving provision, which the company was expected to resist. Men worked under the old room-and-pillar system, where death often dropped from overhead. Under this system, men dug out open work "rooms" between pillars of coal left standing to support the roof.

One to two thousand coal miners were killed every year in that period, most of them by rock falls. Mechanization was still in the future. Men had to undercut the coal with pickaxes before blasting. This meant that miners often had to work on their knees or while lying on their sides. It also meant that it was harder for them to get away in time when slate began falling.

This safety resolution was unanimously adopted after warm speeches. "The biggest danger comes from the foreman, who cares nothing for safety," said one speaker.

Another resolution gave the union the right to inspect and test the company scales that weighed the miners' output. Men were paid by their tonnage, and the company was accused of cheating them with crooked scales.

Talk then turned to the presidential elections of 1908. The three rivals were William Howard Taft, the fat millionaire from Cincinnati, on the Republican ticket; William Jennings Bryan, the "silver-tongued" Democrat; and Eugene Victor Debs, the Socialist Party candidate. Taft was elected a month later by Wall Street millions, but no one had a good word for him at the miners' meeting. One speaker reminded us that Taft had condemned Filipino patriots to death when he was governor-general of the Philippines. Other miners jeered at Taft as "Old Injunction Bill." That nickname came from the strike-breaking injunctions that Taft had issued when he was a federal district judge.

Debs and Bryan were favorites at the union meeting. The Socialist Party had much influence in the coalfields at that time, with some

union districts headed by party members. The idea that the people should own all the mines was widely accepted by the nation's coal diggers. And many members of the Tuscarawas Valley local had heard Debs call for the ousting of capitalists from the country's factories, railroads and mines at a big mass meeting in Wheeling, West Virginia not far away.

Debs was regarded as a beloved fellow worker by most of the men at this meeting, although some of Debs's admirers had illusions about Bryan.

One Bryan man put his case this way: "I want Socialism," he said, "and I know it is coming. I'd like to vote for Debs. But I know Debs can't win this November. His time is coming later. But Bryan can win in November. And when Bryan enters the White House we will have a president who believes in government ownership of railroads, and who is against the bankers and strikebreaking injunctions."

Another Bryan man argued that the capitalists would never allow Debs to be sworn in if he won the election. They will use the army against him, he said.

A Debs man replied that when the workers elect Debs they will be strong enough to protect him from his enemies.

There was a lot more talking, but I remember best what Jim said. "Bryan may sound good," said Jim, "but working people must not depend on capitalist politicians. That's why I'm voting for Debs. Debs is a worker. He is one of us. He went to prison for laboring men in a railroad strike. The only good government is a workers' government." When America gets a workers' government, Jim said, a worker will preside in the White House, and miners, railroad workers and steel workers will sit in Congress.

I never forgot what Jim said: "The only good government is a workers' government."

That meeting was a landmark in my young life.

I've often wished that Jim was with me during our last presidential election. I know how he would have voted. Debs, "the beloved fellow worker," who went to jail for his fellow strikers, is gone. But Jim would have loved Gus Hall, the Ohio steel worker, and Angela Davis, the California teacher, who spent years in jail for the working class. In 1980, they were leading the battle for a workers' government.

19 · Steel

I began thinking of becoming a writer when I was working on the Tuscarawas River dam. I was writing many letters—about Bob, the Black Civil War veteran; Slim Jackson, the Black man from South Carolina who chased the boss off the dam; Harris, the Black boxer and other men I was working with. The letters went to my family and friends. But I wanted to tell bigger audiences about my fellow workers. They were fascinating individuals and they were my people. I was more interested in them than in the "great men" others wrote about. And I longed for the time when I could put the life around me into a newspaper or magazine and perhaps into a book.

My desire to become a writer increased when I joined my family in Dover, the steel town, where I finally sold my labor to America's biggest industrial corporation. I found no Black workers there.

Northern factories and mills were closed to Afro-Americans in 1908 and 1909. But I felt the cruelty of monopoly and the helplessness of nonunion labor. And I wanted to put my feelings into print.

My new home was in a smoky steel town of nine thousand people. The smoke smudged every yard of wallpaper in the town. It belched in huge clouds from the blast furnace overlooking our main street. The blast furnace employed several hundred men from eastern and southern Europe. And it was the first place where I looked for a job, though I didn't relish the furnace's 12-hour day and its 84-hour week.

I went there because I knew the timekeeper, who doubled as employment manager. He was an affable young man who belonged to my father's church and was a Sunday School teacher.

"I'd like to help you," he said, "but there's nothing doing. This is dirty and dangerous work. It kills men sometimes. We hire Hunkies and Wops to do it. They work very hard. They got to. This is all they can get."

By "Hunkies" he meant Hungarians, Slovaks, Poles, Serbs, Croatians, Romanians, Russians and Ukrainians. By "Wops" he meant Italians.

I had better luck at the U.S. Steel Corporation plant on the riverbank, where few immigrants were working. This sheet mill, like a giant, dominated the town. It had a thousand men with a billion-dollar company and the Morgan banking monopoly behind it. The mill was filling a big Japanese order when I applied. I went on the labor gang under a department superintendent whom we called "Smiling Sam."

Smiling Sam won his nickname by pushing us with a grin. He came grinning to my buddy Adolph and me one day when we were loading steel sheets on a railroad car. The sheets were only six feet long by three wide. But they were heavier than they seemed. Adolph and I— one at each end—were swinging them on the car when Smiling Sam arrived. "A little faster, boys," he murmured. "A little faster or they'll put Hunkies in your place." The grin spread over his chubby face as he made this threat.

These steel sheets were dangerous. Their edges cut like dirty knives. They cut my canvas gloves to pieces. I wore out two pairs a week. But Adolph was more severely injured. His left hand was cut so nastily that it swelled to twice normal size. The pain was so severe that he slept little for many nights. The company's doctor said, "This is an ugly case of blood poisoning. I may have to amputate."

I was terribly worried. Adolph was a close friend. We liked the same books. I taught him how to play chess, and we often spent evenings together.

My father found a better doctor, and Adolph recovered. But he never went back to the mill. And he never got a cent from U.S. Steel.

Old J.P. Morgan—the banker, king of Wall Street and the founder of U.S. Steel—once said that $10 a week was enough for an American worker. Morgan must have been thinking of what he paid in his mills when he said this. For $10—minus ten cents ($9.90)—was my official pay for a sixty-hour week at sixteen and a half cents an hour. But I actually netted less. When I subtracted the sixteen cents I paid for two pairs of canvas gloves, at eight cents a pair, only $9.74 was left.

Overtime work raised my total pay a little. We had eight hours of compulsory overtime a week without fail. We did it at a time-and-a-quarter rate. This gave me another $1.65.

Overtime work always came in four-hour chunks, but we never knew in advance when it was coming. Smiling Sam would burst upon us at four o'clock—an hour before quitting time—and say, "You're working until nine tonight."

Our dinner buckets were empty by then. "If he had told us yesterday, we'd have brought more sandwiches," angry workers would say.

This left us with two choices—to starve or to eat in the little mill restaurant. We got fifteen minutes of company time for this. The restaurant was a private venture of Smiling Sam's and other superintendents'. I was too hungry to resist. So I spent twenty cents—about a quarter of the evening's earnings—for a bowl of Smiling Sam's soup. This was a high price for soup in 1909.

We had little time for eating during the day, I breakfasted before six, began work at six-thirty and ate nothing until our twenty-five minute lunch.

The men used to have a thirty-minute lunch, until the company took five minutes off the noonbreak. This daily five minutes added up to half an hour a week, which we got back on Saturday, when we quit at four-thirty instead of five.

That steel mill's technology would be considered very backward today. The present automatic rolls that roll out many hundreds of yards of strip steel without stopping did not exist seventy years and more ago. Our little six-foot sheets were rolled by men called "roughers." The roughers worked in teams of two—one on each side of a pair of rolls. The rolls were two heavy steel cyliners, between which the hot metal passed. There was a long line of rolls and roughers in our biggest building. Each rougher was equipped with a pair of long steel tongs with which he passed the sheets back and forth between the rolls.

It was easy to spoil a sheet by rolling it too thin, and roughers were proud of their skill. I often talked to Harry, a gray-haired rougher with a sad but friendly face, while I loaded his finished sheets on a flat hand truck. Harry was a veteran of the Amalgamated Association of Iron, Steel and Tin Workers, a union of skilled men, which would eventually be absorbed by the United Steel Workers during the great union-building campaign of the 1930s.

"The sheet-steel men were the last union men in steel," said Harry proudly. "The Amalgamated survived in Dover nine years after it was busted in Homestead in the long strike of 1892. We lasted until 1901, when J.P. Morgan took over. We stayed on strike then a long while before they starved us back to work.

"When the strike ended we kept the eight-hour day. The skilled sheet workers were the only men in the steel industry to keep it. U.S. Steel was afraid to take it away."

I left U.S. Steel after seeing a fellow worker crippled for life. I was pushing a hand truck when a slingload of steel crashed down near me. A member of the labor gang named Ernie was pinned underneath. He screamed madly for moments, then passed out. One leg was amputated that night. His family, with two little ones, was left without a breadwinner. But not a line appeared in the local newspaper. I ardently wished that I were on its staff to tell this tragic story.

The company was clearly to blame. A defective cable had snapped, and the maimed worker filed suit. But U.S. Steel had a policy of never paying compensation to an injured worker. Its attorney denied any responsibility. He argued that the victim should sue the maintenance men who had failed to correct the defect. The case was still in the courts when I left Dover months later.

I got work in a metal fabricating plant in Dover when my parents insisted I quit the sheet mill. It was a sixty-hour job that paid the same sixteen-and-a-half-cents an hour as the mill, but without any overtime. The main product was a housewife's iron with a patented cast-iron cover to conserve the heat.

I ran a little riveting machine that clamped the cover to the heating iron. This was monotonous work, but I enjoyed the companionship of the men around me.

The fellow worker I liked best was Ted, a jolly chap of twenty-three or twenty-four years. Ted had come home to his parents from the Rocky Mountains, but his heart was still in the big hills. He had worked in the copper and silver mines for several years and said he was soon going back. "There's a sweet girl in Denver I'm going to marry," he said. He showed me one of her loving letters with much pride.

Ted boasted of the "big money" he used to make—all of four dollars a day sometimes. He spoke very warmly of the hard-rock men he worked with, and of their union—the Western Federation of Miners.

"That's a fighting union," he said. You never get anything from the bosses without fighting.

"We had the greatest union leader in the United States," Ted said. "That was Bill Haywood. We called him 'Big Bill'. There's no one like

Big Bill. He can fight with a gun or with his fist, and when he speaks, his voice fills the biggest halls in the West. That's why the copper bosses framed him on a murder charge. But we got him out. I'd go to hell and back for Big Bill."

That was my introduction to William D. Haywood, who was to lead gigantic textile strikes in Lawrence, Massachusetts, and Paterson, New Jersey, to lead the IWW (Industrial Workers of the World) in its biggest battles for years, and to join the Communist Party. I'm very glad I was able to hear him speak and to talk with him several times before he left for Moscow, where he died. Part of his ashes were buried in the Kremlin wall, the remainder in Chicago's Waldheim cemetery.

The superintendent and paymaster of our plant were a pair of thieves. They ran a little real estate business together. We used to hear them talk about it. But the business didn't give them all they wanted, so they stole part of our wages.

Our pay envelopes were short—by twenty-five cents, fifty cents or seventy-five cents—on almost every payday.

This stealing had started before I was hired. Ted and I and other militants always protested until we got our money back. But this petty larceny continued to nick the wages of other men until one payday when the crooks tried to make a bigger haul. On that day none of the hundred or more men got a cent.

"I didn't have time to go to the bank," the arrogant superintendent explained.

"All right, then, we'll strike," shouted Ted. "We'll strike," cried other men who were filling the boss's office. We gave the boss until the next morning to produce the money. Then all the men but five company suckers went out together.

My father, the pastor of the Moravian Church, was surprised. "Isn't the plant working?" he asked. "We're on strike," I replied. Father was puzzled. He knew nothing about labor questions. His background was farmwork. "Why are you striking?" he asked. "Because they didn't pay us," I said.

"They didn't! They can't do that!" Father cried, bringing his big fist down on the table with a bang. "That's robbery! I'm going to give that superintendent a piece of my mind."

But Father's intervention wasn't necessary. The boss sent word next day that the money was ready. He paid for the time we were out. We insisted on that at Ted's advice. The petty larceny stopped after that.

20 · Cub reporter

In May, 1909, a second daily newspaper was opening in Dover, our little Ohio mill town of nine thousand people. I quit my factory job and was hired as the paper's only reporter. This was one of America's smallest dailies. I shared a tiny office with the young editor and his assistant. Only twenty years old, I was green as the grass in spring. I was what was called a "cub" reporter. Ed Rinderknecht, the editor, was very friendly, however. He showed me how to run a typewriter, a machine I had never touched before. It was an early model, with two banks of keys—one for capital letters, the other for lowercase letters. And he gave me instructions while I gasped for breath in a dense cloud of smoke.

The smoke came from the vile Pittsburgh stogies that Norman Haglock, the assistant, was chain-smoking. A pile of "dead soldiers,"

My Shaping-up Years

as cigar butts were called, overflowed the spittoon beside him. Those stogies were long, thin cigars made from the cheapest tobacco leaf.

"I want you to get everyone's name in the paper," Ed told me. "That brings circulation. So listen to everyone. The town's wide-open to you."

It wasn't quite "wide-open," however. I saw roadblocks in the way as Ed's instructions continued. Ed was advertising manager as well as editor. He cautioned me to report nothing the merchants and the brewery owner didn't like. "We can't live without their goodwill," he said.

"Be especially careful when you write about the brewery," Ed went on. "It's our best advertiser. It's owner doesn't like the dry talk that's going around." The issue of prohibition was coming before the county voters in the fall.

I ran into another roadblock when I told Ed I expected to get good stories from my friends in the big U.S. Steel plant in which I had been working. The editor didn't share my enthusiasm. "Better check with management before you write what workers tell you," he said. "The steel mill runs this town."

My young editor didn't tell me how to get everyone's name in the paper. So I worked out my reporter's beat by myself. I found that half a dozen barbershops were havens for gossips, who came to chat with friends. These gossips kept me posted on weddings, funerals, social parties and travelers. With their help I wrote a column of personal items every day. Anyone who visited a neighboring town was likely to find his name in my column.

One such social item proved very distressing to a young pharmacist in Dover's leading drugstore. The column reported that he was "enjoying an entertaining evening with friends" in Massillon, Ohio. I got this from a barbershop gossip, who had failed to tell me that the Massilon "friends" belonged to what is sometimes called the "oldest profession." Others knew this, however. There was much vulgar snickering when the young man's name was mentioned. He threatened me with violence, and I told him to use his fists on the mischievous gossip who had given me the item.

I used to visit the biggest barbershop at 11 A.M., when its best customer was arriving. This was the superintendent of the blast furnace, who came in sweating for his daily shave and hot toweling. I always asked him how the work was going. And one Monday he answered, "All right, except for one poor fellow, an Austrian Hunky.

This poor Hunky lost his arm at the shoulder, when he fell across the railroad tracks as a switch engine was coming in."

That's all I got from the blast furnace boss before the hot towel enveloped his face. So I went to the hospital, where the crippled young man lay unconscious. His face was white as a sheet. Much of his blood had drained away before they brought him in. The blast furnace had no doctor to stop the flow.

I inquired at the workers' boarding houses near the plant and found the victim's brother, who spoke English. "I'm taking John home," he told me. "We may starve in the Carpathian mountains, but we won't be killed." Then he told how his brother had been injured.

"It happened because we were very tired," he said. "That's how John was hurt." John was quitting work with the men on his shift. They had been working twice as long as the regular twelve–hour turn. This was the terrible "long turn" of twenty-four hours. Men worked without rest from seven A.M. Sunday to seven A.M. Monday. Every blast-furnace man worked the long turn every second weekend, when day men shifted to nightwork.

"We were dead on our feet when the seven-o'clock whistle blew," the brother said. "We were crowded together like sheep as we went out along the tracks. Some one bumped into John without knowing what he was doing. John fell over a rail before the engine could stop. It wouldn't have happened if we were not tired out."

The horror I felt must have gotten into the story I laid on Norman Haglock's desk. He began editing it mechanically, chopping out adjectives as his eye went down the first page. Then he put down his pencil and took the stogie from his mouth long enough to say, "The company won't like this, Arthur." He phoned the blast-furnace office for the company version and wrote a short paragraph. It merely said that the man lost his arm when he stumbled and fell on the tracks, and the company was "taking good care of him."

The "care" ended after John left the hospital.

I managed to get the long turn into another story, however. The magistrate's court was on my beat. A blast-furnace worker from eastern Europe had been found sleeping on the grass in front of one of the churches. A slight smell of liquor was on his breath. He told the judge that he had taken one "shot" in a bar to brace himself after finishing the long turn of twenty-four hours. The grass looked inviting on his way back to his boardinghouse. He was very tired and fell asleep as he lay down for a moment's rest.

The pastor of the church interceded for him. The judge was sympathetic and discharged the tired worker. And Norman let the long turn remain in my story, although he edited out the twenty-four hours.

The two editors gave me little direction. After my morning round of the barbershops, the magistrate's court, the hospital, two or three leading doctors, and sometimes the churches, I was usually able to pick my own assignments for the rest of the day. I loved the baseball games most of all. Dover had no professional ball team, but I wrote enthusiastic stories about the sandlot games. The youthful stars enjoyed seeing their home-run hits in headlines for the first time. They invited me to their social parties, where I got many items for my column of personal notes. And my big day came when I met Cy Young, the great big-league pitcher with the record number of games won.

Cy was then with Cleveland, and one Sunday he visited his home-town—Paoli, a small village near Dover. The great man graciously agreed to pitch for the village boys against a Dover team. I stood near

the home base and was thrilled by Cy's accuracy and speed. The ball always hit the exact spot where the young catcher's mitt was waiting. And glorious moments came when I clasped Cy's big hand after Paoli's victory. I asked him how his arm held out so marvelously after twenty years in the big league's pitching boxes.

"That's simple," Cy replied. "I use my head to save my arm. I study the batter and fool him with slow balls when he expects fast ones. I've seen too many pitchers throw their arms away.

This was my first interview with a famous person, and my editor nodded approval the next day.

The biggest meeting I reported was a debate on Christianity. The opposing sides were represented by the Dover Methodist preacher and a Mr. Charlesworth, a professional critic of religious beliefs from Kentucky. He edited a paper called *The Blue Grass Blade*.

The debate was staged in the city opera house by the Buckeye Secular Union. This was a society of unbelievers, who rejected the Bible and rebelled against the active influence of the clergy in public affairs. There were a number of such agnostic groups in the Middle West at that time. They were followers of Robert Ingersoll, the well-known agnostic lecturer and Republican politician.

The Dover unbelievers were not social rebels. They accepted the capitalist system. They were led by a Mr. Toomey, a rich carriage manufacturer in his eighties, who paid nonunion wages. He attacked religion and exploited workers at the same time, as some leaders of the French Revolution had done.

The opera house was packed before the debate began. This surprised me, because the Buckeye Secular Union had a small membership. But I found as I mixed with the crowd that the hall was filled with supporters and foes of the preacher, who was a controversial figure. He was leading a hot campaign for "No" votes against whiskey, wine, beer and barrooms in the county in the coming October elections.

This endeared the preacher to the supporters of prohibition. But it embittered workers, who liked to relax at a bar after a hard ten- to twelve-hour workday.

The preacher opened the debate by praising the Bible as "the word of God" after he offered a prayer to the "God of love."

The Kentucky editor replied that no "Christian government" ever pretended to follow Jesus' plea to "love thy neighbor as thyself." They wouldn't make wars on their neighbors if they loved them, he said. Nor did any "Christian businessmen" love their competitors. They wouldn't drive them into bankruptcy if they did. As for himself, he said, he believed in following a sensible policy of "enlightened selfishness." This brought an approving smile from his sponsor, Mr. Toomey, the nonunion manufacturer, who sat on the platform.

The champion of unbelief then turned to the Bible. Did the preacher really believe that the Garden of Eden had a "talking snake"? he inquired. And what about the story of Noah's ark, which he called a fairytale. Did the preacher think that this tiny boat could carry specimens of all the animals in Africa, Asia, Europe and the Americas during a flood that covered the world? "Elephants are heavy," he said.

This part of the debate was a forerunner of the dramatic battle between Clarence Darrow and William Jennings Bryan at the trial in Dayton, Tennessee, in 1925 of John Thomas Scopes, a young teacher who'd been teaching evolution. But the Dover debate soon sank to a lower level.

Charlesworth, a heavy, blond man with a harsh, bellowing voice, began denouncing all preachers as frauds. They are after "your money," he asserted. Their motto is "No pay, no preach."

This abusive attack brought hisses and catcalls from the preacher's many supporters. And the preacher had a sharp comeback. "I wanted to give the ticket money to charity," he said, "but Mr. Charlesworth refused."

"That is a lie," Charlesworth bellowed back. The rest of the debate made little sense. Argument gave way to name-calling. Neither side won. And when I wrote my story, Norman penciled out almost everything that might possibly offend the churches or Mr. Toomey. Little was left for the printer to set.

When the votes were counted in November, the preacher's side— the dry side—won by a small margin.

Meanwhile my friends in the U.S. Steel plant were feeding me news. But only one story was printed. That was about the installation of a bigger and faster traveling crane. I interviewed the proud general manager after getting the tip from my friends. My editor was happy to quote him. But no story about injured steel workers survived Norman's editing. And I was most disappointed when an interview with an organizer of the Amalgamated Association of Iron, Steel and Tin Workers fell into the stogie–smoker's wastebasket.

I had met the organizer through my friend Harry, a veteran of the 1901 Dover strike, which the company had busted. The organizer gave me exciting news about a strike of several thousand sheet-steel workers in western Pennsylvania, which both Dover papers were ignoring. This was news—real news—in a sheet-steel town. But it wasn't fit to print. "U.S. Steel wouldn't like it," I was told.

My reporter's apprenticeship came to an end in late summer, when our paper folded. It went out of business because advertisers were not willing to support two dailies in a small city. We were bought out by the other daily—a successful enterprise. I remember our last day well. Ed Rinderknecht, my young editor, had just finished cleaning his desk when his eye fell on the spittoon overflowing with stogie butts by Norman's chair. "Better throw that stuff out, Norman, before the new owners take over," he said.

"No, Ed," replied Norman. "The sales agreement said they were buying everything. Let's give them their money's worth."

My months on the paper hadn't been wasted. I learned the ABC's of the reporter's trade. I lost some of my shyness and got used to interviewing all sorts of people. I even learned to stick it out at an autopsy when my stomach felt very sick. Surgeons were extracting bullets from a body found alongside the railroad tracks. In the pockets were a loaded pistol and a bottle of "knockout drops." We never found out who he was or who killed him.

Most important of all, I had been getting a deeper understanding of American society in a steel-mill community, where, as my editor said once, "The mill runs this town."

I was offered a job with the other daily. The editor, a former Cleveland newspaper man, said he would help me to get on the staff of one of the Cleveland papers if I worked with him in Dover for a while. Instead I went back to Moravian College, which I had left two years before because of eye trouble.

21 · College

With the help of a scholarship, I resumed my studies in Bethlehem. Moravian College was then an old-fashioned institution, with about fifty students. Most of them were preparing for the clergy in the Moravian Church. Many came from rural, German-language communities in the Middle West. There were several white Southerners. And all were thinking along conventional capitalist lines.

I was the college rebel—the only student with a radical social outlook. I had little time to try to change anyone's thinking, however. I was stricken with pleural pneumonia in October and lay in the college sickroom until spring because of a medical error.

My doctor was a highly respected Bethlehem physician, but he did not detect the pleurisy that affected my lungs. He lacked an X-ray machine, like almost all doctors of his time. In general his methods of diagnosis were no more advanced than his transportation technique. He disliked the new vehicle—the automobile. "I hate its smell," he told me. He drove out to see me behind a coachman and a team of sleek black horses, the outfit probably costing much more than a car.

He visited me every day, no matter how busy he might be. And I have affectionate memories of this kindly man in spite of his mistake. He sent me no bill, and he helped to keep me alive by his warm, encouraging manner.

I owe much more to my mother, however. She left my father and my younger brother, Jim, in Dover and nursed me tenderly through winter and early spring. I forgot my pain as she sat beside me reading novels and poems to me in her soft, expressive voice. Her favorites included Alfred Tennyson's long narrative poems about the knights of the legendary King Arthur and their sweethearts. And she told me fascinating stories about her childhood and family.

Her heroine was her grandmother, Charlotte Sophia Reinke, my great-grandmother, after whom Mother was named. My great-grandmother was a fighter for women's rights long ahead of her time. She fought for the right to select her own husband, against heavy odds, in the early years of the last century.

Mother was proud of this story, which she got from her father. The scene of the battle was a Moravian girls' school in Bethlehem, which Mother herself attended as a child. My great-grandmother was a pupil there when my great-grandfather's eyes fell upon her.

My great-grandfather, Samuel Reinke, a Moravian preacher, was twice the girl's age. His first wife had died, leaving several children. He needed a helpmate badly. He saw what he wanted in young Charlotte, but he didn't propose to her directly. That wasn't the way things were done in early Bethlehem. He went to her father, Christian Gottlieb Hueffel, a bishop of the Moravian Church.

The bishop, who was to become one of my great-great-grandparents, agreed. Without asking Charlotte Sophia how she felt about it, he ordered her to prepare for wedlock. "But my grandmother had a mind of her own," Mother told me. She was enjoying life with her girl friends. She wasn't marrying Sam Reinke. That was final.

My great-great-grandfather was outraged. Such defiance was unheard of in this tightly controlled religious community. He thundered until his teenage daughter was in tears. But she wasn't in love with Samuel Reinke. She wouldn't marry him, she said.

But the bishop had another weapon to bring surrender. If she continued to disobey him, he said, he would put her name in the church's lottery box. Only one other name, Samuel Reinke's, would go in. The result was a sure thing.

The Moravian Brethren's marriage lottery had been established when the Bethlehem colony was founded in the 1740s by members of the Moravian Church, who came from Europe. Samuel Reinke's grandfather—my great-great-great-grandfather, Abraham Reinke, a Swede—was one of the founders. They set up a society—the Christian Economy—where men and women worked together and shared the product of their toil.

This was a sensible way of settling the wilderness. But the settlers brought backward ideas about women from Europe. Women could not be elected to the governing Council of Elders. And—worst of all—they could not choose their own husbands.

Nor could young men pick their life partners in Bethlehem's early years. Mother reminded me of what Benjamin Franklin said about this in his *Autobiography,* which she read aloud to me in my childhood. When Franklin visited Bethlehem in 1755, he was told what a young bachelor had to do when he wanted a wife. The young man first asked the advice of the male elders. The latter then consulted the older women. The elders of both sexes then selected the bride from among the unmarried young women. And if there was any doubt which of two or three girls was most suitable, they put the names in the marriage lottery box.

What Franklin didn't mention was the theory behind the lottery. The theory was that God himself picked the winner.

In time, men won the right to pick their wives, if the fathers gave their consent. But the marriage lottery was still used occasionally against reluctant brides-to-be, long after the collective work system faded. And Bishop Hueffel was confident of winning when he told Charlotte Sophia that her name was going into the lottery box.

To the bishop's amazement his daughter still said no. She would not accept the lottery's decision, she told her furious father.

This was rebellion against the Church as well as against parental authority. Bishop Hueffel was aghast. He was an important man in the Moravian Brethren's community. He had come to Bethlehem from the Moravian Church's international headquarters in Herrnhut, Saxony to serve as superintendent of its "American Province," as the Brethren's organization in the United States was called.

But my great-great-grandfather had one last weapon—a cruel one.

He had been called back to Saxony to sit on the Brethren's International Council of Elders. A new wife awaited him in Herrnhut. And he returned to his daughter's dormitory room with an ultimatum, which I quote from the words that Mother got from her father.

"If you will not marry this worthy man," he told Charlotte Sophia, "I will take you back to Germany, where you will be subject to a new stepmother."

The prospect was terrifying. The threat of becoming a household drudge—of scrubbing floors, peeling potatoes, washing dishes under the orders of a woman she had not met, and whom she did not love—overwhelmed Charlotte Sophia. She married Samuel Reinke, bore my grandfather, Clement Reinke, and became my mother's heroine.

Mother thinks her grandmother became happy in time. Mother remembers her grandfather, Samuel Reinke, as a loving and artistic old man. He is referred to in the *History of Bethlehem* by Bishop Mortimer Levering, as the "venerable bishop," who painted "some treasured views of Bethlehem."

I became sicker and sicker as the winter wore on. By February, 1910 I had wasted away to skin and bones. But I listened eagerly to news that was coming in about the class struggle in the Bethlehem Steel plant. The first reports came during a visit from Mother's first cousin, Will Bischoff, a plump and self-satisfied steel boss. Will was a complete company man. He had entered the plant at sixteen at a wage of sixty cents a day and had worked upward. He was now an open-hearth superintendent. His hero was Charles M. Schwab, the chief owner of the plant, who had entertained him in his three-million-dollar palace on New York City's Riverside Drive.

Schwab was a smiling trickster and a ruthless boss at the same time. He had acquired the art of union-busting as superintendent of Andrew Carnegie's works at Homestead, Pennsylvania, and as president of the U.S. Steel Corporation before coming to Bethlehem. He boasted to Will about his tactics, and Will admired him immensely.

Will told us that a strike might be coming. "The men are never satisfied," he said. The machinists, he told us, were making most of the trouble. But Will wasn't worried. "Schwab will promise the men anything to get them back," he said. "Then they'll be under his thumb again."

I learned that overtime pay was a very sore point with the men. They used to get time-and-a-half pay for overtime hours, and wanted it back. I heard about this from a classmate, who picked up a machinists' leaflet that he read to Mother and me.

The leaflet said that Schwab had wiped out all overtime rates in 1907 on the pretext that he was losing money during the depression that year. But there was no depression in 1910, as the leaflet pointed out. Schwab's profits were swelling faster than ever before. The huge plant on the Lehigh River was filling big orders from the Argentine Navy for armor plate and heavy artillery. The big naval guns, which gave Bethlehem its reputation, were fashioned with the help of skilled machinists, who were toiling thirteen hours a day—from 7 A.M. to 8 P.M. The machinists followed this tough schedule seven days a week, without getting any overtime rates. And many of the other workers had a twelve-hour day and an eighty-four-hour week.

Free Sundays were almost unknown in this plant of ten thousand men, the leaflet said. "That's wicked!" Mother exclaimed. "The sabbath was made for worship and rest."

The strike began when Schwab fired a committee of machinists who had come to his office with demands. But he quickly shifted his tactics when work on the naval guns stopped. He welcomed a second committee with smiles and cigars, and made the pledges that Will predicted. He assured the machinists that their grievances would be satisfactorily adjusted after they returned to work. But the machinists didn't trust this tricky capitalist anymore. They were joining the International Association of Machinists (IAM), a member of the American Federation of Labor (AFL).

The machinists were no longer alone. The open-hearth men, who turned pig iron into steel, were coming out. Crane men, foundrymen and other skilled and semi-skilled men were leaving the plant. The army of laborers was joining the strike. All were calling for overtime rates, Sunday holidays and other demands, under the leadership of Dave Williams—the militant representative of the IAM—the strike chairman.

In a week the big plant was shut down for the first time since smoke began coming from its stacks in 1855. The 108-day strike that followed made a deep impression on me at a formative time of my life. It was my first contact with a big struggle in steel.

I kept in touch with the struggle through the bedside reports I got from classmates who were getting their first lessons in the class struggle.

Schwab was coming out openly as an enemy of labor. In reply to a strikers' letter, containing their demands, Schwab told the press that "under no circumstances will we deal with men on a strike or a body of men recognizing organized labor."

The workers' answer was mass picketing. The call for mass picketing came from two thousand strikers who packed a meeting hall while many other workers waited outside. And Schwab struck back with brute force when the governor of Pennsylvania sent a company of mounted police to help him.

The troopers belonged to the notorious Pennsylvania Constabulary. This outfit was always on call as a professional strikebreaker. Its men were heavily armed with pistols, rifles and clubs. And one of my classmates, the son of a Minnesota farmer, came to tell me about them.

"I saw them riding into a column of steelworkers," he said. "They began knocking men down with their clubs. I saw one poor fellow lying under a horse. His head was bloody. I think the horse stepped on him. Then the police began shooting and I ran."

Another striker was shot dead a few days later. The killing was just an "accident," a Philadelphia newspaper said. The policeman who fired wasn't trying to hit anyone, the story asserted. The victim's family, however, never collected a cent of damages from the company or the state.

The strikers' lines held together for a long while. Then hunger and terror began to win. The men had no experience in unionism and they got little help from outside. One by one they began drifting back.

One very big trouble was the lack of help from outside. The American Federation of Labor was weak in 1910, but much could have been done if its president, Samuel Gompers, had mobilized support. Gompers made some fairly good statements against the Bethlehem Steel Company. But he organized little practical help. And the bureaucratic leaders of the AFL's craft unions were not much interested in the semi-skilled and unskilled mill workers.

"I think we'd have won with AFL help," a veteran of the strike told me, nine years later. This man was a fellow member of Hope Lodge 79, my machinist local in Seattle, where I worked before the Seattle general strike of 1919. "We could have turned Bethlehem into a union town if Sam Gompers had made an urgent appeal to the AFL unions to help us," my friend said.

I was almost dead when my illness was correctly diagnosed by a hospital surgeon and two operations saved my life. When I returned to college, Bethlehem was still sharply divided over the recent strike. The steelworkers were ground under Schwab's iron heel and were bitter about it. The middle class, in general, was on the company's side. And I was rebuked by a professor when I praised an article in the *Survey* magazine that was on the strikers' side. "That magazine supports trade unionism," the professor hotly replied.

I was making friends among steelworkers meanwhile. A favorite stopping place was a Greek boardinghouse on the Lehigh River near the mill. Here I drank Turkish coffee, gave volunteer English lessons and listened to workers' stories from the plant.

"We're all Socialists," said Homer Guili, a young worker whom I liked best of all. "Have you read Frederick Engels?" he once asked me. I hadn't, but I found a copy of Engels' *Socialism, Utopian and Scientific* in the Bethlehem Public Library and read it through twice before I saw Homer again. That's how my reading of Marxism began.

Inside the sign: WE STRIKE FOR BREAD

22 • *New York reporter*

As my college days were ending, I thought of getting work on a labor paper. The best prospect seemed to be the New York *Call,* a Socialist daily. But before I asked for a job I sent the editors a poem against the Bethlehem Steel Company. It described life in the mills, with its endless hours, as a nightmare, and it predicted a workers' uprising and victory.

The editors rejected my blank verse without comment. I have no copy of my effusion. It may have been poor poetry. But the abrupt turndown discouraged me from seeking a *Call* job. I looked elsewhere. And by September, 1912, I was a reporter for a New York City news agency.

This was the New York City News Association, a cooperative news service owned by the Associated Press and twelve newspapers, which covered events in Manhattan and the Bronx. I did not become a full staff member at once. I started on the "extra list," while the city editor was trying me out. This meant I had to shape up, as longshoremen would say, for an occasional assignment every morning and evening.

It also meant two hungry months. I often said my life was saved by "Hitchcock's Beef and Beans." That was the name of a little basement beanery on upper Park Row, often called "Newspaper Row," near Brooklyn Bridge. There ten cents bought a plate of navy beans and a scrap of beef. I bought two plates of beans when I had the dimes to do it.

My first assignment was to John D. Rockefeller's church, in the East Fifties. The founder of the oil monopoly had installed a new pastor, as a baron might have installed a new priest in his chapel in the Middle Ages. The new pastor was a Dr. Wolfkin. I was to report his first sermon. I knew Rockefeller was the real story, so I kept my eyes on the world's richest man as he ambled into a front pew with his son and heir, John D. Rockefeller, Jr., beside him. And I saw them nodding their approval as Dr. Wolfkin's discourse began.

The oil baron's spiritual adviser was assuring the congregation that his sermons would deal only with "spiritual" things. That was his "mission," he said. He did not intend to talk about "worldly" matters from this Baptist pulpit. They had no place in the house of God, he declared.

This meant that the morals of the oil monopoly were safe from criticism in Rockefeller's home church. This assurance was given at a time when there was lots of such criticism. The U.S. Supreme Court had pretended to dissolve Rockefeller's Standard Oil trust as an illegal organization the year before. And some clergymen had refused to accept Rockefeller gifts on the grounds that the money was "tainted."

I thought I had a good story as I transcribed it on a wax duplicating sheet. But the remarks of the pastor that won Rockefeller's approval did not survive the editor's pencil.

I had better luck with an Election Day story. I was sent to the

polling places on New York's crowded lower East Side to investigate reports that the Democratic Party's Tammany Hall bosses were "stuffing ballots." This was long before modern voting machines came in. I was met by angry poll watchers from the Socialist Party who had been pushed out of balloting halls, where many workers were trying to vote for Eugene V. Debs, the Socialist presidential candidate. One watcher had a black eye, another a bruised cheek, and several were arrested; I got a few paragraphs into the papers on election brutality.

Sometimes I spent the day in the state's Criminal Court Building, as an assistant to the chief City News reporter. This was "Pop" Flannery, a white-haired and popular oldtimer with a flaming red face that came from many whiskeys daily. The big story then was the Rosenthal murder case, which made more headlines than any other killing in the city's history.

Rosenthal, a professional gambler, had been gunned down that summer by four gangsters, near Times Square, when he failed to split his winnings with Police Lieutenant Becker, the head of the anti-gambling "Strong Arm" squad. The gunmen were convicted and electrocuted without much difficulty. But Becker had the corrupt Police Department behind him. And three years and two murder trials followed before he was electrocuted.

My job was to collect the latest news on this sensational case, while Pop Flannery made his morning and afternoon rounds of the four bars on the corners facing the courthouse.

Crime news got a bigger newspaper play than international events, before World War I. Crime reporters were located in every section of the city at night. I gained an intimate knowledge of New York, filling in as a relief man when a City News crime man had his weekly night off. And I was finally given a regular staff job as the night reporter in the Greenwich Village and Chelsea districts on Manhattan's West Side.

My main news spots were the Women's Night Court at Ninth Street and Sixth Avenue, and two police stations—one on Charles Street, in the Village, and the other on West 17th Street, in an Irish community.

I was taken around the district for two nights by my predecessor—Ollie Olcott, an elderly reporter who was retiring. Ollie was a broken-down alcoholic. One drink made him helpless. I was instructed by the assistant night city editor, Tom Meade, to snatch Ollie's glass away before he downed it. Tom, a real humanist, became an active Communist later.

I tramped around the district ten hours a night, six nights a week, from five P.M. to three A.M. We had no union to shorten the shift. The American Newspaper Guild was twenty years away.

I learned much about police ties with the underworld in those nocturnal tours. The upper part of my district was still called the "Tenderloin." The term dated back to the time when it was the center of the nightlife of millionaire playboys. O. Henry got some of his best stories in the Tenderloin. Delmonico's, the exclusive dining house of society's Four Hundred, at the turn of the century was within its borders. The gilt-edged gambling halls and brothels of the financial aristocracy were in the Tenderloin at that time.

Billy Reitmeyer, the New York *World* man, who covered the district for twenty years, had many tales about police payoffs when the Tenderloin was in its prime. The sucker who bought poker chips in the palatial halls of chance was financing the police captain as well as the professional gambler.

And the cop who collected the monthly payoffs from the brothels' madames was probably the best-paid man in his precinct below the rank of captain. After visiting a brothel he walked away with a juicy tip for himself, in addition to a roll of bills for the captain.

The captain's collector was known as the "getter." And the getter of those days, whom Reitmeyer named, was "Con," short for Cornelius, a cop I knew well. Con's big-money days vanished when the nightlife moved further uptown. So he turned to a new career by studying to pass the sergeant's examination.

Rank-and-file cops made many complaints to me about their working conditions. They were constantly harassed by the inspector's "fly cops," who spied on them. They enjoyed only one full day off every month. And they had to spend eight hours on reserve duty in the squad room twice a week, in addition to their daily eight hours on the street.

I spent much time with them in the squad room. They were a much better source of news than the precinct's brass. I was not only gathering press items from them, however; I was also exploring the police mind. In getting their life stories I was learning why they had joined the force and what they thought about organized labor.

In the Charles Street police station, an old Irish detective named Boyle took me far back in New York labor history.

Boyle had been president of the streetcar union in 1886, when the power was furnished by horses. He led his union in the city's first May

Day parade that year, when 30,000 union members marched through the streets for the eight-hour day. He had a clipping from the New York *Sun* of May 2, 1886, that gave this figure. He was very proud of it.

"That was a big labor year," the old detective told me. "We almost elected a labor mayor in '86. Our candidate had the votes but he was counted out by Tammany Hall."

This was an historic campaign. It was the only time in the city's history when the entire trade union movement united behind a labor candidate.

That candidate was Henry George, the author of *Progress and Poverty* and the father of the Single Tax theory. Both the unions and the Socialists were behind George. He accepted labor's program for the shorter workday and other reforms. And he was winning the election. He was well ahead of Hewitt, Tammany's millionaire candidate, Boyle said, until ten o'clock at night, when a flood of Hewitt votes was pulled out of the ballot boxes.

"We couldn't beat Dick Croker's ballot-box stuffers," the old Irishman said. Croker was the Tammany boss. He retired to Ireland with his millions and later built a castle.

The West Seventeenth Street station was a temporary home for the precinct while a new building was rising. It was a converted stable. Horses were still kept in the basement and smells enveloped the lieutenant's desk.

A crude wooden stairway behind the desk ran up to the squad room. Under the stairway, where it met the floor, was the spot where old Eddie Sherwood, one of the lieutenants, kept his bottle. He pulled it out every forty-five minutes—I once timed him—flashed a grin and gave the police toast, "Success to crime!" as the whiskey went down.

Eddie was the only lieutenant in the precinct who wasn't Irish. The New York Police Department was overwhelmingly Irish, but this precinct seemed most Irish of all. The cops on the beat spoke longingly of the green fields of Erin when they stopped for a chat with me. "My family would never have left Ireland if we had had enough to eat," one cop said. And old Sergeant O'Connell put it this way: "My father couldn't make a living in Ireland because he wasn't an English landlord."

The dean of the precinct's Irish was old Joe Ivory, who was usually grinning. He used to tell me stories about the banshees—the Irish evil spirits—and the good "little people," who lived deep down in the Irish earth. I suspect he still believed in them, though he joked when he talked about them.

But old Joe lost his good humor when he talked about police commissioners. He hated them all. "They're all rich society gentlemen, who don't give a damn about us," he said.

The commissioner old Joe most despised was Theodore Roosevelt, who became President of the United States after President McKinley was assassinated in 1901. Roosevelt had been in charge of the city's police in the late 1890s.

Teddy was a fool," said old Joe. "I think he was personally honest, but the crooks were all around him with their hands out for money. They didn't make me a captain because I wouldn't give them six thousand dollars. That's why I'm still a lieutenant."

The man I liked best was John Connolly, an Irishman in his middle thirties. He was the only man in this precinct with a trade-union background. He had joined the Bridge and Structural Iron Workers Union after coming to New York from Ireland. He spent several years bolting steel beams together on the city's rising skyscrapers. Bold men were needed in this dangerous trade; many men fell to their death from the dizzy heights at which they worked. John said, "I was never afraid when I was walking on a narrow piece of steel hundreds of feet above the street."

But the ironworkers' perils weren't only on the job. They also came during physical battles with "snakes." That's what iron workers called scabs and other company agents.

John was placed on an anti-snake committee by the union leaders. The committee was made up of well-muscled young men. They confronted the snakes in the early morning at nonunion construction sites. At first victories were easy. Then the snakes began coming in big groups, with guards to protect them. There were bitter battles, which the union men usually won. But committee members became marked men.

"The snakes tried to kill me three times," said John. "The first attempt was made by a gunman, who fired two shots at me on Eighth Avenue when I was on my way home. I couldn't identify him in the dark," John went on. "But I know it was a snake. I had no other enemies."

Another night two snakes jumped out of a doorway near John's home and attacked him with heavy clubs. John ducked when one of the snakes swung at him, and he missed. "I knocked him down with a stick," said John, "but the other snake knocked me down with his club. And he was about to crush my skull when one of my friends came up. The snake ran away.

"Here's where he hit me," said John, putting his finger on a jagged white scar above his left eye. "I met that snake again when I was a cop. He had become a bouncer in a big Tenderloin bar."

John had a third narrow escape on a skyscraper, when a foreman told him to work on a scaffold. The scaffold was a deathtrap. John was about to step on it when a fellow worker stopped him. Something didn't look right. His friend investigated and found that one end of the scaffold was rigged to drop and send a man headlong to his death as soon as a foot touched it.

The foreman who set this deathtrap vanished before he could be questioned. He had worked for scab contractors before he was hired by John's employer.

This murderous foreman was not the only snake who got into John's crew. John found another of these reptiles on his gang when he was working on a high chimney in Brooklyn. This snake had scabbed in the last ironworkers' strike. But that wasn't all the men had against him. He was a leader in a "snake union." That was John's name for the company union, one of America's first.

This snake was treated as an outcast. "No one ate lunch with him," said John. "None of us worked beside him if we could help it."

And no one came to help the snake when he was hanging by his fingers screaming. He had slipped. He wasn't a good ironworker. He had missed his footing on a slippery steel beam and caught hold of the edge of the chimney as he was plunging downward.

He couldn't pull himself up. He was paralyzed with fright. He was dangling over death, waiting for him 300 feet below.

"It was a terrible sight," said John. "He was screaming like a madman. I couldn't help feeling sorry for him, though he was a damned snake. But I didn't try to help him. I was afraid of the rest of the men. And one of the men leaned over him and shouted in his face, "Die, you damned snake! Die, and to hell with you!"

And the snake surely would have died, said John, if the foreman hadn't heard his cries and put out a hand to save him.

John joined the cops during a depression, after he was out of work for months. He was worried about his family, and the Democratic district leader got him on the force. "But I'm still a union man at heart," he told me. And he said that he made a financial contribution to the defense of the secretary-treasurer of the Bridge and Structural Iron Workers and his brother "in that bombing trial in Los Angeles two years ago."

John was referring to the trial of the McNamara brothers, which had stirred the labor movement in 1911. They were convicted of bombing the Los Angeles *Times,* an anti-union paper, on evidence supplied by the Burns Brothers detective agency. Some printers died in the blast. J. J. McNamara, the union leader, was sentenced to fifteen years' imprisonment. His brother, J.B. McNamara, received a life term.

John's union sympathies were about to be tested. The test came in the first big strike in his precinct since he had joined the police force. This was also the first strike I reported in New York. The strike began in early January, 1913, when thousands of "white-goods" or underwear workers walked out of their sweatshops in Chelsea and other New York districts.

The strike was called by the International Ladies Garment Workers Union, which was more militant then than today. The workers— many fifteen- and sixteen-year-old girls—responded eagerly.

John was very enthusiastic as we watched long picket columns marching in front of the loft buildings that housed the sweatshops. We talked to dozens of pickets. They told John and me that the bosses promised "good jobs" to girls if they would spend their nights with them. There were no good jobs, however. Few girls got more than a dollar a day. They were thin and hungry-looking. They were demanding 20 percent wage increases, a fifty-four-hour week instead of sixty hours, union recognition and other needed things.

"There's going to be trouble," predicted John as we drank coffee together at the end of his eight-hour tour. A man from the bosses' association had visited the station house that night. He came out smiling after an hour with the captain. The captain will do what he's paid for, said John.

The trouble came the next day. Goons were attacking the pickets when I arrived in Chelsea. They were slapping them and cuffing them and handing them to cops, who pushed them into the patrol wagon while the sergeant stood by.

I recognized one of these brutes from his picture as he slapped a tiny girl picket and thrust her into the arms of a cop. He was a 220-pound heavyweight—Tom Kennedy. He had been hailed in the sports columns as the "Great White Hope," who would beat Jack Johnson, the Black heavyweight champion. But Tom Kennedy had been whipped a week earlier by Al Palzer, another aspiring Great White Hope. So Kennedy was reduced to selling his muscle to the bosses for pork-and-beans money.

I got a story about him into one of the sports pages the next day. It was headlined something like this: "White Hope Fighting Girls Half His Size." Kennedy sent word through a cop that he was "going to get" me. But he didn't show up on the picket line again.

Meanwhile John, the former ironworker, was making no arrests. "What the hell's the matter, John?" the sergeant was growling. But John wouldn't lay his hands on a single picket. Instead he pulled some goons away from their victims when the sergeant wasn't looking. "To hell with the sergeant," he told me. "I won't help the goddamn snakes."

One couldn't help loving the brave girl pickets. They came back to the struggle after the union paid the magistrate's fines. They sang about their coming victory as they tramped the Chelsea streets.

I was phoning strike stories to the Socialist *Call*. And the stories were getting bigger. The white-goods sweatshops had become a national scandal. There was talk of a congressional investigation. Prominent women were joining the picket lines. I saw policemen pushing Fola La Follette, the daughter of Senator Robert La Follette of Wisconsin, into a patrol wagon. Leonora Boyd O'Reilly, the beloved Irish-American leader, was grabbed a few minutes later. I got good interviews with both of them in the West Seventeenth Street station.

But best of all were the girl pickets. "I'd rather be dead than be a scab," a little Italian-American girl told me. And the little Jewish girl beside her said, "This is bad as czarist Russia, but I'm staying out until we win." She was limping from an injury to her hip she had received when she was thrown into a patrol wagon some days before.

John was still passing the test a week after the strike began. But he was feeling the pressure. The sergeant was not merely growling. He was threatening. "He told me I was looking for trouble," said John. "But to hell with him! I want these girls to win."

The pressure next came from the captain himself. A lieutenant told John that the captain said, "Connolly's days on the force are numbered if he doesn't act like a cop." Reports came that the captain was desperate. The size of his payoff depended on the success of his strikebreaking, it was said. But strikebreaking was failing. And John was finally called in by the captain himself.

John told me about the meeting that night. "You got four nice children, John," the captain said. "You want to take care of them. That's why I'm giving you another chance to be a real cop. It's your last chance, John."

I could see John was worried. "You can always be an ironworker again," I told him. "That's right," he replied, "I've got a withdrawal card from the Structural Iron Workers; I can rejoin anytime. And I can hold my own with any ironworker again." Then he began worrying. His former employer had quit the business. What would his wife say when a job was hard to find? And at that time the ironworkers had no pension system like the cops'.

"But to hell with it," added John. "I won't help the snakes." In spite of those brave words I was worried. The union man and the cop were fighting for his soul inside the blue uniform. And I feared the cop was winning.

The cop did defeat the union man in that internal struggle, after the captain called John in again. And a sullen John Connolly was taking frail teenagers from the goons and pushing them into the patrol wagon when I arrived in Chelsea at five o'clock. He didn't look at me, and I turned away sore at heart. I felt as bad as if a good friend had died.

Meanwhile mass picketing was winning in spite of the goons and the cops. In the middle of February the bosses' association finally caved in after all their hopes of getting scabs came to nothing. The strikers held big open-air celebrations after their six-week battle. They had won a fifty-two hour week, wage increases and a preferential union shop—giving preference to unionists in hiring.

And this victory, in the first mass struggle I had seen, increased my confidence in the power of the working class.

I often passed John, but I didn't speak. Other cops told me this hurt John, but I couldn't forgive him. And then one night he came weeping to me.

I was walking under the Sixth Avenue elevated line at three a.m., on my way home, when a uniformed policeman staggered out of an overnight bar. He was very drunk. I recognized John Connolly as he slumped against an elevated pillar beside me. He was crying like a baby. "Shields," he moaned, "you know what I am. I'm just a goddamned snake." The tears were running down his face.

23 · Women of the streets

I saw many tragedies as a crime reporter. I'm thinking, as I write, of the misery in the Irish slums in Hell's Kitchen on Manhattan's West Side. I remember the old grandmother in a patched dress who was weeping as she knelt on a bare floor in her apartment, before the images of three saints. There was nothing else in that naked railroad flat; it had been stripped clean by the sheriffs, who had dumped her possessions on the street when she couldn't pay her rent. Her husband was dead. There was no one to help her.

The agony of a young navy sailor is also imbedded in my mind. He was crying in delirium for his mother as he writhed on the pavement under the Sixth Avenue El with a bullet in his bowels. He was shot in a fight with a pimp, who had butted in when he was talking to a girl of the streets. The pimp had a richer customer for her, the cops said.

But the saddest place in my district was the Women's Night Court. That three-story brick building on Sixth Avenue and Ninth Street was a den of broken lives. There young women—who were captives not only of the pimps but of the Vice Squad detectives—were sent to prison on charges of selling sex.

Some writers called them "white slaves." New York was overwhelmingly white seventy years ago.

I learned how these women's lives were broken when I was covering the Night Court in 1912 and 1913. The city was a deadly place for unemployed women who had no families to help them. There was no welfare or relief system. Pimps were always lying in wait for hungry women. And I never found, in the judges who sent them to prison, a particle of sympathy for the pimps' captives.

When I entered the court for the first time, the magistrate, a sleek man in his forties, was scowling at a woman of twenty years. She had been brought in by a Vice Squad detective, a rosy-cheeked young man in a flashy suit, who had picked her up on Seventh Avenue. The pimp's lawyer made no defense and the defendant said nothing. "What's the use?" her expression seemed to say.

After sentencing her to three months in prison, the judge looked at the press row and smiled. He smiled again when he noticed a new reporter. And he invited me to his chambers during the next recess.

His Honor began by assuring me that he was a very good friend of the press. Then he gave me some paternal advice. "You're very young," he said. "I want to help you. You don't look like a New Yorker. But you can make good in this city if you keep away from whiskey and these women."

The judge spoke with contempt of all women of the streets. "None are any good," he said. "Some writers say they were driven into this life by poverty. That isn't so. They are simply depraved creatures."

I couldn't accept this inhuman judgment. And I wondered during a later court session if his Honor was listening to what a young defendant said after he told her to "be a good girl when you come out of prison in six months."

"How can I be good on what the dime store pays me," she replied as the matron was leading her away.

I wanted that dramatic dialogue emblazoned in every newspaper. Behind it was the tragedy of starvation wages that drove girls into sex slavery. My editors didn't use it but they gave a good play to a visit by President Woodrow Wilson's two daughters, who came to the Night

Court to study the sexual side of the city's underworld. The White House ladies sat on each side of the magistraie and looked down on their unfortunate sisters below.

I soon noticed that pimps were seldom arrested. Vice Squad men cracked down on the slaves rather than the slave masters. Nor did I ever hear a magistrate denounce filthy pimps as "depraved creatures."

I also noticed that almost all the defendants were women of the streets. They came from the very bottom of the sexual underworld. Women from apartment-house brothels were seldom brought to court. One reason was they were not in the public eye like the women of the streets. There wasn't the same outcry against them. But a more important reason was the brothel prices were higher than prices on the street. This meant bigger payoffs to the police.

Tiny offices across the street from the Night Court housed the pimps' lawyers, who stood at the foot of the legal profession. I never heard a pimp's lawyer talk about human rights. I never, indeed, heard one make any argument in open court. They relied on plea bargaining for lower sentences instead. And they had cozy relations with Vice Squad men.

One of the pimp's advocates often started chats with me, which I tried to end quickly. He was a tiny man with graying hair who liked to talk of his early days, when he had a "nice clean job." He had sold hail insurance to Iowa farmers. "No better people in the world," he would say.

This attorney for procurers was defensive, however, about his present job. "Everyone has to make a living," he once said, looking at me in a pleading way. Another time he stopped me as I was leaving the courthouse. His voice was thick with whiskey. I had trouble understanding him. But I finally got this: "You boys don't like me. I know that. But I'll tell you one thing. Vice Squad men are worse than pimps. They get the big money. Just look at their diamond stickpins."

Vice Squad men were utterly callous about their captives. "I'll go back to Times Square and grab another one," a young detective said to Billy Bolger, the *Sun* reporter, and me, after his prisoner had been sent away. "I always work on Times Square," he added.

"The women must know you now," remarked Bolger.

"Oh, no," the plainclothesman replied. "There's always a new crop."

"What happens to the old crop?" asked Bolger.

"They're in some cemetery. They don't last long in this business."

Vice Squad men testified in set phrases that ended like this: "She solicited me. I gave her three dollars and arrested her."

I was skeptical about this testimony. So I questioned a squad man about it. He was a tall, rawboned fellow who posed as a longshoreman and netted his captives along the West Side docks. I picked him because he was the least sophisticated man on the squad.

"I said I did the soliciting," he told me, "the first time I testified. The judge gave me hell and dismissed the woman. I didn't make that mistake again."

The official guardians of virtue made other mistakes, however. Progressive papers and magazines reported that a number of "respectable women" had been arrested as prostitutes.

I met this cop again when I returned from the West in 1919. His assignment had changed. He had become a police stoolpigeon. I was attending a dockworkers' meeting in the Red Hook waterfront section of Brooklyn. In the back row I spotted this former Vice Squad detective. I passed the word to the IWW leaders who had called the meeting. And everyone was asked to look carefully at the spy as he was taken out.

Another Vice Squad man named Jones put his takings into Brooklyn real estate. I discovered this in 1924, when my wife, Esther, and I were living in a four-story house on Columbia Heights overlooking the harbor. The rental agent said the house was owned by a Mr. Jones. The name meant nothing to me until I went to the basement to use the pay-in-the-slot telephone. At the instrument was the former Night Court detective I had known a dozen years before. He was talking about a second house he had acquired.

We moved out as soon as possible.

The smell of those Vice Squad men stays with me still. These sex wolves who grafted on the unfortunate women of the streets were despised by most cops. "They have the dirtiest jobs on the force," an old sergeant from the Chelsea district told me. "I get angry when I'm ordered to help them."

I'm proud I knew one man who rebelled against this filthy assignment. That was John Flanagan, the famous hammer-thrower, whose memory I cherish.

John Flanagan belonged to a group of Irish athletes who were called "the Pride of the Force." All were Olympic gold medalists. Among them was Pat ("Babe") McDonald, the gigantic shot-putter, who took the big iron ball in his hand and tossed it farther than any other man could. Another was Matt McGrath, who succeeded Flanagan as hammer-throwing champion. The other two were Martin Sheridan, the world's greatest discus-thrower, and Mel Sheppard, who led the world's runners in the 800-meter and 1500-meter races. Mel was called a "human greyhound" by sports writers.

These gold medalists were relieved of police duties while in their athletic prime. John Flanagan, for instance, never made an arrest. Their pictures were taken with mayors and police commissioners. They marched in the vanguard in police parades. They were the darlings of the sports pages. And they were given all the time they needed to keep in condition and to prepare for athletic contests.

John Flanagan was the most famous of all. He won the Olympic championship three times in succession. He triumphed in Paris in 1900. He got a second gold medal in St. Louis in 1904, and a third in London in 1908, when he broke all his old records.

I met John Flanagan from time to time through his younger cousin, Jimmie (Seamus) Hayes, a good friend of mine. Jimmie was a teamster with a progressive outlook. We swam and hiked together. And he took me sometimes to Celtic Park in Brooklyn, an Irish sports center, where John and other members of the Irish-American Athletic Club did their training.

John helped to organize the Irish club after he left the New York Athletic Club. He left it, he told me, because it was dominated by "rich swells," who patronized the Irish athletes.

John was proud of his athletic skills, which he had acquired by years of hard work. He had developed a new hammer-throwing technique, and Jimmie persuaded him to tell me about it. The hammer is a 16-pound iron ball at the end of a chain. Before John's time the hammer-throwers used to whirl the ball around twice before letting go. But John began whirling it three times. This sent the sphere further on its flight. Other athletes soon adopted the Flanagan technique.

John also told me why he had joined the force. He had no steady income as an amateur athlete. He could not give paid exhibitions and keep his amateur standing. The part-time jobs he took sometimes were not paying the family's bills. And he was about to take a full-time job, which would limit his training, when a high police official came to see him.

The department needed John as an "ornament to the Force", the visitor said. "Your time will be your own," he assured John.

John liked to live over again the London Olympics, the biggest one until then, as we drank coffee in a restaurant near the park. There he had broken the world hammer-throwing record. King Edward VII and his queen were in the reviewing stand as Flanagan and other sons of Erin went by. And John proudly told me, "I raised the green Irish flag of the Irish-American Athletic Club as we paraded in front of the English king."

John and his fellow gold medalists were heaped with honors after their ship docked in New York. President Theodore Roosevelt entertained the Olympic winners—mostly members of the Irish American Athletic Club—at his home in Oyster Bay, Long Island. A big dinner followed at the Waldorf-Astoria Hotel. And John laughed as he lifted his hand and said, "I almost wore it out signing autographs in the next month." His hand was twice as big as mine.

John held the championship longer than any hammer-thrower before or since. He was very proud of that. But the years began taking their toll. Matt McGrath, a younger man, threw the iron ball a bit farther than John at the Stockholm Olympics in 1912. John continued his training, however. And he was educating a number of Irish youngsters in his art when I visited him at Celtic Park for the last time.

In the meantime a new police commissioner had been appointed. He was a stuffy swell who wasn't interested in any sport but golf. "These athletes will have to earn their money as cops," the commissioner was heard to say. And soon the blows fell.

Babe McDonald was transferred to traffic duty, where he towered over the crowds on Times Square. Mel Sheppard and Matt McGrath were put on patrolmen's beats. Martin Sheridan became a detective on routine crime assignments. None were given time for training, and Sheridan's waistline was bulging when I saw him a year later.

Flanagan's turn came at last.

"I got a call from John late one night last week," said Jimmie Hayes. "I was home in bed. I was much surprised. It was after midnight, and John keeps regular hours."

Jimmie was still more surprised when his cousin asked him to come to an Irish bar in Manhattan's West Thirties. John had never been a drinking man, but he was sitting in a back room with a whiskey bottle in front of him.

"Sit down, Seamus," he said. "You're the cousin I love best. You know John Flanagan, Seamus. They built a statue to him in Ireland. But what is John Flanagan doing now, Seamus? He's chasing who-ores on Seventh Avenue. That's what they will say, Seamus."

John hadn't chased anyone. He had refused to make any arrests when assigned to the Vice Squad. His young cousin reminded him of that. "But that's what they will say," replied John. "He's chasing who-ores on Seventh Avenue." He laid his face on the table and cried like a baby.

This went on for two hours, while the whiskey went down. "And what is John Flanagan doing now," he kept repeating. "He's chasing who-ores on Seventh Avenue."

At last the bottle was empty. John was drunk, but steady on his feet, as he led the way to the Hell's Kitchen station house on West 39th Street, to which he was officially attached.

The lieutenant on the desk—an old Irishman—gave John a warm greeting. "Come behind the desk, John, and rest while I get some black coffee," he said.

"No thank you," replied John. "I came to say good—by." And without another word John unpinned his police shield and laid it on the desk.

Jimmie then took John home and stayed with him until he was in bed. Then he went back to the police station to tell the lieutenant that John would write his formal resignation the next day.

"He'll be all right in the morning," the lieutenant said. "He did this because he was drunk."

"No," replied Jimmie, "he got drunk to do it."

John went back to Ireland a few weeks later. He acquired a little farm and worked it until he died. He was too clean a man to stay on the cops. But—as Jimmie said to me—John wasn't really a cop.

24 · *Faking the news*

As a reporter, I learned early not to believe all I read in the papers. Many years later I would frequently see reality turned upside down in the capitalist press stories about the socialist countries, when I worked there as a correspondent for the *Daily World*.

The fiction sometimes is done by an editor so that an honest reporter's facts are suppressed. I recall, for example, a story I once wrote for a paper in Oakland, California. It told how an unemployed woman had put her head in a gas oven until she died. The gas oven was left out of my story on the printed page. She merely died suddenly, the story said. "We couldn't use what you wrote," the head of the copy desk explained. "The gas company raises too much hell."

It's also true that less honest reporters are not always the only authors of the fictions they pass on to their readers. I remember how a certain New York *Herald Tribune* man got his anti-labor fables during the Little Steel strike of 1937. He got them on the golf links, where he played with the steel bosses every morning.

I also saw much faking in my early days as a crime and accident reporter in New York. The best stories were true stories. The facts I uncovered were more dramatic than the imaginings of others. But facts required digging. And some reporters found it easier to blend fiction with fact.

This was called "piping a story." That is, piping gas into the facts.

This "piping" went on daily while I was covering the upper West Side of Manhattan for my news agency. My district included Broadway from 42nd to 110th Sts. I worked independently, while seven other reporters, representing seven morning papers, worked in a group together.

The group's leader was Mike, an old *Herald* man with a domineering manner and a rich imagination. Mike seldom went out on a story. When another reporter brought one in, he gave the facts to Mike before calling his own paper. Mike then phoned a piped-up story to the *Herald,* while the man who had given him the facts listened with a notebook and pencil in his hand. The facts became raw material, and Mike's imagination did the rest. Thus the story of the arrest of a burglar suspect might end with a violent struggle between the prisoner and a cop, which was pure fiction.

Mike became the crime editor of *The New York Times* after the *Herald* folded.

Mike could depend on only two members of his crew for steady work. One of the take-it-easy men was Eddie, the *Tribune* reporter. Eddie spent much time in nightclubs and rathskellers, where drinks were on the house. His office often couldn't reach him. Eddie got word that he was to be fired. He had as rich an imagination as Mike's and he put it to work on a big current story to save his job.

A deputy street-cleaning commissioner, Rofrano, had vanished while awaiting trial on manslaughter charges. Rofrano was a well-known politician and the newspapers were featuring the mystery. Police were hunting him, and Eddie joined the hunt.

Eddie's hunting ground was the Broad Channel–Jamaica Bay area on the city's outskirts. He told his city editor that Rofrano had been seen there and he was given time to investigate. Eddie had picked this area because his father, a retired policeman, lived there, and friends would back up his story.

His friends included bar owners and other small business men—all of them Eddie's drinking companions. They were glad to be quoted by the *Tribune.* Yes, they had seen Rofrano. One witness saw him walking along the water's edge of Jamaica Bay in the direction of an abandoned fisherman's shack.

Eddie slogged through mud to the shack and "found" remnants of fresh food. Then he entered the *Tribune*'s newsroom in muddy trousers with a pocket full of notes. A rewrite man typed out a two-column scoop. The city editor was pleased. Eddie's job was saved.

The story was a masterpiece of pipe-dreaming. Eddie confessed this to me later. He was too proud of his success to keep the secret.

In Harlem, where I worked during the last quarter of 1913 and the first half of 1914, the piping was done by Billy, a 29-year-old reporter who was in charge of the *Herald*'s two-man bureau. I shared offices with Billy and often heard him phoning his tales to a rewrite man.

I was covering the West Side, from 110th Street to the northern tip of the island. This district was all white and mainly middle class at that time. A colleague from my agency had the working-class East Side of this area. This included the Black people in Harlem's Lenox Avenue district and tens of thousands of Italian immigrant families who lived in crowded tenement houses on the East Harlem streets.

Police treated the Black people cruelly and my colleague told me about atrocities he had witnessed. One summer evening several Black youths were talking and laughing peacefully together in front of a drugstore at 130th Street and Lenox Avenue. A white plainclothesman came upon them, a folded newspaper in his hand. Inside was a blackjack. In moments, two youths were clubbed to the ground.

"Why did you do this?" asked the reporter.

"To make them afraid of the police," the detective replied. "That's how we keep order in Harlem."

Billy didn't tell many fables about Blacks, however. The *Herald* was so racist that it kept almost all Black stories—good or bad—from its columns. Billy concentrated his lies against Italians instead. And East Harlem was presented to *Herald* readers as a breeding place for gangsters.

Billy was personally an affable chap. That can be said for him. He also went to Mass and confession regularly at his home church in Freeport, Long Island. So he informed me. But Billy let nothing interfere with his ambitions as a sensational reporter. Nor was he restrained by the fact that many victims of his fabrications observed the rites of the church as well as he did.

Billy's faking followed a definite plan. Each street in East Harlem was inhabited by thousands of people, who lived in tenement houses on the long blocks that led to the East River. Of course there were crimes from time to time, among so many people. But every shooting became a gang shooting in Billy's stories.

Thus, a shooting on 104th Street would be described as the work of "the 104th Street gang," though Billy had no evidence of this. A shooting on 108th Street had been done by 108th Street mobsters . . . and so on.

Billy wrote wildly exaggerated accounts of each incident for a local paper, *The Harlem Home News,* which carried local store advertisements and was distributed free from door to door. The clippings of these stories were then filed and indexed under *name, address* and *crime.*

These terribly inflated *Home News* stories then became raw material for big *Herald* features. And from time to time Billy gathered a group of these inflated "gang" stories together and inflated them still further for a major expose in the *Herald* of a "Harlem crime wave".

The piping wasn't over, however, when Billy phoned his Harlem crime-wave story to a *Herald* rewrite man. Billy's fictions then became raw material for another piper to work on. The rewrite man, Dick, was given all the space he needed, and he had the imagination to fill it. Dick was paid at space rates, so Billy's stores were a windfall for him.

I've often thought since of the damage that men like Billy and Dick were doing. There were others like them in Boston, Chicago, Philadelphia and other cities. They and their newspapers were fostering the prejudices that made it possible to send innocent men like Nicola Sacco and Bartolomeo Vanzettii to their death on false murder charges.

25 • Paterson

The first revolutionary orator I heard was Eugene V. Debs, the great Socialist leader. The drums of the class struggle were sounding as he appealed for help for striking West Virginia coal miners. They were in the midst of a historic life and death struggle with company gunmen on Paint and Cabin creeks. Many were killed, on both sides, before the miners won.

Debs was at the height of his fame in 1913. He had won nearly a million votes, in addition to those that were not counted, in his campaign for the U.S. presidency in November 1912. That was before women had the suffrage. And he carried the audience with him. He seemed to be talking to me personally as he leaned over the edge of the platform with his eyes on the faces before him. Debs needed no microphone. His musical voice filled the theater where he was speaking as he talked of his West Virginia comrades.

Many miners were in the Socialist Party at that time.

"John D. Rockefeller has one billion dollars," said Debs, "but not one comrade. I would not trade one of my comrades for all of his blood-stained dollars."

That was a favorite remark of Debs's. I heard him use it again later.

Debs's speech almost led me into the Socialist Party. Unfortunately I did not meet the revolutionary left wing of the party. The spirit of Debs was sadly missing at the next Socialist meeting I attended. The speaker, Morris Hillquit, a wealthy lawyer, didn't talk about workers. He spoke of the party's influence in professional circles instead.

Meanwhile the drums of the class struggle were sounding from Paterson, New Jersey, nearby. A mass strike of oppressed silk workers had begun. It was led by the "Wobblies," as members of the IWW were called. They had led a victorious strike of twenty-five thousand woolen workers in Lawrence, Massachusetts, the year before. And William D. Haywood, the IWW leader, was coming to New York to speak about the struggle.

Bill Haywood was one of my heroes. He came from the Rocky Mountains, where he had led big strikes against the copper- and silver-mining bosses. He had become almost a legendary figure. He was said to have battled company thugs himself with fist and gun. He had been framed by Pinkerton detectives on false murder charges. But he had won his freedom in a national defense campaign in which Debs had played a big part.

Haywood was better known as Big Bill. And everything about him was big when he took the platform in the *Jewish Forward* hall on New York's lower East Side. The bigness wasn't just in height and breadth of shoulders, nor in his voice that rolled like a big bass drum. I felt as I looked and listened that I was in the presence of workers' power. I saw it before me as he spoke with the utmost conviction of the strength of workers who are banded together.

Big Bill spoke proudly about the courage of the silk strikers. "A hundred policemen are clubbing and arresting our pickets," he said. "They club sixteen-year-old girls and old men. But they can't drive them back to work.

"The newspapers accuse us of violence," Haywood continued. "But our only violence is the violence of folded arms. Twenty-five thousand workers have withdrawn their labor power from the silk mills and dye houses. And all the king's horses and all the king's men can't put those looms to work again without meeting our demands."

This adaptation of Mother Goose's *Humpty Dumpty* lines brought loud applause.

Big Bill liked to put ideas into rhyme. And the hall rang with applause again when he spoke of the coming eight-hour day with its

> *"eight hours of work, eight hours of play,*
> *eight hours of sleep and EIGHT DOLLARS A DAY."*

The last words crashed like thunder. Eight dollars was twice the pay of a highly skilled worker at that time.

Big Bill was a compelling speaker. His words still sound in my ears as he spoke of workers' power. "Our weapon is solidarity," he said. "We unite all the silk workers into one big industrial union, regardless of their different skills. That gives workers power like this—" As he said this he held up his right hand with fingers outspread, then brought the fingers together in a mighty fist.

"There's no power like the power of workers when they're united," Big Bill said. "That power will change the world. It will put the capitalists in overalls and bring happiness to all working people."

Big Bill closed with those lines. I joined a long file of workers who shook Haywood's big hand after the meeting. There were many Socialist workers among them. Big Bill was a member of the Socialist Party's executive committee in 1913, but he was expelled from the committee later that year, after a campaign by the party's middle-class right-wingers. Haywood never rejected all political action, as did many IWW leaders. And he joined the Communist Party soon after it was born.

The speaker I loved most was Elizabeth Gurley Flynn, one of the Paterson strike leaders, whom I heard the next Sunday. I did not hear her in Paterson, however. No big strike meetings were allowed in the silk city by Police Chief Bimson, who served as boss muscleman for the silk manufacturers. The streets were deserted when I arrived. "Everyone's in Haledon," I was told.

Haledon, a neighboring town, had a Socialist mayor, who welcomed silk strikers. I had trouble squeezing through the men and women who filled several acres of city land. Fifteen to twenty-thousand strikers and sympathizers were applauding a beautiful young woman, whose passionate voice reached everyone in the crowd.

She spoke from a high platform heaped with gorgeous flowers. But violets and roses paled before this twenty-one-year-old beauty. And I fell in love with Elizabeth Gurley Flynn at first sight.

I wasn't her only captive. No other woman speaker except Mother Jones won so many hearts as Elizabeth Gurley Flynn. She won them in struggles against big exploiters, not in quiet lecture halls. She inspired tens of thousands of workers in battle in the logging camps of the Pacific Northwest, in the hard-rock mining towns of the Rocky Mountains, in the great woolen strike in Lawrence, and on many other stormy fronts.

I couldn't hear everything that Elizabeth Gurley Flynn said. As men and women applauded, there was a babel of voices around me in many languages. But her appeals for solidarity against the common enemy—the silk bosses—came through like bugle calls. And there was a dramatic scene when Elizabeth called an Italian girl she knew to the platform. This was a pale, thin teenager of sixteen or seventeen years.

Elizabeth embraced her and then said, "The silk bosses are killing Angelica. They are working her to death. They put her on four looms instead of two. She's working twice as hard as before."

The speaker was interrupted by a tumult of voices. "They did that to me," a woman beside me was shouting. The strike began as a revolt against the new four-loom system. When quiet came, Elizabeth said, "But that isn't all the silk bosses did to Angelica. They didn't give her enough to eat." Angelica, she said, was the only support of a sick mother and her younger brothers and sisters. Her father was dead. Her family was hungry. The family seldom ate meat. "She's also striking," Elizabeth said, "for a raise to give her family enough to eat."

I don't remember what Angelica was paid. But I recall Elizabeth telling us that some girls were getting only $1.85 a week.

The silk bosses are robbers, Elizabeth continued. The cars they are driving, the diamonds their wives are wearing, the rich food their families are eating, their winter vacations in Florida's sunshine—all come from the labors of Angelica and twenty-five thousand other silk workers. "And when you win the raises you are fighting for," she said, "you'll get back only a little of what you produced. But these raises are just a beginning. The time is coming when you will run these plants for yourselves."

Elizabeth Gurley Flynn's confidence in the revolutionary future led her into the Communist Party later. She was the Party's beloved chairman when she died, fifty-one years after the silk strike.

The silk strike drew me to Paterson on my free days, but I'm not giving the strike history here. That is splendidly done in Elizabeth's autobiography, *Rebel Girl*. I'm only presenting some pages from a visitor's notebook. I must add that these visits had nothing to do with my job as a New York crime reporter. But I served as a voluntary correspondent, sometimes, for the *Call,* the New York Socialist daily, though I wasn't a party member. I was attracted to the IWW instead.

I visited strike headquarters on my next trip. It was in an old building near the mills. A two-horse truckload of food was unloading as I arrived. It came from New York sympathizers.

I arrived at noon, as picket lines were changing. An organizer was telling pickets how to avoid arrest. "The jails are full enough now," he said. "Don't go too near the mills, where the cops are waiting. Catch the scabs some distance away."

"There aren't enough scabs to produce anything," the organizer told me. "But the battle could go against us if more scabs got in."

The organizer, Ewald Koettgen, was a silk weaver, about forty years old. He was a tall, gaunt man with deep lines in his face. I was told that he never rested. He was out with the pickets at six in the morning and not home again until late at night. But he relaxed for several minutes as we talked together.

"You asked where the silk workers came from," he said. "There are at least twenty nationalities in the plants. But the majority are German, Italian and Jewish. My people are German."

When I asked why I saw no Black workers, he replied, "That's not the fault of the IWW. It's the fault of the silk bosses. They won't hire Black men and women. The IWW welcomes Black workers. We have many Black members on the Philadelphia docks."

Ewold Koettgen was happiest when talking about the IWW. "The strikers are united in one big industrial union for the first time," he said. "That's the secret of our solidarity." His eyes filled with pride as he said this. "The American Federation of Labor never got anywhere in Paterson," he continued. "It failed because it kept the silk workers divided. It split skilled workers into different unions according to their different skills and left unskilled workers out in the cold."

"What will your industrial unions do after the revolution?" I inquired.

"They will manage the country's industries for the benefit of all the people," he replied.

Most IWW theoreticians expected capitalism to collapse in a

general strike, but Ewald Koettgen didn't discuss the organization's revolutionary tactics during our short conversation. Nor did he refer to the IWW's rejection of the need for a revolutionary party. I did not notice that, however. I was so enthused by the IWW's fighting spirit that such questions didn't enter my young head.

I told the organizer that I was thinking of joining the IWW, but he didn't encourage me after I described my job as a crime reporter. "This is a movement of industrial workers," he said. "If you get a job in a plant, we'll take you in. Meanwhile, we welcome you as a friend."

This delayed my membership for six years.

Our talk was interrupted by a lawyer—a Socialist volunteer from New York—who came for bail money. More than a hundred men and women strikers were in the city prison. "It's a hellhole," the lawyer was saying. The men were sleeping on the floor of the "bull pen," the big room. Several men had been savagely clubbed before they were brought in. One man's scalp was still bleeding, the lawyer said. "And," he added bitterly, "he's getting no medical care."

The bleeding man was one of the few freed that day. The rest remained in the hellhole until more bail money came from friends outside.

This is the same prison where John Reed, the future author of *Ten Days That Shook the World,* the story of the Russian revolution, was confined. His dramatic report of the Paterson strike in *The Masses* started his career as a revolutionary journalist and historian.

I saw Chief Bimson's clubbers at work on my next visit to Paterson. I had become very friendly with Harry, a young German dyehouse worker, whom I had met through Ewald Koettgen. I was visiting Harry's home in late afternoon of a hot spring day. We were sitting on the front steps, as were other people in this tenement-house block. Across the street was a long silk mill, whose grimy brick front looked like a prison wall. A handful of scabs began coming out as the mill whistle blew. The people on the steps were muttering their hatred of scabs.

At that moment a column of police appeared on the street. "Disperse those pickets," a sergeant was shouting. My friend's mother screamed as a cop grabbed Harry by the shirt collar. Another cop was jerking me to my feet when I flashed my press card in his face. It was signed by the New York police commisioner. "I've got your numbers and will write you both up if you make any trouble," I yelled.

The two cops were confused and let us go, but an old woman was knocked off the steps of a neighboring house by another blue-jacketed thug. Several men were clubbed. Ten or more men and women were arrested. And I rushed to a telephone to catch the *Call*'s early edition.

"That was a typical police attack," said Ewald Koettgen when we told him about it.

More than a thousand strikers were arrested during the long struggle. And Patrick Quinlan, an IWW organizer, spent three and a half years in a New Jersey penitentiary on false charges of "inciting to riot"—at a strike meeting where he hadn't spoken.

All the strike leaders were arrested on various charges—Haywood several times. Elizabeth Flynn and Carlo Tresca (a popular speaker in the Italian language) were indicted on fake inciting-to-riot charges. But both were saved from Quinlan's fate when trial juries disagreed.

I'm sorry I couldn't attend Elizabeth's second trial in 1915. It was a farce to remember. The prosecutor's "evidence" came from a string of Paterson cops, who testified one after the other. Some of these blue-coated witnesses were almost illiterate. Yet all had memorized the same piece. All repeated exactly the same words which they said Elizabeth had used in a speech to strikers two and a half years earlier. This was a memory miracle. The jury, however, didn't believe in this miracle, and a "not guilty" verdict was returned in several minutes.

Terror wasn't what defeated the silk strikers; they were starved—literally starved—back to work after five months of heroic struggle. The American labor movement was still too weak and divided to give its embattled brothers and sisters sufficient support, while the silk bosses were being helped by the bankers.

This defeat was a sad lesson to me. I had been so impressed by the strikers' magnificent solidarity that I thought they were invincible. But Ewald Koettgen, whom I met as the strike was ending, told me not to be discouraged. This was only one battle. "More battles are coming. The class struggle will go on until final victory," he said.

Ewald Koettgen himself went on fighting. I met him again in Paterson in another silk strike eleven years later. His hair was graying and the lines in his face were deeper, but he was still confident of the workers' future.

26 · Culture

My father, Thomas Shields, died in Port Washington, Ohio, a rural village on the Tuscarawas River, as I was entering my twenty-sixth year. He was an affectionate parent, and he had given his four sons happy childhoods, with the help of my mother. He enjoyed playing games with us. He was a good chess player, and I remember my mother begging him to work on his sermon when we were playing together on a Saturday. "I will, Lottie, when we finish this game," he would reply. But the temptation for another game was often too strong to resist.

Father had little formal education. Rural schools were open only three months a year in his native North Carolina community. His background in a poor farmer's home did not give him an understanding of trade unions. He never opposed them, however. He respected people who worked with their hands. He liked to be with them. They liked him. And tears were shed at his funeral by poor farmers and railroad workers.

Father was buried in the Moravian cemetery in Gnadenhutten, a few miles up the Tuscarawas. His grave lies near the tall, white monument to ninety Native Americans of the Delaware Tribe who were massacred by a mob of white racists in 1782.

Mother was left with a tiny pension. My youngest brother, Jim, then quit school to work sixty hours a week on a bridge that was going up over the Tuscarawas. His job consisted of wheeling gravel up a ramp and dumping it into a concrete mixer. This was tough work for a sixteen-year-old boy, but Jim stuck to it for months, until Mother moved to Bethlehem, Pennsylvania, where she had relatives and friends. There Jim got a scholarship at Moravian College and spent his summers in the Bethlehem Steel Company plant, where he worked eighty-four hours a week.

Mother took in lodgers for several years, then moved into a church home for aged women. This was called the "Widows House." It had been built of enormous stones in the middle of the eighteenth century by the Moravian Brethren.

I was working in a barren cultural atmosphere meanwhile as a New York crime reporter. Among the hundreds of policemen I talked to, only three ever mentioned a book. One—Lt. O'Connor—spoke enthusiastically about a book on police rules that he had written. Another lieutenant once referred to O. Henry. "He knew his crooks," this police official said. That was his only literary comment. The third cop, a very Irish patrolman named Devlin, was in a higher cultural class. He knew many Irish songs and ballads by heart. And he had the utmost admiration for Jonathan Swift. He knew all the characters in *Gulliver's Travels* as well as if they lived in his home. He loved Swift's greatest satire, the *Modest Proposal,* with its advice to Irish landlords to fatten, cook and eat their tenants' babies instead of letting them starve to death. Devlin wasn't a real cop. He finally quit the force to follow the carpenter's trade.

Nor did the crime reporters I worked with often open a book. Many came from poor families, but they lacked a rounded working-class background. Many of them had started their journalistic careers as office errand boys. They had contempt for a college education and they despised the United States' first School of Journalism, which was established at Columbia University by Joseph Pulitzer, owner of the New York *World.*

I once attended a lecture at the Columbia School of Journalism as the guest of a girl student. The lecture was given by Arthur Brisbane, the chief editor of the Hearst papers. Brisbane warned the students not to overestimate the intelligence of their readers. "If you want the lady in the big house to read what you write, you must write for her washerwoman," he said.

Brisbane also advised us to use few adjectives. "When you report a wedding, don't say the bride is beautiful. Describe her beauty instead."

One must always give the reader a picture, Brisbane declared.

This was good advice. But Brisbane had nothing to give me except technique. His daily columns in the Hearst press were collections of capitalist banalities. A critic once called them "Brisbanalities." This talented man had sold his soul to William Randolph Hearst and he became a millionaire several times over. His father, Albert Brisbane, a leading follower of Fourier, the French utopian Socialist, would not, I think, have been proud of his son.

I was learning much from the theater. George Bernard Shaw was a Broadway favorite in the century's teen years. I remember seeing seven Shaw productions in one season. I especially enjoyed *The Doctor's Dilemma, Man and Superman, Arms and the Man, Androcles and the Lion* and *Pygmalion,* in which Mrs. Patrick Campbell had the stellar role.

Shakespeare also appeared on Broadway more frequently than today. I had the pleasure of seeing *Hamlet, Macbeth, Julius Caesar, The Merry Wives of Windsor, Henry VIII* and other dramas by the greatest playwright, for seventy-five cents or less.

Sometimes tickets cost only fifty cents. These low prices seem a fabulous bargain today. They seated me in the top galleries that rose four stories above the orchestra floor.

I was introduced to Ibsen's plays by a neighbor, soon after coming to New York. My neighbor, Andrew Myhr, was a pharmacist in the Red Hook waterfront section of Brooklyn. Andrew, a native of Oslo, had a rich Norwegian culture. He liked to read aloud and I would listen for hours while he declaimed the lines of *Ghosts, Rosmersholm, An Enemy of the People* and other Ibsen dramas. I was much influenced by the courage of Dr. Stockman in *An Enemy of The People.* He was not afraid to stand alone against deceit and corruption. But, looking back, I can see the doctor's mistake. He should have enrolled others in his struggle against the polluted baths. I have learned since that social victories are not won without allies.

My favorite poets were Keats, Shelley, Byron and "Bobby" Burns. I remember many lines of Shelley's "Ode to the West Wind." I can also reproduce some of Keats' sonnets exactly. I succumbed for a while to the magic melody of Swinburne. But I finally got the smell of death in Swinburne and dropped him after finding Walt Whitman.

Whitman is the joyous poet of life—of the life that bubbled in the veins of the men and women of his country who worked with their hands. His people were my people. I thought of the Black men I worked with on the Tuscarawas River dam when I read Walt's description of the Black teamster who drove the dray from the stoneyard. Walt's ferrymen, his farmers, his woodcutters were people I knew. His Civil War poems brought back Bob Edwards, Captain Cunning and other veterans I lived with or worked with. I was enchanted by the vividness of the pictures Walt painted in *Leaves of Grass* and by the musical though irregular rhythm of his lines. And I lived with Walt's poetry daily a long time after I found him.

I did not find Walt until I began reading *The Masses,* a brilliant left literary anti-war magazine, which John Reed helped to edit. The good gray poet had been almost forgotten for a generation. I never heard his name as a child. He was not mentioned in my high school's *History of Literature.* No copy of *Leaves of Grass* was in the public library in York, Pennsylvania. Nor were there any references to my country's greatest poet in the magazines that came to my home.

Many critics have attributed the boycotting of Whitman to Walt's frankness about sex at a time when sex was seldom written about. But I think the main reason for the boycott was Walt's abounding faith in democracy and in the people. Whitman proclaimed his confidence in the common man when our country was being taken over by the titans of big business. They not only despised the people, they feared them as well.

I was also much influenced by revolutionary novelists, including Maxim Gorky and Upton Sinclair. And a proud evening came when I was sent to interview Sinclair, who was temporarily lodging in my territory.

This was a few days after the Ludlow Massacre of April 20, 1914, when Rockefeller gunmen killed eleven tiny children, several women and a dozen or more striking coal miners at Ludlow, Colorado. The author of *The Jungle* was leading a funeral march in the daylight hours in front of the 26 Broadway office of John D. Rockefeller, Sr., the aged billionaire, and his son, John D. Jr.

I sat with the famous Socialist novelist for an hour while he discussed the Ludlow crime. I do not have a copy of my notes, but I remember that he told me that he was not denouncing the Rock-efellers merely because they were guilty individuals. He was demon-strating against them as the leading representatives of the murderous capitalist system, which put dollars before human lives.

Unfortunately little that I reported was published.

Sinclair was very cordial. He took my address and sent me copies of some of his books, including *Manassas,* an exciting Civil War novel.

I was glad when I was taken off the crime beat. But I wasn't happy in my new assignment. I was sent back to the Criminal Court Building, where I had worked once before. My chief news sources between trials were the prosecutors, who got their jobs through politicians. They were a heartless lot. They showed no mercy to poor defendants, but dealt softly with rich men. And I finally met a portly old man who was known as "The Fixer." The Fixer handled the bribes that passed from some defense lawyers to cops and prosecutors.

My fellow reporters were cynics, who shut their eyes to corruption. "We can't stop it, so why not let sleeping dogs lie?" an old timer explained.

These reporters were kind to fellow workers, however. I was nominally the assistant to Pop Flannery, the news agency's bibulous court reporter. But I did all of Pop's work and sent in my stories in Pop's name. And my fellow workers helped me, because they didn't want Pop to be fired.

I was soon transferred to the news agency's office as a rewrite man. There I worked with men who had wider cultural interests. Some were frustrated writers. One desk man was working on a play for the left-wing Provincetown Theatre, where later Eugene O'Neill developed. Another desk man, Porter Crane, a former sailor on sailing ships, wrote excellent verses. A general assignment man, Howard Seitz, had written a novel that was published. He was disliked by Hardenberg, the general manager, because he urged his fellow workers to build a newspaper workers' union. Old Jim Corrigan, the agency's chief reporter in the Federal Building, was applying for a patent on a miniature, one-man submarine, which he named the *Brian Boru,* after an ancient Irish king.

Two men warmly encouraged my interest in working-class strug-gles. One was O'Connell, a middle-aged Irishman with a distinguished reportorial record. He was the first newspaperman to get interviews with the survivors of the *Titanic,* after the "unsinkable" giant liner, struck an iceberg and went down. The other was Tom Meade, the assistant night editor, who eventually joined the Communist Party.

Tom Meade, O'Connell and I worked together like a team during a long streetcar strike in 1916. Tom assigned O'Connell to cover the strike, while I took his bulletins by telephone and wrote the news stories.

The strikers, who had no union until then, were rebelling under the leadership of the Amalgamated Association of Street and Electric Railway Employees. Their grievances were low wages, unjust firings and the split-shift system. The split shift idled many men during the slow midday period and kept them from home for fourteen to fifteen hours daily.

This was a bitter struggle. I spent much time with pickets when off duty. O'Connell was usually with me. His County Mayo accent helped us with the strikers, who were overwhelmingly Irish. We were accepted as friends. And one night I saw a scab pulled off a car on the Third Avenue line and hurled headlong on the pavement.

The scab had been recruited by the Bergoff strikebreaking agency, a murderous outfit. An attempt was made to recruit me, too. I was visiting a Bronx carbarn one day when a Bergoff boss—a tall, hard-faced fellow—grabbed my arm. "I got a good job for you, son," he said.

"What are you paying?" I inquired.

"Six dollars a day—and all you can make," he added with a wink. The "all you can make" would be the passengers' fares.

I gave this item on the scabs' bonus to the socialist *Call,* while O'Connell got it into the commercial press through our agency.

The strikers won on some lines, but lost recognition later. New York's transit workers did not build a strong, enduring organization until the CIO Transport Workers arose in the 1930s.

Big strikes, some very bloody, were going on in many communities in the century's teen years. I followed them through the Socialist and IWW press. In Minnesota, thirty thousand iron miners walked out of the pits of the giant U.S. Steel Corporation under the IWW banner in 1916. They resisted company gunmen and starvation for many weeks, but were finally forced back to work. Elizabeth Gurley Flynn, whom I had admired in the big IWW silk strike in Paterson in 1913, was one of the leaders.

In Bayonne, New Jersey, thousands of oil-refinery workers struck in 1915 against sickening working conditions and wages that barely kept their families alive. Almost all were immigrant workers from eastern and southern Europe. They were fighting back against the Rockefellers' Standard Oil Company and against Tidewater Oil, in which the Getty family was interested.

I wanted to rush to Bayonne, which was not far away. I was stirred by press reports and by the brilliant and blistering drawings of John D. Rockefeller, Sr., in the *Call.* They came from the brush of Robert Minor, America's greatest cartoonist, whom I was to know well after he became a Communist leader. I could not get away from New York for many days, however. I was kept back by compulsory overtime.

By the time I finally reached Bayonne, several strikers had been murdered. They had been shot down by Bergoff gunmen from behind a wooden stockade made of heavy beams several inches thick.

Strikes in basic industries were treated like insurrections by the authorities in those days.

The strikers' attempts to build a union were shattered. They were forced back into semi-slavery again. I had no time to make an investigation of the butchery. But certain facts were clear. This was a case of killing for maximum profits, like the killings at Ludlow. The high profits came from the sale of immense quantities of oil to warring Europe, from the expanding US. automobile industry and from low, nonunion wages

27 · At sea

In August 1916 I got a leave of absence from my job as a news agency rewrite man and shipped out for England on a small British cargo vessel.

I was lured to the sea by scores of ship stories, including Joseph Conrad's maritime novels. I also wanted to visit the country whose literature I had grown up with. And I was anxious to learn what British workers thought of the war that was bathing Europe in blood.

My ship, the *Bovic,* was tied to a White Star line dock on Manhattan's West Side. The *Bovic* was a 4,000-ton coal burner. She used to carry cattle. She was now hauling grain and British army supplies to Salford, a port city on the Manchester ship canal. I signed on as an ordinary seaman at £4 a month, and was berthed in the crowded fo'c'sle with a crew of Englishmen, Scots, Irishmen, Norwegians and one Australian. I was the only American and was called "Yank."

I got my first lesson in seamanship while still in New York Harbor.

The German Kaiser's submarines, the deadly U-boats, were sinking one British ship out of every four or five in Atlantic waters in 1916. We were testing the launching of the lifeboats that might save us if a torpedo struck. We did this by swinging the boats out over the water as they hung from the davits. I hauled at the lines with other sailors while the bosun's mate, a white-whiskered sailor, sang a chanty.

The chanties were sailors' work songs. They were sung on British sailing ships while men hauled at the rigging together. The songs began disappearing as steamships came in. But our white-whiskered bosun's mate had spent most of his long life on wind-powered ships And when we grabbed the lines he began singing:

> *As I was going down Paradise Street,*
> *Blow, blow, blow the man down,*
> *A sweet little lassie there did I meet,*
> *Blow, blow, blow the man down.*

We all pulled together at *Blow the man down*. The first stanza is the only one I remember exactly. But the sailor's romance went on in the alternate lines, while we threw our weight on the ropes at each *Blow the man down*. And the story of the love night on Paradise Street was still going on when the last lifeboat had been swung over the water and swung back.

The bosun's mate was a popular old man, who never hurried us. He had charge of our work for two days, while the bosun was recovering from a shoreside drinking bout. "I know many chanties," he told me. "I began learning them on a square-rigged ship in the Australian trade nearly fifty years ago. They made our work easier. You're always working, on a square-rigger," he said.

Square-riggers were coming back during the war to replace the ships the U-boats were sinking. And each one was a fascinating sight. I was on watch on the forepeak at night when my first square-rigger hove into view. Its broad sails were shining in the moonlight like the wings of a great white bird, rising out of the water. It was a thing of beauty I cannot forget.

The moonlight flashed back from the waves in many colors. The lookouts had no other lamp than the moon. The ship's lights were out, and all smoking was forbidden, except behind dark windows or belowdecks.

The fo'c'sle was my home for two weeks. A dozen men lived in this tiny room belowdecks in the bow of the ship. We slept there, played checkers there, and washed our bodies from buckets that slopped on the floor. And we dined on planks laid on trestles between two rows of bunks.

The steward fed us austerely. We breakfasted on tea, bread and oatmeal, which was called "bergoo." We lunched and supped on tea, bread and hash containing little meat. That was on weekdays. The Sunday menu included beef stew and plum pudding.

"Food was worse before the war," an old Scottish salt said. And I thought of John Masefield's *Salt Water Ballads,* where a sailor was *chewing salted horse and biting flinty bread.*

My shipmates were good men to live with. I never heard a quarrel, though they argued about many things, including military tactics. I remember one dispute about the Battle of Gallipoli on the Dardanelles Strait between the Mediterranean and the Black Sea in 1915. One of my shipmates, a young man from Melbourne, Australia, had been in the front lines of the British forces that tried to capture the strategic straits.

"I fell with a bit of shrapnel in my chest just after we landed on the beach," he said.

"That was a damn fool adventure by Winston Churchill, who planned Gallipoli," the Scot remarked.

"You're bloody right," another seaman said. Two more anti-Churchill men chimed in.

But the Gallipoli veteran made a half-hearted defense of Churchill's plan. "Victory would have given us Constantinople," he said. "And we might have won. We were supposed to attack before dawn, but the officers were drinking. We started too late, when the Turkish gunners could see us. That's why I was hit."

I enjoyed working on the deck with these friendly men. The skies were cloudless that first week. Soft winds caressed us. The work wasn't hard. My shipmates set a reasonable pace. My night watches were fascinating. And I vigorously objected when I was shifted to the captain's and mates' galley, at a small raise in pay, to replace a sick man.

I washed dishes, scrubbed the galley deck, brewed coffee, made the officers' beds, served their tea and polished the brass on their cabin doors. This job let me eat the captain's roast beef and it gave me an inside view of class distinctions in our little world at sea.

Not all officers were snobs. The captain, an Irishman, always made a friendly remark when I mounted the bridge with his tea. He once said that he wanted more fog. "It hides us from the U-boats," he explained. Another time he told me that his last ship had been torpedoed—"But every man was saved by the lifeboats, I'm glad to say."

The chief engineer, on the other hand, never said anything when I came with his tea. That didn't mean he was trying to snub me. He snubbed everyone, without trying. I never heard him speak to anyone, high or low, except the ship's cat, which he fondled. And he dined alone in silence, with the chief steward waiting on his table.

A couple of officers, however, openly displayed their contempt for the lower ranks. A crude example of stuffy arrogance was given by a petty officer; a PO in training to become a mate. He cried out in horror when he saw me carrying a big tray to the fo'c'sle, where I still lived at night. It was laden with roast beef, fruits and pastries for the able

seamen and ordinaries. "Give them nothing," the young PO cried. "Don't you know they're all bloody lower class?"

Ironically, the White Star Line paid its able seamen more than it gave their detractor. ABs got £8 a month—POs only £7.

Class differences also stared me in the face when the pompous chief steward was getting his tea. The chief steward, a Welshman, was swelled up with his importance. I got on well with him, but I was not allowed to serve him. My rank wasn't high enough. That honor was

given to Ralph Cloudsdale, the second steward, a pale, slim man from
London. The chief's teatime came when he woke from his after-lunch
nap. Woe to Cloudsdale if he wasn't at hand with the tea. That
happened one day as I was passing the chief's cabin. An angry call—
"Cloudsdale!"—was coming from within. The cry became louder
when Cloudsdale didn't answer. It ended in a roar that sounded all
over the ship. It was answered by a distant patter of feet and a faint
"Yes, sir. Coming, sir." And moments later the truant appeared with a
cup in his hand.

"Don't let this happen again, Cloudsdale," the chief said as the cup
was going to his lips.

At home in London, Ralph was headwaiter in a fashionable West
End hotel, where the tips were very good. This was his first trip to sea.
"I signed the ship's articles," he told me, "to escape the bloody
trenches. You haven't a chance in the trenches. If the shells don't hit
you, the poison gas will. I'd rather run the risk of sinking with this ship
than go through life with my lungs burned out or my arms and legs
blown off.

Many members of the crew felt the same way.

Ralph never talked back to his arrogant chief. That might have
meant the trenches. But some crew members had the courage to fight
back. And I'm glad I was present when four brave firemen confronted
the chief steward with a pan of stinking food.

A young Black fireman from Jamaica was among them. They
brought the notorious "black pan" that carried leftovers from the
captain's and mates' table to firemen on British ships. This was a
black, circular iron dish, about fourteen inches wide and three and a
half inches deep. It was filled with scraps of stale meat and vegetables
that smelled up the galley.

The chief steward was responsible for this putrid mess. But the
firemen went over his head. "We must see the captain," they said.

The captain smelled the mess as he was coming in. "What's the
trouble?" he asked as he stood back near the door. The firemen didn't
answer in words. They simply held the black pan up near the skipper's
nose.

The steward took advantage of their silence to do the speaking.
"They say this isn't enough for four men," he told the captain. That
was a crude distortion. The deputation of four represented twelve
hard-working men, who fed the hungry furnaces.

But the captain had been given his cue. And he backed out, saying, "It seems enough for four men."

The angry fireman replied by heaving the black pan over the side. It hit a green wave and went under. They looked at the bridge and caught the skipper's eye. Their food was better after this.

My chum was Bob Gill, a young Irish sailor who kept his shipmates laughing with merry songs and jokes. Behind his fun was a rich Irish culture. I owe much to him for introducing me to the literary geniuses of modern Ireland, whom I had not known until then.

Bob recited their magic lines to me at night as we sat on an army truck that was tied to the after deck. His recitations made an indelible impression on me. I remember every haunting line of William Butler Yeats' poem, *The Lake Isle of Innisfree* and most of James Clarence Mangan's revolutionary poem, *My Dark Rosaleen*. And the tragic beauty of John Millington Synge's play, *Riders to the Sea*, is with me still. Bob would have loved Sean O'Casey, whose genius flowered a little later.

Our recitation parties changed to concerts when two recruits joined our cultural circle. They were the navy gunners who stood watch by a clumsy old 4.7-inch gun on the stern nearby. Both were good singers. Blews, the chief gunner, sang British North Country love songs with a soft, tenor voice. Scotty McKie, the gunner's mate, gave us *Scots, Wah Ha' Wi' Wallace Bled, Comin' Through the Rye* and other Bobby Burns' masterpieces. And Bob alternated Irish love songs with Irish revolutionary ballads. One of his favorites was John Keegan Casey's *Risin' of the Moon*, with its chorus:

> *At the risin' of the moon,*
> *At the risin' of the moon*
> *Our pikes must be together*
> *At the risin' of the moon.*

All three singers joined in each other's songs. English, Scottish and Irish accents blended together. And Bob remarked that our concerts were acquiring an international flavor.

We were nearing England at last. "These waters are the graveyard of many ships," Blews said one night. And half an hour later our concert was interrupted by a cry from the crow's nest overhead. "Submarine! Submarine! I see a submarine," the lookout was shouting. What looked like a periscope was breaking the surface of the moonlit sea two hundred yards ahead.

There was no time to turn the ship around for the stern gun to fire. The lifeboats were lowered with speed. Each man slid down a rope to his place without going after his duffle bag. There wasn't any panic. If anyone was scared, he didn't show it. The captain was the last man to leave the ship.

"Can you pull an oar?" the bosun asked me. I proudly nodded. Our little fleet was pulling away with enough food and water to last us until we should be picked up.

And I was giving a good-by glance at the *Bovic* when the old bosun's mate whooped in delight. "Hurray, boys! It's only driftwood," he said.

The captain congratulated us when we were back on deck. "You behaved like good men," he told us. "I'll tell the Admiralty about you."

I did not know how lucky we were until we reached the Manchester ship canal next day. We learned that another British ship had gone down in the same waters soon after our false alarm.

Bob and I shared lodgings in Salford after signing off the *Bovic*. A room was hard to get, but we finally found clean bunks in a home for dock workers. The place was full of tired men. They were toiling overtime to take the place of dockers in the trenches. "I worked twenty-four hours last Sunday," an elderly man told me.

"So did I," said a still older man.

Many ships waited long for dock crews. Work on the *Bovic* didn't begin for a week.

I wanted to spend more time with the dockers, but Bob took me on visit to his Irish revolutionary friends in Salford and Manchester instead. This was only five months after the Easter Week uprising in Dublin, when less than a thousand Irish rebels had risen against the British Empire. The rebels knew they couldn't win that battle. Their plans for a national uprising had been betrayed. But they fought for a week, nevertheless, to demonstrate Ireland's determination to win independence.

Bob and I visited half a dozen veterans of the Irish liberation struggles in the next week. The one I like best was Jack, a former Dublin tram conductor, who had taken part in the Easter Week battle. Jack barely escaped capture after his last bullet was spent. He showed me the scar of a bullet wound in his upper left arm. It had healed without medical care. He didn't dare go to a doctor, because all friendly doctors were under British military observation.

Jack's hero was James Connolly, the rebels' military commander. Jack had been defending the Dublin Post Office, the rebels' headquarters, when Connolly fell, badly wounded, a few feet away. His ankle was shattered by an expanding bullet. "The pain must have been terrible," Jack said. "But Connolly never groaned a bit. He just continued giving orders while his ankle was bandaged."

The tram conductor said the Connolly was the best of the sixteen leaders who died before British firing squads after the battle. The executioners tied the crippled commander to a stretcher and propped it up before they shot his heart to pieces.

"I would gladly have died for him," Bob's friend said. "I became a trade unionist in the big strike that swept over Ireland in 1913. It was led by Jim Larkin and Jim Connolly. I've read everything that Connolly wrote since then. He was a Socialist. He always said that Ireland must become a workers' republic."

I'm sorry to say that Bob didn't share the tram conductor's clear working-class outlook. Bob belonged to the Irish Republican Brotherhood. This group had a fighting alliance with Connolly's armed union men, but it was led by middle-class intellectuals. The martyr Bob loved best was Padraic Pearse, the poet and IRB leader, who signed the Easter Week independence manifesto as president of the short-lived revolutionary regime.

Bob admired Connolly as a brave military leader. But the Irish Workers' Republic meant little to him. Bob was a romantic nationalist who dreamed that happy days would come when the green flag flew over the island. I could not convince him that Ireland would not be free until Connolly's Socialist ideas were victorious.

I lived with the Easter Week rising for a week. The climax came at a gathering of 500 men and women in Salford. On the surface this was just a concert to raise funds for the families of hundreds of Easter Week prisoners. It was more than that, however. It was a revolutionary demonstration.

I felt the Irish people's anger when a soloist sang *The Wearin' of the Green* and the entire audience joined in the chorus: *"They're hangin' men and women for the wearin' of the green."*

After the concert the people talked of more rebellions to come. Easter Week had been the first battle. Next time Dublin would not be alone. The Irish East and the Irish West would rise together against the oppressor.

I heard a lot of this talk as I sat with a pint of half-and-half in a smoke-filled pub near the ship canal. And the predictions were soon fulfilled. I rejoiced in New York in 1917 when I heard that an Irish general strike had smashed Britain's last attempt to impose military conscription in Ireland. I assumed that Bob and the tram conductor were in the armed struggles that followed in the next years. I grieved when the British split the independence movement in 1921 and kept the six northern counties under the Union Jack. But two thirds of the Irish people had finally won political independence, and the green flag flew over the island's twenty-six southern counties.

Unfortunately Jim Connolly, the founder of the Irish Socialist Party, and his closest associates were dead. And the independence struggles did not bring the workers' republic that Connolly had worked for. British capital was still dominating the green island when I visited Dublin many years after.

The workers' republic has not been forgotten, however. It is the goal of the vanguard of the Irish working class that is led by the Irish Communist Party and its allies. And I have the utmost confidence that the hopes of Jim Connolly, Jim Larkin and the Dublin tram conductor will be fulfilled—perhaps in my time.

Bob and I parted with mutual regret a day or two after the concert. Bob was shipping out again—and not just as a sailor. He was a revolutionary courier—a link between the Irish Republican Brotherhood and its Irish-American supporters. But I didn't learn this until we met in New York the following year.

I took the train to London. In Salford and Manchester, I had learned much about the struggles of the people in Britain's oldest colony. Now I would find out what the British people were thinking about in wartime, in the capital of the empire whose leaders still ruled much of the world.

28 · *Wartime London*

Blacked-out London was a ghostly sight at night in the fall of 1916. Windows were shuttered or heavily curtained. Street lamps were out, except for tiny ones at intersections. They were covered above and cast the dimmest light on the paving four feet below. People passed like shadows. Tall shadows were often Anzacs, as Australian and New Zealand troops were called. They were favorites of the street girls, because they got several times the pay of British Tommies.

The girls hunted in pairs. I would stand aside as a captured Anzac went by in the dark with a girl hanging on each arm.

I had many chats with the Anzacs. All were disillusioned about the war. "We owe nothing to the empire," a New Zealander remarked. "All we got, we got by ourselves."

"I was a fool to enlist," said another Anzac, who was recovering from a bayonet thrust in his shoulder. "I didn't have to go. Conscription was defeated by a referendum vote in Australia. But I was foolish. I came from the outback lands of New South Wales, where we grow nothing but sheep. I was tired of sheep and joined the army to see the world."

"What did you see?"

"Just hell," he replied.

And he gave me this picture of trench warfare in France. "You sit under shellfire for days. Then comes the order to attack. You run through machine-gunfire to the enemy trench. You throw your grenade. You jump in, and it's kill or be killed. Sometimes the enemy attacks. It's hell either way. Half my company is dead or wounded, and I'll soon be in hell again."

Our talk ended in a Lipton tea parlor, where he showed me a picture of the girl he left behind. "I was a fool to leave her," he said.

I got a taste of war when London became a battlefront. The world's first aerial bombing of a giant city began shortly before midnight, a week after I arrived. The bombs fell from the gondola of a long, cigar-shaped airship—an invention of Count Zeppelin. They dropped from a height of 4,000 feet, a mile and a half from my room on Gower Street, in the heart of London.

With a reporter's bad luck I slept through the bombardment, as did many other people in my part of London. The bombs were small by World War II standards. But I followed the route of the raid the next morning. The trail was marked by wrecked houses. Bombs had struck every three or four blocks.

The brick walls of a two-story house were still standing at the first bomb site I visited. But the inside was full of twisted timber. The bomb had hit the bedroom, where the husband, a young carpenter, and his wife were sleeping. "They were good people," a neighbor told me. "I helped to carry their bodies out."

The press said that about a hundred people were killed. Fatalities were probably higher, but even so they were only a fraction of the deaths in average bombing raids in World War II. But most people I talked to were terrified. One old man was still trembling as he told how screaming women "rushed out of their homes in their shifts and shimmies" after the first blast.

The children were least frightened. A four-yard crater was blasted out of the ground beside another wrecked house I visited. Water was oozing into the pit, and two lads of six or seven years were sailing a toy boat in the pool that was rising.

Farther up the road, a dozen men and women were digging into the wreckage of a big brick house. The family of four who lived there had not been heard of since the bombing. I volunteered to help. A London bobby—a policeman—inspected my seaman's papers and welcomed me into the group. Pickaxe, shovel and crowbar were provided. We found no bodies but finally unearthed a fine library. And I felt like one of the gravediggers in Hamlet as a set of Shakespeare in rich leather bindings came out of the rubble.

After digging for three hours, I shared a Red Cross lunch and listened to my fellow workers. There were some cries for revenge, but they didn't sound the dominant note. Most of the diggers were talking peace. "No one is winning this war," one woman said. "I think they will have to make peace."

"I want my man back," another woman exclaimed.

"I lost my son in France," an elderly man murmured. "He meant more to me than those colonies they are fighting about."

We quit digging when the bobby got word that the occupants of this house had left London before the raid. A retired army sergeant, with whom I had been digging, then invited me to his home, where his wife, a motherly woman, served us tea and muffins.

The sergeant and his wife were an ardent win-the-war couple. The sergeant, a lean, wrinkled veteran of sixty or more, was proud of his long service under the Union Jack. He had joined the army at seventeen, was a drummer boy at first, then fought for the empire in Asia and Africa. "I marched with Field Marshal Kitchener against the city of Khartoum in 1898," he said. "We conquered those white-robed dervishes in one big battle on the Nile. They couldn't stand up against our artillery. The Nile became the empire's longest river. The whole Sudan was British again."

My host didn't dream that the empire would ever break up. He talked on and on about Britain's colonial victories while my cup was refilled and my plate of muffins replenished. I finally got him back to the bombing and he said, "Don't worry about the Zeppelins. They only kill people. They do no military damage. The Kaiser can't win."

I slept through the next Zeppelin raid and missed a spectacular sight. The Zeppelin was over one of London's suburbs when a British shell hit it, igniting the flammable gas inside the long silvery casing. The airship burst into flames in the heavens like an exploding comet.

"I never saw such beautiful colors," an English journalist told me. "The flames illuminated the landscape for many miles around."

I had brought a letter to this journalist from *The New York Times* ship-news reporter, "Skipper" Williams, who knew him well. I was offered a job on his paper, the London *Daily News*. "We would like to have an American with us," the British editor said. "You would write about the American scene. That would help us. Your president, Mr. Wilson, is on our side, and I think we will soon be fighting together."

This looked like a fine opportunity for a young newspaperman, but I wasn't tempted a bit. I knew what he wanted. He wanted to use me for war propaganda.

Meanwhile I was enjoying the company of people I met on the street. I talked to dozens of soldiers and sailors and rank-and-file civilians. Most of them came from the working class. They were very friendly to this lonely young American. And I developed a warm affection for rank-and-file British people, which I've kept ever since.

I was also probing the people's attitude to the war. Most of them were sick of it. Many I talked to had lost brothers, sweethearts, husbands or sons in the trenches. And the hate-the-Germans propaganda was not rousing all the anger that had flamed up a year or two before. They did not feel that their country was fighting for its existence, as the British people would feel in the next generation, in the war against Hitler and fascism.

I was enjoying the sights of London at the same time. I visited music halls, where one sat at a table with a mug of beer and took in a floor show for a trivial price. Some Gilbert and Sullivan bits were done well; I remember a satirical skit that made fun of men whose wives were busy at war work while papas tended the kids. It was amusing, but, I thought, unfair.

One of my first visits was to that famous feudal fortress, the Tower of London. A grim sight there was the broad-bladed axe and the chopping block where the head of King Charles I was struck off after the Revolution of 1648-49. I also paced back and forth in the narrow stone cell where Sir Walter Raleigh, the colorful courtier, explorer, poet and scholar, was confined. I've often wondered how he was able to write his bulky *History of the World* by dim candlelight in that gloomy den, before he laid his head on the block.

In the historic British Museum, I tried to find out where Karl Marx sat while he was digging up raw material for *Das Kapital.* The young attendant could not help me. But I was shown fine specimens of pottery and bronze craftsmanship by England's early inhabitants, the Iberian people, who came long before the Celts and Saxons.

I also visited *The Old Curiosity Shop* and other landmarks described by Charles Dickens, whose writings I love. And I gave some time to the slums of London's East End. I was inspired to do this by Jack London's fine study of East End misery, *The People of the Abyss.*

Jack London had buried himself in this sea of suffering for three months. Disguised as an unemployed marine fireman, he climbed the stairs of East End sweatshops, walked the streets with homeless workers at night, and came out with a classic socialist document.

I lacked time for a thorough investigation. But vivid pictures of human distress still linger in my mind. I began by making a rough comparison between the people I saw on the streets in the affluent West End, and the East End slum dwellers. In a ten-mile walk from West to East, I found the people shrinking in size. They lost inches of stature before I reach the end of Whitechapel Road. Generations of undernourishment had taken a savage toll.

Jack made his study in 1902, when King Edward VII, Victoria's eldest son, was crowned in Westminster Abbey. That was one of the empire's lush years. The wealth of India and other colonies was pouring into London. The rich were becoming richer, but the British poor were shamefully neglected. I came in wartime, fourteen years later. The able-bodied poor were finding war jobs. But the sick, the weak, the old, the workers' widows were at the mercy of the most brutal exploiters. And I remember the pitiful spectacle of a ragged woman of forty or fifty years who limped out of an East End alley and accosted me. Her price was only three sixpence pieces, she pleaded.

Sweatshops are sweatshops, whether in Britain or the U.S.A. And I almost thought I was inside one of New York's little nonunion slave dens when I found a dozen women making pants in an old stone building near Whitechapel Road. They were operating Singer sewing machines at a long table, under electric lamps glaring down from overhead. The dirty windows were closed. The air was foul. One young woman was coughing, and spitting into a cuspidor. No boss was in sight, so I lost no time. "What do they pay you, lady?" I asked an elderly women who looked up at the visitor.

"You might as well know," she replied. "I got twenty-three shillings last week." That was about $5.50 in U.S. money in 1916.

"Can you live on twenty-three shillings?" I inquired in a tone that did not hide my surprise.

"I don't think I could if my brother didn't help me. He's a docker."

"How many hours a day are you working?"

"They'll tell you," she said, "that we work from seven to six. But last night they kept me until eight."

At that moment steps sounded from the corridor outside. The women bent over their machines as an angry young man burst in with a long pair of garment shears in one hand and a pair of pants in the other.

"Who worked on this?" the boss shouted as he held the pants high. Then he saw me and glared, and I hastily explained that I wanted a job.

"What's your trade?" the boss shouted.

"I'm a seaman."

The boss snorted in disgust. "What's a seaman doing in a garment shop? You wouldn't be worth ten shillings a week to me, maybe not five. Don't take up my time. We're working for an army contractor."

It was nearly six o'clock. I waited outside for more than an hour, until the workers came out. Then I asked them why they didn't join a union and get better conditions. "I'd like to," the elderly woman said, "but the union leaders are not interested in little shops." Meanwhile she had to keep this job. Her husband was dead and she was supporting a crippled son. He had been knocked down by a runaway horse some years before.

I was about to leave London—my bag was packed—when I met a college classmate, Kenneth Hamilton, who had a wartime job with the international YMCA. In his office was a British photographer named Hackett, who asked me what Theodore Roosevelt, my former president, was doing. "I don't like Teddy," he said, "and I'll tell you why."

Hackett said he had met Roosevelt in a British West African colony in 1909, when Teddy was hunting big game. "I was invited to join his safari to take pictures," he said. "Teddy told me he was collecting specimens of rare animals for the Museum of Natural History in New York. But I found that he was more interested in killing than collecting.

"Once I saw Teddy empty the magazine of his repeating rifle into a herd of quagga. They were big, harmless animals. He killed and wounded many, The carcasses were left on the African plains for the jackals and vultures."

The quagga, a first cousin of the zebra, has been extinct for several decades. It was wiped out by irresponsible hunters. Hackett's story has never been written, so far as I know. But I think of those massacred quagga when I see the equestrian statue of Teddy Roosevelt on Central Park West in front of the Museum of Natural History, where he is lauded as a friend of wildlife and a true conservationist.

My next stop was Liverpool, Britain's second biggest port. There I lodged in a seamen's boardinghouse while I looked for a homebound ship. The house was kept by a big Irish woman, with the help of two daughters. Both were war widows. One had three children, the other four.

This boardinghouse was filled with men from many lands who sailed on British ships. My roommates were two young marine firemen from Odessa, the Ukrainian Black Sea port. The older man, who spoke English, was very friendly. We talked about the workers' movement and he said, "We have many strikes in Odessa. The police can't stop us. We don't like the czar in Odessa."

They sat at the dinner table with a tall young Norwegian, a big, chubby Dane, two Portuguese, several English and Irish seamen, and a short, potbellied Belgian who was more English than the English. He boasted that he always shipped out as a bosun.

The pompous bosun was our military expert. He told us several times that the British Army had never been beaten. It had the best military formation the world had ever seen. That was the famous hollow square, which had won many victories in the empire's colonial wars.

"The hollow square has never been broken," he asserted very loudly one day, with a glance around the table to see who dared to disagree. I felt like quoting Rudyard Kipling: *But for all the odds ag'in you, Fuzzy Wuz, you bruk the British square.* I might also have reminded our expert that the hollow square was never used in trench warfare; that would have been suicide. But I held my peace, as did others who knew better.

I did not join the diners for several days. My funds had almost vanished. I was living on one meal a day—a tiny loaf of whole wheat bread that cost tuppence ha'penny—five cents—at a neighborhood bakery. I was not seated at the table until I gave the big Irish landlady my one good suit. It came to breakfast the next morning on the back of the young Norwegian, who was keeping company with one of the war widows.

I finally signed up on the S.S. *Finland,* a U.S. passenger and cargo ship, as a third-class steward. Nearly all my fellow workers were English. We scrubbed floors and slept in the "glory hole," a long room deep down belowdecks, where about fifty bunks were crowded close together. The glory hole was full of romping rats. A big one scampered over my chest one night. That happened often in nonunion days.

Our food could be described as slops. Everything was cooked and overcooked together in a big pot. But my English shipmates complained more about the tea. It was cheap, tasteless stuff. Not quite all of us suffered, however. We soon found that the pantryman was serving much better tea to half a dozen members of our gang who were his personal friends. They had sailed together many times.

We took action under a capable leader—Rob, an English, lightweight boxer, whose trade was stamped on his face. His nose had been broken, his lips were thickened and he wore cauliflower ears. But his fighting spirit was still there. He rolled his sleeves up over his bulging biceps, led us into the pantry, dropped a fistful of high quality tea into a pot while the pantryman was screaming, and poured in boiling water.

The pantryman, a skinny, mustached Englishman of forty or forty-five years tried to grab the pot. He gave up when Rob flourished his fists and said, "Let's settle this man to man." We drank good tea after that.

We docked in New York in late November, and I went back to my job on the news agency. I had learned much in three months in Britain

and at sea. My stay in Britain had filled me with hatred of war. I was much concerned with the likelihood that my country would be in the bloodbath before long.

The sea trips brought me still closer to the working class. The men I lived and worked with had my affection and respect. The journeys on the *Bovic* and *Finland* took me farther along the road I was to follow.

29 · *Last frontier*

Like many other Americans, I was bitterly opposed to President Wilson's declaration of war against Germany in March 1917. I rejected Wilson's propaganda that this was a "war for democracy." I knew that U.S. imperialism was no better than Kaiser Wilhelm's. I had heard old soldiers tell of wiping out entire villages of civilians in the Philippines and I had seen plenty of strikebreaking. I went to anti-war meetings and spoke freely to my fellow-workers. But I knew this wasn't enough. I felt frustrated. And I welcomed an opportunity to go to Alaska when it came.

I had been eager to see Alaska—America's final frontier—since I began reading Jack London at fourteen. My desire increased when I read my brother Walter's letters from the Arctic, where he had been working for eight years. Walter had slept in the snow when the thermometer registered sixty-five below. He had been storm-bound in lonely cabins for days. He had broken new trails in the icy wilderness between Nome and the northern coast. He had mushed thousands of miles by dog and reindeer sled since I saw him. I wanted to join him. So I took a train to Seattle when he wired me to come to Nome as his assistant.

Walter, my oldest brother, was superintendent of the Northern Eskimo school district, which covered thousands of square miles between Nome and Point Barrow on the Arctic Ocean. He was also in charge of the expanding Eskimo reindeer industry.

I arrived on the last ship from Seattle, in October 1917, just before the winter freeze. Nome has no harbor. It was built on the shore of the Bering Sea during the gold rush. We anchored two miles out. The fog was heavy, and I could not see the town. But I could hear the howling of the malamutes, the Eskimo sled dogs, as I waited for Walter, coming out in a lighter to take me in.

Malamutes never bark. Their speech is a moaning howl like that of their ancestors, the Arctic wolves. It comes from perpetual hunger. And we were encircled by moaning beasts when we set foot on the sands.

I found myself in a village of low frame houses strung along the shore. Nome had dwindled to a tiny fraction of its former size. The booming gold-rush capital of Rex Beach's novels was no more. Tex Rickard's gambling hall, where thousands of dollars had changed hands at night, was gone. Of thirty thousand people who had camped on the sands in 1900, only thirteen hundred were left. This included three hundred Eskimos on the Nome sandspit. The rest had gone with the gold they washed from the beach.

"Don't judge Nome by its size," Walter cautioned me that night. It was still an important gold town. There was still much treasure in nearby creeks. Nome was the seat of a territorial judicial district, with a U.S. judge and six U.S. marshals. It also had two daily papers—the *Nugget,* representing commercial interests, and the Nome *Industrial Worker,* which was owned by the gold miners' union.

"You will find good friends in the union hall," Walter said.

We were enjoying a reindeer roast in Walter's home on the beach. With him was his wife, Julia, and the six-year-old twins, Tommy and Sarah.

As we dined, Walter talked enthusiastically about the reindeer herds and reindeer herdsmen. "I'm proud of these men," he said. The first herds were formed at the turn of the century with twelve hundred deer from Siberia. They were imported to replace the game that whites were killing. The Eskimos were instructed in reindeer culture by herders from Norway's Lapland. But now, said Walter, the pupils know as much as their teachers. The herds had multiplied more than a hundredfold. Two hundred thousand deer were grazing on the tundra. There should be a million before long.

"Someday," said Walter, "reindeer meat will be a popular dish on tables outside Alaska."

The Eskimo herders' future looked bright as I listened. The herders were protected from competition by government contracts forbidding the sale of female breeding deer to whites. But there was one nasty shadow on the future, Walter said. The shadow was cast by the richest man in Nome.

This was Jofet Lindberg, the owner of the Pioneer Mining Company, who had worked with reindeer in his native Norway. Lindberg came to Nome during the gold rush, and at once began acting like an invading gangster. Like many others who sought quick riches in gold, he hired goons to jump prospectors' claims and he bribed government officials to alter the records. He became a millionaire. Now this ruthless crook was launching a private reindeer syndicate. He wanted to turn the independent Eskimo herders into Lindberg employees. And he was bringing suit in federal court to cancel government contracts that banned sales of female deer to whites.

"What are you doing to stop Lindberg?" I inquired.

"We've organized an Eskimo Reindeer Men's Association to defend the herders. It's uniting the Eskimos of northwest Alaska for the first time.

"And I'm starting a little magazine to promote reindeer culture. I'm calling it *The Eskimo*. I want you to edit it."

The Eskimo's first number was soon off the press. I wrote a feature story about it for the Associated Press. And many subscriptions came with the first dogsled mail teams from outside.

One of Walter's friends, Tom, a Danish-American miner, showed me the sights on my second day in town.

"Millions of dollars were washed from these sands," Tom said as we strolled along the beach. They were washed out with rockers. A rocker, he explained, was like a tub on a rocking chair's rockers. The miner filled it with water and sand, and rocked it until the gold sank to the bottom.

But the richest gold strikes were not on this beach, Tom said. Much richer was the Third Beach line two miles inland, where surf pounded ages ago. This treasure trove had been discovered by a prospector named Brown. And Tom told me Brown's story.

Brown planted his stakes, recorded his claim, took his first bag of gold to the assayer's office and fell asleep happy. But Brown wasn't happy next morning. His stakes had been replaced by Lindberg's stakes. And the recorder said he had no record of Brown's claim.

Then Brown went hunting for Lindberg. They met on the main street. Both were big men, but Brown landed the first swing and jumped on the claim jumper with both feet. Then he told Lindberg that he'd kill him if there was any more trouble.

Brown kept his claim and retired with a million. I met him when he visited Nome in 1918 to greet old friends.

But there was only one Brown. Most prospectors never made wages, Tom said. And many of the lucky ones were eaten up by wolves—big ones like Lindberg or little ones.

"Only one big wolf is left," my guide said. "That's Lindberg. But I'll take you to one of the little wolves. This is Yorkie's place." Tom pushed open a door that was decorated with a painted cigar. It was the poorest apology for a tobacco shop I've seen. A pile of Bull Durham bags, a box of cheap cigars, some plugs of chewing tobacco, some tins of smoking tobacco and some stale candy were in a dirty glass show case. There were no customers. The tobacco shop was a front for what was going on in the back room.

Tom turned to a nervous old man, who stood by a rear door. "It's all right, Yorkie, we're just looking around," he said as we stepped inside. There I found myself between two long tables that filled the back room. At one table a dealer was passing out poker chips. But the big excitement was at the blackjack table.

The dealer was winning. A blackjack dealer has an advantage. The odd card is in his favor. Alaska used no paper money then, and coins were rattling as the dealer packed them into rounded grooves cut into a heavy, twenty-by-twenty-inch board at his right hand. The grooves for double eagles ($20 gold pieces), eagles, $5 gold coins and silver dollars were filling up. I felt sorry for a young army sergeant who had come on the ship with me. He was a likable chap and he shook his head sadly as his last double eagle was grooved away.

"Poor fellow," whispered Tom. "He hadn't a chance."

The dealer was a big man with a fleshy, expressionless face. He seldom said anything—just let the cards speak for themselves and scooped the eagles and double eagles in. I asked Tom about him when we went outside. "He's a bad one," said Tom. "He comes here in fall to get the money the miners saved during their summer in the camps on the creeks. Some men have nothing left for their boat tickets when they walk out of this den. But the robber goes out with a fat wad. It gets fatter on the Mexican border, where he runs another gambling joint. Then he comes back to Nome and fattens it again. He sure is a bad one. The union has warned all the miners against him."

Tom then promised to take me to "the best thing in town." And he led me to a long, one-story building with NOME MINERS' UNION painted over the door. "This is the furthest North local union of the AFL's Mine, Mill and Smelter Workers," explained Tom. "Mine, Mill . . ." he added, "is the present name of the Western Federation of Miners that Big Bill Haywood led." And he assured me, "You will find a lot of Big Bill's spirit inside."

The hall was full of men. The placer mining season was over. The winter freeze had begun. Half the men were bound for the outside, on the ship that was waiting offshore. The rest—real "sourdoughs"— would winter in Nome. But, sourdoughs or not, the miners were union brothers. I enjoyed the warm atmosphere in the hall as men from different mining camps clasped hands and exchanged experiences. And I got a hearty welcome as Tom introduced me around.

These gold diggers were bold spirits from many lands. Ole Olsen, a big, flaxen-haired man, the first one I talked to, had been a weight-lifting champion in Norway. "I came as a prospector," Ole told me, "but I found little pay dirt. So I sold my labor to the bosses, like a lot of my brothers here."

Ole introduced me to many Norwegians, Swedes and Danes. The Scandinavians formed the largest group in the hall. But I also met Irishmen, Scots, Welshmen and Canadians, as well as a Pole and a couple of Ukrainians.

White men from the United States were a minority. There were no Black or Hispanic men. I was to meet only one Black man during my Arctic travels. This was a roadhouse keeper on a dogsled trail a hundred miles from Nome, who was popular for his excellent reindeer stew and his jolly stories. The Black migration from the South, that began in World War I, hadn't reached Alaska.

Tom next took me to the office of the Nome *Industrial Worker,* in the same building as the union. I wanted to meet the editor, John McGivney, an Irishman. Walter had told me about him. "Mack is the best-read man in Nome," Walter said. "He knows English literature intimately, from Shakespeare on. He's an excellent writer. And he has a fascinating history. He joined the gold rush twenty years ago."

But McGivney wasn't in. He was packing up for his first visit outside in twenty years. His winter replacement also wasn't in. So I did the next best thing. I leafed through the files of the *Industrial Worker,* and liked what I saw. The big American strikes were getting sympathetic attention. The paper was supporting the Russian workers against the counter-revolutionary Kerensky. And I found no hurrahs for President Wilson or the U.S. role in the World War.

"This paper tells us what the miners are thinking," Tom said.

That night one of Nome's leading merchants called at our home with an invitation. He begged Walter to join the Arctic Brotherhood, a private upper-class club. Walter politely turned down the invitation, as he had turned it down several times before. The merchant then turned to me. "We want you with us, Arthur," he said. "You'll meet all the best people in the Arctic Brotherhood."

I asked our visitor to tell me more about the "best people."

"There are two kinds of people in Nome," he replied. "There are the roughnecks who mine the gold. They're not the kind of people you want to know. They're not the people who run this town. Many are not even Americans. The people you want to meet are the merchants, the mine owners, the attorneys, the federal officials, the dentist and doctor. You'll find many of them in the Arctic Brotherhood."

The members gathered once a month, he said, to discuss public questions and to refresh themselves. They wore formal costumes when they came together. "But don't worry about that," he added. "I can give you a good black suit at a very reasonable price."

I told him I would think about it, but my thinking was already done. I knew which side I was on.

30 · Revolution

The winter freeze was turning Nome into an isolated Arctic outpost by early November. The last ship steamed away as ice began spreading on the Bering Sea. Dog teams were mushing on newly fallen snow. But the postman's first mail from the outside was not due until Christmas. Our only tie to the rest of the world was through a wireless station. It carried brief reports, which were often distorted, from the capitalist news agencies.

The news from Russia was especially distorted. All we knew was that a struggle was going on between Russia's workers and Kerensky's capitalist forces. Then a bolt of lightning flashed through the fog. I was walking along the beach one day when a miner yelled to me to come to the union hall. "There's revolution in Russia!" he cried out. Inside he showed me an earth-shaking bulletin to the *Industrial Worker*. The Winter Palace in Petrograd had fallen on November 7th. The Bolsheviks had won! I was too full of triumph for words.

The Bolshevik victory divided Nome along class lines. Miners were enthusiastic; capitalists were upset. The Arctic Brotherhood, the upper-class club, called a special meeting. Mayor Lomen was the main speaker. This uprising must be suppressed, he said. No property was safe when revolution spread.

The mayor was feeling better when my brother Walter met him next day. He was comforted by the hope that the Bolsheviks would fail. Workers and peasants are too ignorant to control a country, he said.

Lomen, an old Norwegian, was a lawyer for Jofet Lindberg's Pioneer Mining Company. Lindberg, who had won his first million by jumping prospectors' claims, was outside for the winter.

The miners celebrated the Russian workers' victory at a special union meeting, to which I was invited. There was only one subject on the agenda—the Revolution. The hall was crowded when I arrived. A miner in work trousers and a flannel shirt was in the chair. He spoke English well, with a Ukrainian accent. He began by saying that he might not stay much longer with his Nome brothers. "I love you all," he said, "but I want to be with my people. They threw off the chains of the hated czar last winter. Now they are throwing off the chains of the capitalists, too. They are the first people in the world to do that. What I've dreamed about for years has come true."

Applause made him stop for a while. Then he said, "Don't forget, brothers, the Russian workers are your neighbors. It's only a short distance across the Bering Sea to Russian land."

The "neighbors" idea went over big. "We neighbors have the same kind of enemies. We must stick together," said Martin Kennelly, the local union president, a militant young Irishman, who spoke next.

An old Scottish miner quoted the historic appeal that Karl Marx and Frederick Engels made to "workers of all countries" to "unite." He was one of several good Marxists in the Nome miners' union.

Several speakers said they feared that President Wilson would invade revolutionary Russia. We must stop that, they said. Everyone agreed, and the meeting ended with the passage of a strong American-Russian solidarity resolution.

The name of Lenin—the Bolshevik leader and the head of the revolutionary government—began coming over the air waves. The words "Lenin" and "Peace" were coupled together. Lenin was urging all warring nations to make peace.

The peace bulletins in the *Industrial Worker* stirred Nome workers profoundly. But most dispatches about Russia were lies. Among these lies were Associated Press bulletins in the *Nugget,* the local capitalist paper, which indicated that the workers' state would be overthrown.

But the truth reached us at last. It came in a copy of a Seattle workers' paper. This paper was also called the *Industrial Worker.* It was not connected with the Nome *Industrial Worker,* but was published by the IWW, and reflected its revolutionary outlook. It ran a long interview with the crew of a Soviet ship—the *Shilka*—which the Nome miners' paper reprinted. The interview described the gains Russian workers were making and emphasized the strength of the revolutionary regime.

The *Shilka* was the first Soviet ship to visit the United States. It anchored in Seattle harbor on December 21, 1917, only six weeks after the fall of the Winter Palace. Behind this visit is a story of international working-class solidarity that I often wrote about in later years. A number of Seattle dockworkers had appealed to maritime workers in Vladivostok to send speakers to tell them about the revolution. Vladivostok's Bolsheviks responded by sending The *Shilka,* a transport in the czar's navy that had been turned into a merchant ship.

Police confined the Soviet crew to the ship for a while, but the seamen were soon freed, at the demand of the AFL and IWW unions. Seattle labor spoke with a powerful voice at that time. *Shilka* seamen began speaking at big mass meetings. And before the *Shilka* sailed, Seattle workers became the best-informed Americans about the Russian revolution.

The story of the *Shilka* reached Nome in a U.S. mail sled after an eight weeks' mush from Valdez in southern Alaska. It was now midwinter. By this time the strength of the new workers' republic had been demonstrated to the entire world. Kolchak, the czarist general, had been defeated, although bigger battles loomed ahead.

Nome miners celebrated the *Shilka*'s visit at another special meeting. Fifteen to twenty enthusiastic speakers took the floor. The one I liked best was the Ukrainian miner who said, "Soviet Russia is the only country, brothers, that sends workers as ambassadors."

When the *Shilka* left on January 8, 1918, we did not know that she carried a letter to Lenin that described the terrible persecution of IWW members and other militant workers by the wartime government. Thousands were being arrested, and some were being murdered in terroristic attacks on workers' organizations.

This letter had been written by Roy Brown, a lumberjack, Seattle's IWW leader. I worked with Roy in Chicago three years later, when he was elected to the national chairmanship of the IWW. He joined the Communist Party soon afterwards. The letter was hidden in a lifebelt on the *Shilka* by Commissar Kryukov, the crew's political leader, so police searchers wouldn't find it.

The IWW letter was answered by Lenin in his famous *Letter to American Workers,* which ends with the triumphant declaration that "we are invincible because the proletarian revolution is invincible." It was often reprinted. In the latest U.S. edition (New Outlook Publishers, 1970), Lenin's message is introduced by Gus Hall, the general secretary of the Communist Party, USA. And it is followed by this writer's story of the ship that carried the Seattle workers' letter to Lenin.

I met Commissar Kryukov at his home in Leningrad fifty-four years after his American trip. He was a grand old man, with his grandchildren around him. His chest was covered with medals awarded for his courage and skill in the defense of his hero city against the Hitlerite hordes. And he spoke with the utmost admiration of Roy Brown and other workers he had met in Seattle.

31 · Reindeer

I did my first mushing during a thirty-mile run to a reindeer herd. My brother Walter was with me. He let me take the reins, and all went well until the dogs realized that they had an inexperienced driver. Then the fighting began.

Our team leader, a big dog, had much outside blood. This made him alien to the eight malamutes behind him. A malamute would nip him and the team would become a tangle of harness and furry brutes until Walter cracked his long whip near their ears. He never struck them, but they got the warning. And then we'd be mushing again.

It was ten degrees below zero, but we were dressed for the weather. We wore long woolen underwear, two pairs of wool trousers, two pairs of wool socks inside our deep reindeer-hide mukluks. Heavy sweaters and jackets covered our upper bodies. Reindeer-hide parkas enveloped us from head to knee. And our hands were stuffed into woolen mittens inside long fur gauntlets.

Walter and I took turns driving.

The driver stood on runners extending a foot behind the sled and held on to handlebars that rose waist high.

The other man mushed alongside at about five miles an hour. That was easier than it seems. Our mukluks were soled with *ugoruk* (big seal) skin, which slid along the hard snow.

"Ten below is the best mushing temperature," Walter said. "It's not too cold, and the snow is hard as sand underfoot."

We spent the night on the floor of an Eskimo igloo in a small village near the herd. The sun had set before we arrived. All we could see of the igloo by moonlight was a rounded roof rising above ground to half a man's height. It was made of walrus-hide stretched over a framework of driftwood and was covered with turf.

The rest of the igloo was underground. We entered through the "cache," a hole in the frozen earth about four feet wide and four and a half deep. The cache was also a refrigerator. Its sides were hung with frozen meat. On the side opposite the entrance, at the bottom, was a low tunnel. We crawled through it on hands and knees into a small room filled with life.

This was living room, bedroom and kitchen combined. In the center, two small boys were playing with a malamute puppy that was tethered to a knife stuck in the ground. At one side a man was weaving a fishnet. On the other a woman was chewing a reindeer hide to break down the tissues and bring the flexibility garments require. A reindeer stew was simmering meanwhile in an iron pot that rested on hot driftwood coals on the floor.

The iron pot had come from Nome a few years earlier. Before that the only cooking utensil was a wooden bowl, scooped out by hand. It held water, which boiled after hot stones were dropped in.

The family worked and played by the light of an oil lamp. The lamp was a shallow dish carved out of soft rock, about ten inches long and eight wide. The wick was made from absorbent grasses, and it was placed along one side. This gave a flame about one inch high, which heated a slab of seal blubber that hung above it, bringing about an oil drip that replenished the fuel.

The reindeer stew was delicious. It was supplemented by bacon and baked beans, which Walter had brought from Nome. The bacon was served in big chunks and we relished it as much as the Eskimos, who eat lots of fat meat in winter.

Our dogs, meanwhile, were dining on frozen salmon. Each swallowed his daily ration in one long gulp. The salmon had been netted in a nearby river in summer, then split and sun-dried on high lines near the igloo.

The sun hadn't risen when we reached the herd after a reindeer and bacon breakfast. A thousand deer were sleeping in the snow. But bucks, does and stags leaped up together when the herdsmen walked among them to select bucks for butchering.

Walter did some of the killing. It was done with a low-caliber rifle. The target was a spot between the eyes and the horn. Walter never missed. A thousand deer fled wildly after each shot, but they were quickly rounded up by the herdsmen's dogs. These dogs were not malamutes. Their ancestors had been rounding up deer for ages in Norway's Lapland, and some had come to Alaska with the Lapps who were training the Eskimo herdsmen. So they knew exactly what to do. Each dog picked out a deer in the vanguard of the runaways and leaped at him, yelping and nipping. In minutes the deer were huddled together again. Soon twenty deer were dragged away to be skinned and cut up for the Nome trade.

Walter was off in December on a long mushing trip to his northern schools, leaving me in charge of the office. As he was packing his sled he said, "I'd like you to stage a reindeer race while I'm away. Start it from Nome. The white men say that it can't be done. The dogs will panic the deer, they say. I want you to show they are wrong. I want to convince Scotty Allan especially. He's the champion dog racer and throws a lot of weight in this town."

The white men who drove dog teams laughed when I announced the race in the pages of the *Nugget* and the *Industrial Worker*. I scheduled it for Christmas Eve, when the town would be full of merry-makers and their malamutes. I knew the malamutes would make trouble, but the success I expected would be more impressive. All depended on getting the best racing teams. I gave the job of recruiting them to Marcus Ezazruk, a young Eskimo herder Walter highly respected.

The trouble came, as expected. The malamutes were leaping at the deer with loud howls when our seven teams assembled in front of Scotty Allan's hardware store. But the Eskimo drivers lashed back the savage invaders, and five of the seven teams broke away from the dogs when I blew my whistle at twelve noon.

The race was to Fort Davis and back—a total of eight miles. The seven teams were close together on the way out. But Ham—Marcus Ezazruk's deer—and Kobuk, his nearest rival, pulled ahead on the way home. Ham and Kobuk were running nose to nose until within a mile of Nome. Then Ham began gaining by inches. And Ham was a couple of sled-lengths ahead when he crossed the victory line.

The winner was much applauded. Ther *Industrial Worker* gave him a front-page story, with a lead that said: "Marcus Ezazruk, driving Ham, brought home the bacon." Scotty Allan, a real sportsman, admitted to me, "I don't think any dogs in Nome could have caught up with Ham, except perhaps some of my best."

Walter was pleased when he returned. "This will encourage white people to use sled deer," he said.

Christmas Eve closed with a jolly beer-quaffing party in the miners' union hall, to which I was invited. No formal entertainment was planned. Each man did his own thing, as the spirit moved him. Two old-timers, who had sailed the seas in wind jammers before they went into mining, sang a series of chanties. An old Swedish miner did handsprings and cartwheels with the agility of a youth. Another old-timer told stories about Jack London, whom he had mushed with in the upper Yukon country, twenty years earlier. And best of all was the Ukrainian who sang revolutionary songs in his own language, to the tune of his accordion, as he danced around the hall.

Walter's family and I celebrated Christmas with a ptarmigan feast. I've never tasted anything better. These luscious little birds are fatter and juicier than quail. They came in a box of frozen game from Walter's Eskimo friends in Mary's Igloo, a village ninety miles inland.

The Board of Trade saloon, the biggest in town, was packed tight on New Year's Eve. Men in heavy furs were waiting outside, where it was sixteen below. They had come to say farewell to the old year and to drink Nome dry. Alaska was going dry on January 1, 1918, by order of the Territorial Legislature. Inside, men were packed many deep in front of the long bar. I met prospectors from the Kyukuk Trail and the Kugorok country and other distant spots, who had been mushing in for days. Their moaning dogs were tied up outside.

Thousands of dollars' worth of quality stuff was going down hundreds of throats, at giveaway prices. Champagne was drunk by men who had never tasted it before. Canadian Club was selling at two drinks for two bits (twenty-five cents). I saw the burly owner of the Wild Goose Mining Company putting down ten or eleven Canadian Clubs in thirty or forty minutes. He was still on his feet as the last one went down. He could not have fallen if he had tried. He was squeezed in too tightly.

Men were still coming in when the big clock on the wall began tolling the midnight hour. Alaska was now officially dry. But the twelfth stroke had not sounded when a tall Danish miner climbed a stepladder and set the clock back four hours.

The drinking went on for another four hours, with no one becoming sloppy. Some men were singing, others were laughing, but only one man seemed drunk as I looked over the crowd. That was old Mayor Lomen. He put down his glass and climbed on the bar with the help of Tex, a lanky marshal from the Lone Star State.

"Speech! Speech!" a City Hall flunky was crying.

The mayor began by saying, "We're doing all right tonight. We don't need any damn prohibition." He wanted to say more, but he lost his balance and would have tumbled if Tex hadn't helped him down.

That was a night of class peace. The dividing line between rich and poor was forgotten while capitalists and workers drank together. But the drums of the class struggle were sounding again after the birth of the New Year. Alaska's eight-hour-day law had just been declared unconstitutional. That was a heavy blow. The eight-hour limit had been overwhelmingly voted in by a Territorial referendum in 1917, with an eighty-four percent majority.

My friends in the gold miners' union had worked hard for this victory. They had been telling me with joy that the cruel ten-hour shift in the gravel pits on the creek banks would be no more. They forgot that the mine owner had a friend in the U.S. District Court in Nome.

That friend was the judge himself. Mayor Lomen, the attorney for Jofet Lindberg's Pioneer Mining Company was a buddy of Judge Holtsheimer. They wined, dined and schemed together. And Holtsheimer gave the bosses what they wanted. He decided that the eight-hour law infringed on the rights of individuals who wanted to work longer hours.

"We know who Holtsheimer is," said Martin Kennelly, the young president of the miners' union, when we met next day. "He's the mouthpiece of Lomen and Lindberg. You'll hear our answer to him at our next meeting."

The hall was full of angry men when I came in. "The bosses have declared war on our union," said Kennelly as he opened the meeting. "We won't mine gold without the eight-hour day we voted for," a miner shouted. Others chimed in. The strike vote was unanimous. The struggle would start when the winter freeze ended in late spring.

"Lindberg will bring scabs on the first ship," a speaker warned. "We know that," Kennelly replied. "We'll take care of the scabs when they come in."

32 · Nome in winter

I often think back fondly of the Northern Lights that flashed across Alaska's winter skies at night. They were long silvery streaks of incredible beauty. I don't miss the dark daytime, however. I seldom saw the sun in Nome's midwinter. It climbed over the horizon for only three hours a day, but that meant little. The Bering Sea fog blotted out the heavenly rays, and all we got was Arctic twilight.

Most of Nome's social life went out with the sun. The gold creeks, which brought life to town, were solid ice from top to bottom. No dredges or sluice boxes were working. Almost all the lively young miners wintered outside Alaska, while the old sourdoughs lived austerely in little cabins until spring payrolls came again. Under these circumstances, the town lost much of its working-class character in winter and became top heavy with federal marshals, who had little to do; with courthouse officials and attachés, who waited for occasional trials; with merchants, lawyers and their wives and with idle mine owners.

But worst of all was the imbalance of the sexes. The white part of our town had been overwhelmingly masculine, ever since Nome was born on an empty beach during the gold rush in 1898. Among a thousand whites one could almost count on one's fingers all the teachers, secretaries and other unmarried women—aside from five who followed what is sometimes called the "oldest profession." The five lived in a little Nome byway called "the Alley."

Nome's unmarried women could have had their pick of many men. I remember the broken-hearted longings of Martin, a sixty-year old Danish miner. He was madly in love with the chief marshal's secretary, who was less than half his age. Martin would not have been a bad catch. He was still very strong. He got full-time wages all summer, and had several thousand dollars from his diggings during the gold rush twenty years earlier. He used part of his savings to buy a small house across the street from the marshal's office, so he could watch his beloved as she came and went. I used to see his broad, bearded face in the window. She wouldn't notice him, however. He told me once that he cried himself to sleep at night.

Some matchmakers tried to arrange a romance between the secretary and me. The young lady was attractive, and the matchmakers might have succeeded if her social ideas had not stood in the way. She had the same class outlook on miners as the marshal himself.

Walter was absent on long mushing trips much of the winter. I had charge of the office and spent the evenings with friends. Among these friends was McDonald, the village pharmacist, a native of San Francisco, who also managed Nome's biggest store. Both of us enjoyed poetry and we spent hours reading Walt Whitman, Bobby Burns and Shelley together. And I also relished Mac's biting wit.

Mac was amused by the pretensions of the merchants, lawyers and government officials, who called themselves the "best people." And he did not hide his contempt for their illusions of racial superiority over the town's native people, the Eskimos.

In the past, Eskimo customers stood back in the store while whites were served first. But Mac's rule was "First come, first served." And I saw frustrated women in rich furs grumbling while Eskimo women in deerhide parkas were finishing their shopping.

Mac was a good friend of the miners' union and openly voiced his scorn for all scabs and scabherders. His comments were reported to a well-known scabherder and big bruiser named Kilroy, who had been a mine foreman in South Africa before coming to Nome. "I kept the Blacks in their place," he used to say. Kilroy was scheduled to lead a team of scabs to Jofet Lindberg's biggest mine when the winter freeze ended and the miners' strike began. Meanwhile he lounged around town, posing as a superpatriot. And one day he came into Mac's store looking for trouble. Mac and I were chatting together.

An audience of some of the "best people" and a group of miners was listening as Kilroy began: "I say anyone who doesn't like this war should be run out of town." He looked at Mac and me as he said this.

"If you like this war so much, why aren't you fighting in France?" Mac replied.

"No traitor is going to tell me what to do," the scabherder shouted.

The word "traitor" touched off an explosion. Mac, a little dark-skinned man of forty-five or more, dropped off the high stool on which he was perched behind the cigar counter. A long revolver was in his hand. "Listen, Kilroy," he said, "this is a little leveler I brought from Wyoming. It'll bring the biggest SOB in Nome down to my size."

Mac slammed the gun on the glass showcase as he said this. Kilroy was out of the store before Mac could pick it up again.

Among my very best friends were Harry Osborne, an IWW member and a skilled mechanic, and Morris Pascoff, the village tailor. Both were young revolutionaries who planned to go to Russia to fight and work with the Bolsheviks.

Morris was a popular figure with a warm, jolly personality. He was much in demand as a singer at social affairs. He specialized in love songs, but his dearest love was his Russian homeland. In talking with me, he called himself a Communist-Anarchist. I found nothing anarchistic about him, however. He believed in organization and leadership, and planned to join the Bolsheviks on his return.

But getting away was difficult. Morris couldn't drive a dog team. If he tried to go out on someone else's sled, he would be arrested as a draft evader long before the eight-week trip to southern Alaska ended. So he decided on the northern route. He would hike 150 miles to Cape Prince of Wales and cross the icebound Bering Strait to Soviet territory.

I begged Morris not to risk this. The strait was almost impassable. It was jammed with crazy ice hummocks, and he might run into open leads of water he couldn't cross.

But Morris couldn't be stopped. "I'm afraid they'll send me against the Revolution if I'm drafted," he said. So he loaded a pack with dried salmon and chocolate, stuffed $500 in gold coins in a money belt, and left at night.

He left a week before Nome's draftees were called up. They were sworn in together in front of the courthouse. And Mayor Lomen had just finished a win-the-war speech when someone cried, "Where is Morris Pascoff?"

Meanwhile Morris was footslogging along the beach through ice and snow. He was a vigorous youth, but the permafrost was melting and his feet sank in mucky sands. He had made only about sixty miles, a week later, when he was picked up by the U.S. commissioner at Teller and sent to Fort Davis as a prisoner.

The popular young singer was denounced as a coward and traitor by the officials, merchants and mine owners. This was too much for Walter, who supported the war but respected courage. "There's nothing cowardly about a man who intended to cross Bering Strait," he said.

Now comes a genial ending to the story. I met Morris on the street a month later, in uniform. "They said I was unfit to fight for America," he remarked with a smile. "They condemned me to be fort tailor. I'm getting a hundred dollars a month above my salary, making uniforms for officers. And I'm going home after the war."

I liked to talk with Harry Osborne very much. Harry was a clear-headed working-class revolutionist. He was one of the few white Wobblies I knew who thought about the special problems of Black workers. He told me that he had once pulled a big construction camp out on strike when the boss tried to fire a Black cook on racist grounds. And when we discussed Soviet Russia, he said he would find a way to go there and use his skills in building up the country.

Harry was an expert in several trades, able to get winter jobs when others were unemployed. That winter he used his skills to give a group of men much more work than they expected. Harry left Nome in midwinter with a gang that was moving a gold-mining dredge from one pool to another. That could be done only in winter, when streams were solid ice. The dredges became grounded in the shallows between pools if an attempt to move them was made in summer.

"This job will last only five weeks," said Milton Roper, a Scot from Nova Scotia, another friend of mine, as he left town with the gang. But Harry had different ideas. The job lasted five months instead.

When the gang came back in late Spring I asked Milton what had happened. "It was a very big dredge," said Milton. "We ran into difficulties. Ross, the contractor, didn't know what to do, so he asked Harry to show him. Harry's methods moved the dredge, but it took all winter to do it."

When I asked Harry about it, he replied with a smile, "It was as simple as this. The men needed the job, and Ross, the contractor, was no friend of the working class."

Harry had just signed on as an Arctic sea captain. His ship, a tiny trading schooner, carried only a few tons of cargo. It ran in summer between Nome and Anadyr, a little Soviet port on the Bering Sea. "I'll buy this ship at the season's end," Harry told me. "It needs repairs. I can get it cheap. And next year I'll take it to Siberia, with a crew of six. We'll fight on the side of the Bolsheviks, then go to work to build up the country."

I was delighted when Harry asked me to join the crew. He told me to be ready when he came to Seattle with the ship. And I was deeply disappointed when he arrived in Seattle with bad news in the late fall. The Allied naval patrol had drawn such a tight net along the Siberian coast that our miniature wind-powered ship would have no chance of getting through.

33 · The Eskimo

I got much help from young Eskimo correspondents in editing the monthly journal Walter was publishing. They wrote some of the best stories for *The Eskimo*. So did some of Walter's teachers.

Our little paper was dedicated first of all to the Eskimo-owned reindeer industry Walter was supervising. My correspondents reported the experiences of many reindeer herders on the vast tundras that run from below Nome to the northern coast. Their stories were eagerly read by young herders and helped to improve their work.

I liked best the stories of the herders' battles against wolves, lynx and brown bears. The bears did less damage than other raiders, because their usual haunts were far from the reindeer tundras. But I ran a number of stories about brown raiders who filled their famished bellies with deer meat after their long winter sleeps.

The Alaska brown bear is the biggest predator on the North American continent. He is one and a half times the size of a grizzly. And one of my correspondents—a herder himself—gave me an eyewitness description of a bear raid. The herder's dogs couldn't stop the bruin's charge. He slapped two malamutes down when they leaped at him. One never stirred again. He towered over the does as he began knocking them down. And he was felling his third doe when the herder's bullet hit him.

This was near Cape Prince of Wales but a long way from the salmon-river land where brownie lived. A hungry bear can cover many miles.

Lynx and wolves were far more destructive than bears, and my correspondents disagreed as to which was worse. The big Canadian lynx was almost immune to attacks by the herders' dogs. He was equipped with very deadly weapons on his hind feet. They were long, needlelike claws. And one herder wrote me about a lynx that ripped the life out of his three best dogs before he shot it.

This correspondent insisted that lynx did more damage than wolves. Most others disagreed. The lynx, they said, had one serious weakness. He got bogged down in deep snow and was then helpless before the hunter. Wolves, on the other hand, never bogged down. They also did more killing because they ran in packs, while the lynx was a loner.

But wolves, lynx and bears were all innocent of attacking human beings in our tundra country while I was in Alaska.

A popular figure on the reindeer tundras was the bull caribou. The news that a bull caribou was visiting a reindeer herd was always a choice item in my paper. It meant that the next generation of reindeer would include some big ones. The American caribou is an oversized reindeer, and the herders did all they could to keep a visiting bull with them. They never kept him very long, however. After enjoying his new mates for a while, the bull would wander back to his own kind. Unfortunately he sometimes took some of his reindeer wives with him.

I also ran make-it-yourself pieces by Eskimo craftsmen. Better ways of making fishnets and sleds appeared in our pages. And one tanning expert told how to turn skins into fine leather with a new tanning extract. He got it by scraping young willow bark. The tundra willows grew only three feet high in the soil above permafrost.

An article on Arctic gardening came from Mrs. Elizabeth Forrest, a teacher at Wainwright, on Alaska's extreme northwest coast. Her crop was lettuce. She planted it in a box indoors in late May, transferred it to a tiny greenhouse in late June and enjoyed succulent lettuce until October. The greenhouse was made with five panes of glass. She placed it in tundra soil in the middle of a high snowbank that reflected the almost twenty-four-hour sunshine of the summer months.

The Eskimo also had a broad cultural program. I'm especially proud of our Eskimo folk tales that told the legendary history of the Innuit people, as the Eskimos call themselves. My favorite writer was Joe Sekonik of Kivalina, an Alaskan coast village more than a hundred miles north of the Arctic Circle. Joe was then twenty-eight.

Joe Sekonik had never won glory in the whale hunts. He had never killed a walrus, harpooned a seal or hunted the fierce polar bear. He was a polio victim, who couldn't walk. But he did worthwhile things none the less. He listened to the old men and stored his mind with the tales fathers had been passing down to sons for hundreds of years.

One of Joe Sekonik's stories was so good that I devoted an entire number of *The Eskimo* to it. It told the story of Ki-yi-yak-tua-luk, the founder of Kivalina. All peoples make heroes of their strong men. The Israelites had Samson, who killed thousands of Philistines. The Greeks had Achilles, the Norse people the victorious Argonauts of the sagas. The Afro-American people had John Henry and many other heroes. And Kivalina had Ki-yi-yak-tua-luk, a fabulously strong man.

Ki-yi-yak-tua-luk traveled up and down the tundra and the coast, killing bad men and protecting their victims. His arrows never missed their mark, and one blow of his fist finished the toughest enemies of the people. Thus, an arrogant giant who attacked him was demolished at once.

My paper also used many verses. Some were by Walter, who was an excellent rhymster. And I still laugh when I read his *Song of the Naughty Sled Deer,* as told by Trouble, a lazy deer.

Trouble was too lazy to work. He tangled up the towlines and lay down on the trail when drivers tried to hitch him. And he was happy until his worries began. Then—

> *Sometimes when I'm snorting at*
> *Some very angry herder*
> *I fear he'll see I'm very fat,*
> *And then there may be murder.*
> *I had an awful dream of late:*
> *I saw some steaks upon a plate,*
> *And heard the boys say, as they ate:*
> *"Well, here's the end of Trouble."*

Another one of Walter's reindeer songs was "by" Kobuk, a wise old sled deer he had often driven. Kobuk was complaining about men who drove their sleds over frozen streams. The slippery ice gave more speed than rough tundra, but on the ice the sled deer was in danger of a broken leg. And Kobuk exclaimed:

> *Looks to me men by and by should know*
> *That on ice it's no good to go.*
> *Long-time sled deer, plenty* ipanee*,
> *All the time I savvy what I see,*
> *Man, him* peluk** *brains, it looks to me.*

I once quoted Kobuk during the Soviet-Finnish War of 1939. I was replying in the *Daily Worker* to Lowell Limpus, a writer for the New York *Daily News*. Limpus asserted that Baron Mannerheim's Finnish Army was whipping Soviet troops, with the help of wonderful reindeer. Each deer hauled hundreds of pounds of war supplies a hundred miles a day, he said. These figures were crazy, and Kobuk replied: *"Man, him* peluk *brains it looks to me."*

Limpus called me up to congratulate Kobuk when he read the story.

Since *The Eskimo* was put out by the Eskimo Reindeer Men's Association that Walter founded, we gave much space to its annual conventions, where officers were elected. These conventions were called Reindeer Fairs, because they were accompanied by athletic events and dramatic contests of many kinds.

That winter the Reindeer Fair was held in the center of the Seward Peninsula, on which Nome is located. The convention village—Mary's Igloo—was an ideal meeting spot. In its midst was a huge hot spring that flowed into a steaming pool about twelve feet wide and three deep. The pool was covered with a big tent. I arrived just in time for a plunge before supper with several young Eskimo men. Then we ran out nude together, rolled in deep snow, and were in hot water again before the March ten-degree cold bit in.

Reindeer herders came to the Fair bringing their wives, who were dressed in the best Arctic finery. Mink, fox and squirrel parkas were

*ipanee, old time or old timer;
**peluk, no or nothing.

attractively embroidered, and prizes were given for the best handiwork.

The Fair lasted five days. The foot races, deer races, wrestling bouts and rifle shooting were most exciting. But I was especially interested in the fire-making contest. The ancient bow-drill method was used. The pointed end of a short stick was placed in a small hole in a piece of combustible dry wood. The upper end of the stick fitted into the loop of a tiny bowstring. The stick revolved in the hole as the bow was jerked from side to side at high speed. And the fire-makers were sweating when the first sparks appeared in less than a minute and a half.

I also enjoyed the convention sessions in the big assembly tent. The reindeer herders felt at home when Tautuk, Menepedluk and other elected leaders opened the sessions. They had practiced democracy in village meetings long before the whites came. Many men took the floor. Complaints against a number of herders, whose deer ranged beyond their allotted pasturage, were soon settled. There was plenty of room on the tundra for all herds.

A checkup showed that the rule against selling female breeding deer to whites was generally well enforced. One young herder, who had sold a doe to an agent of the white reindeer syndicate, was threatened with expulsion. He promised not to do it again.

On my way back to Nome, on an easy, well-traveled road, I dined with the only Black man I met in Alaska. He ran a one-man roadhouse, where I had a big meal of soup, reindeer steaks and raisin pie for a dollar. He told me that he went through difficult years after coming to Alaska from California during the gold rush. He was barred from the mines. "We want no Black men," the bosses said. He finally got a job as a cook, saved money and bought the roadhouse. "I get along well with everyone now," he said, "and I'm staying in Alaska until I die."

34 · Gold strike

Northwestern Alaska was reborn in spring. The snow gave way to green grass and Arctic flowers. The frozen gold creeks became torrents of water. The Bering Sea ice went out. And I saw the outside world arriving on the *Victoria,* the first ship from Seattle, late in June.

The class struggle also came in with the ship. The miners began striking for the eight-hour day when the frozen creeks melted. And the bosses hit back. The *Victoria* carried a cargo of strikebreakers. They had been recruited by Jofet Lindberg, the millionaire claim-jumper, who was returning to Nome to break the strike.

But Lindberg's scabs were confronted by pickets from the Nome local of the Mine, Mill and Smelter Workers Union. The pickets were joined by union men returning to Nome. The union muscle was well organized. It was led by my friend Ole Olsen, the former weight-lifting champion. One of Lindberg's goons, a six-footer with a broken nose, hit a picket. But he was a child in Ole's hands. And he made no more trouble after Ole tossed him into icy water at the edge of the beach.

The scabs pleaded that Lindberg had said nothing about a strike. And nearly half of them quit when the union promised them food and lodging until the struggle ended.

The miners won a partial victory in the strike, which lasted all summer. Most of the smaller companies opened their mines with eight-hour-day union contracts. The big companies were hard hit. They were able to open only half their mines, because of a shortage of scabs.

I gave much time to the struggle as a volunteer reporter for the Nome *Industrial Worker.* I teamed up with John McGivney, the witty and scholarly editor of the miners' paper. He had returned on the *Victoria* after his winter in Seattle, where he had written for a left-wing Socialist Party paper.

I had already read his back issues, but our friendship began when he landed. He grinned when he saw me, and showed me the latest copy of the *Literary Digest,* which came on the ship. It contained a featured piece by me, which I didn't know had been printed. It was based on letters I wrote from Nome to a newspaper friend in New York. I made fun of the stuffy politicians, merchants and mine owners, who called themselves the "best people." My letters had been displayed in a full page of the New York *Sunday World,* and then reprinted in the *Digest.*

"Your letters were the talk of the ship," said McGivney. "The 'best people' were angry, but my people, the miners, were delighted."

I'm proud to say that Walter defended me when the "best people" complained. "Your brother is making trouble," they said.

"I liked what you wrote," Walter said to me. "You told the truth about these people."

McGivney and I made a good team as editor and reporter. He enriched my reports from his long Alaska background as he knocked the stories out on a typewriter. He had been editing the miners' paper since 1907, although he had arrived in Alaska during the gold rush in 1897.

My best helper was a Wobbly who arrived on the second ship. He was Bob Nicholson, an athletic young man who had been given free passage by Lindberg's agents, because they expected him to scab. But Bob never even thought of scabbing. The class struggle was in his blood. He came to Alaska for one purpose—to do missionary work among the scabs. I met him in the miners' hall an hour after he landed. Several passengers, whom the Lindberg men had recruited, were with him. They were promised free board and lodging by the miners when they swore they wouldn't scab.

Bob became a reporter's reporter. He met all the incoming ships and visited the scab mines. And he had a narrow escape in one of Lindberg's camps that he was investigating for me. This camp was on a swollen creek some eight or ten miles from Nome. Bob mushed there on foot. It was a difficult hike. His shoepacs sank into the marshy tundra at every step. And when he reached the camp he found that only one of two dredges was working, because of the lack of men.

Bob carried a migratory worker's blanket on his back and was promptly hired. The pay was $5 a day for a ten-hour day, with no assurance of any overtime pay. It was suppertime when he arrived, and Bob began his missionary work over a pork-and-beans meal in the commissary tent.

"What kind of a job is this?" he inquired.

"It stinks like this grub," one of the older men replied.

"The bosses are pushing us all the time," another man added.

Another man spoke up, then another and more. Bob listened to the chorus of complaints about speedup, dirty bedding and bad grub for a while. Then he knew his time had come. He began talking about union wages and the eight-hour day. He felt the men's minds were with him. And he was about to propose that they present their demands to the boss when the boss himself burst into the tent.

The boss was a big, scowling man, who had been listening outside. Two bigger men were with him. "Kick this man's ass out," he shouted.

That meant a beating, and Bob was about to have the fight of his life when several workers jumped up. "Don't touch him," they said.

The majority of the workers were not ready to strike, however. Bob had to go. But half a dozen men went with him as he hiked back to Nome by the Arctic twilight. It was payday—a good time to quit.

Bob met Lindberg on the street a few days later. I was some distance away and only got snatches of the dialogue that followed. I heard the millionaire strikebreaker shouting, "You ought to be in jail. You're a damned contract breaker."

"You're a damned scabherder," Bob replied.

I saw Lindberg clenching his fists, but his goons weren't with him and he backed away, cursing. The miners were laughing about the incident when I visited the union hall later.

This claim-jumping millionaire was a symbol of the corruption and brutality of his class. His arrogance and selfishness came out in a conversation with me some weeks later. We met by accident in front of the courthouse. His face was flushed with whiskey, and he was

unsteady on his feet. He was drunk enough to be very frank. He began by saying, "You're Walter's brother. Tell Walter he's on the wrong side. Jofet Lindberg's reindeer syndicate will win. We're going to take over the reindeer herds, with the government's help. If Walter joins us, he'll get a good job."

Then Lindberg turned to the gold miners' strike. "I know all about you," he told me. "You're on the side of the strikers. Well, I'm not worried about my Alaska mines. They will soon be worked out. The big gold is in Siberia. Jofet Lindberg knows where it is and he's going to get it."

A long, rambling talk about Siberia's gold followed. Lindberg said his prospectors had found rich placer-mining deposits in northeastern Siberia, but the Russian czar had driven them out.

"That's why I turned to the Kaiser," he said. Maybe you heard about that. I wanted the Kaiser to win. I could do business with him."

But Lindberg said the Kaiser lost his chance when America entered the war. The U.S. Army is going to take over eastern Siberia, he assured me. Jofet Lindberg's men are going in with the army, he declared, and they'll get those placer-mining deposits.

He went on talking about the dredges he intended to put on Siberia's rivers and creeks. He was still talking when I left.

This was my first mine strike. It was followed by much bigger ones in later years.

35 · *Farthest West*

I'm sending you to Cape Prince of Wales," Walter said one April morning. "I like the young Eskimo teacher there very much. He's setting a splendid example to my other teachers. I want you to sit in on his classes and write a report on his work."

Cape Prince of Wales is the farthest point west on the American continents. It's so far west that it's almost in the Eastern Hemisphere. The trip meant five days mushing each way. I was to travel with Jesse, a capable young Eskimo. And we were harnessing eight malamutes to a sled when Jesse's eyes fll on Walter's house dog, Brownie.

My companion liked Brownie's looks. He towered over all the dogs in Nome. "I think Brownie would make good sled dog," Jesse said.

"He used to lead a mail team," I remarked. That was a perfect recommendation. The mail teams had the reputation of always going through, regardless of wind and weather. "But Brownie hasn't worked for three years," I cautioned Jesse.

"He will work now," replied Jesse.

But Brownie hadn't been consulted. The traces were slack on his chest as we started. "I think Brownie one big wobble-wobble," said Jesse as Brownie's strike continued. He was calling Brownie a Wobbly.

Brownie's strike was demoralizing his teammates. After ten miles, we had to take him out. Then his energy came back with a bound. He chased a stray reindeer over a hill, came back and chased reindeer and rabbits again. I reckon Brownie traveled forty-five miles that day, while we were making thirty.

The weather was perfect, though the winter cold continued. The streams we crossed were still frozen solid from top to bottom. The moisture in my breath still froze in the air. The tundra was covered now with several inches of good, hard snow. But the spring sun was delightful. There had been little snow before February, and that had made mushing difficult during most of the winter.

After making good progress, mostly northward, we spent the night in an empty cabin. We had a supper of baked beans and reindeer meat, which we thawed and cooked in a deep frying pan. We were much disappointed when our choicest delicacy went down a wrong throat. A pound of fat bacon, which tastes better than cake in Arctic weather, was in our food box. I was lifting the cover of the box off when a team leader, a big dog with reddish brown hair, leaped in and grabbed the bacon.

It was a big solid chunk and hard to swallow. But the thief squatted in the snow, letting the cube of frozen fat go slowly down his gullet. Jesse's mukluks were pounding his belly, but he dug his feet in the snow until the bacon reached his stomach. Then he trotted silently away. And that bacon was a bonus—he had already swallowed his ration of frozen fish.

The cooking was done over a fire of willow branches and alder bushes. This fuel had been left by the last occupant of the cabin, in accordance with an unwritten law of the trail. We cut a new supply for the cabin's next guest. The willows were only three feet high. No woods grow in this permafrost land except along riverbanks.

Jesse and I spent the next night in our sleeping bags in the snow. We lay under a tarpaulin that ran from the sled, which was turned on its side, to pegs driven into the ground. Our dogs, meanwhile, were comfortable under the snow. Their hot breaths melted a hole in the snow above them to give them the air they needed.

The third night brought us to Teller, sixty miles from Nome. Here we were too warm. We slept in the Norwegian Lutheran Mission, behind tightly closed triple windows in a room overheated by a hot stove.

Our route was now turning west. We had met no travelers on the trail. But next morning an Eskimo was mushing just ahead. He was driving a breed of dogs I had heard much of but had not seen before. They were Siberian malamutes.

Siberians had the reputation of outlasting all other dogs on the trail. They had won all long-distance races in recent years. There were eight in this team. I admired their powerful, chunky bodies and the bushy tails curled over their backs. They were pulling more than 800 pounds. This included a 600-pound load, the sled itself and the driver, who stood on the sled runners in the rear. The Siberians' speed never varied. Their only sign of weariness came when their tails began uncoiling in the afternoon.

We slept in an abandoned village after a 35-mile run. This was Tin City, where much tin had been dredged from shallow waters in former years. There were no igloos in Tin City. Eskimos never lived there. The town consisted of empty cabins on the shore of the Bering Sea, 20 miles from Cape Prince of Wales.

An Eskimo youth sighted us before we reached the cape and sprinted back with the tidings. The schoolhouse emptied at once, and we were met by a children's welcoming party. I had never dreamed of such a reception. A hundred or more chubby youngsters in parkas and mukluks danced about us, shouting their greetings. They escorted us to the school, where a lovely girl of eleven or twelve made a welcoming speech in English. A feast of white whale meat, which the Eskimos called *stuk* (I'm guessing at the spelling) came next. Then the young Eskimo teacher showed me the sights of the town.

Cape Prince of Wales had about five hundred people, with no white face among them. The hundred or more igloos were spread along the beach at the point of the cape. A mountain rose behind the town. The cape was the continent's land's end. Across Bering Strait was the Soviet Arctic land, within sight on a clear day. Dense fog, however, blotted out our view.

School was recessed the morning after I arrived, because a big hunt was beginning. The game was the bowhead whale, which weighs dozens of tons, and the children were on the beach with the whaling flotilla.

This was the annual spring hunt. There were two whale-hunting seasons every year—in fall and in spring, when there were open leads of water between the ice floes, where whales came up to blow.

The Cape Prince of Wales flotilla included eight walrus-hide boats called umiaks. Each umiak carried eight hunters, who stood up with paddles in hand when we arrived. In the bow of each boat was a small harpoon gun. I was admiring these weapons when one of the hunters picked up a harpoon gun and smiled at the girl who had made the welcoming speech in the school. He was a big man with a very deep chest and wide shoulders. "This is my father," the girl said with pride. "He has killed many whales."

"He's a famous man," the teacher added as the harpooner sat down in his boat. "He never misses. Last fall he killed the only whale that the hunters brought in."

The teacher then described the hunting methods as the crews were saying good-by to their families. Umiaks are lighter than they seem, he explained. The hunters drag them over the ice to leads of open water. Sometimes they have to drag them several miles. And sometimes each boat cruises in a different open lead.

A winning team, the teacher said, is rewarded with some of the choicest cuts of meat. But no teams are losers. The bulk of the meat and blubber is distributed equally among all the umiak crews. And every village family was given plenty of meat and blubber, whether it had a representative among the hunters or not. In doing this the hunters followed old ancestral traditions.

I also learned that nothing was wasted when the giant sea monsters were cut up. Whale skin became *muktuk,* a delicious dish. Blood was much relished. Intestinal casings were turned into nets. Sinews were used as thread. And whalebone was carved into useful and ornamental things.

At a signal from the famous harpooner the children left, and the teacher took me to the schoolhouse. "The whale hunters are praying for success," he told me. "They are not praying in the missionary's way, and they don't want anyone to hear them."

I sat in the beginners' class that afternoon and enjoyed it immensely. The teacher used dramatic methods. The little pupils were learning simple English verbs. And I remember how the teacher became a fisherman when he was explaining the meaning of the English words,

"I fish." He threw a line with a big hook on the floor and dragged it around until it captured a piece of wood. Then he said, "I fish," as he hauled his catch in. He said, "I fish," several times. The children repeated the words after him. Then he wrote "I fish" on the blackboard and the children copied it on their slates with their slate pencils.

He followed this method with a number of other verbs and held the childrens' attention.

I sat in again with the beginners the next day, when they were learning elementary English nouns. The teacher had a big picture book. He began by showing the picture of a dog. Then he asked the children to say "dog" in English after him. Nearly twenty high-pitched voices rang out together. I noticed that several children were imitating the teacher's pronunciation almost exactly.

The little Eskimos then studied the English names of other animals that are part of the Arctic's life. Among them were whale, seal, fox, bear, snow rabbit and wolf. Their attention never flagged for a minute.

The teacher then wrote the animals' names on the blackboard, and asked his pupils to copy them on their slates. Then he went from desk to desk, checking on their handwriting. After this he drilled them in pronunciation again.

Questions and answers in the Eskimo language came next. One boy asked why they needed English. The teacher replied that they needed it to know what was happening in the big world outside. Then he added with a smile that it would be harder for fur buyers to cheat them when they understood what the traders were saying.

I saw again, when I attended a class in arithmetic, how the teacher's knowledge of his pupils' language helped. From time to time a student was unable to solve a problem—in multiplication, fractions or long division—until the teacher explained the difficulties away in Eskimo.

"I couldn't teach well if I didn't know both languages," the teacher told me. "Eskimo is a rich language. English is, too. But the two languages have nothing in common, and the youngest children would be lost if I didn't help them by using Eskimo."

My brother wanted to recruit more of his teachers from the Eskimo people. But his chiefs in Washington didn't agree. They preferred to send in white teachers from the States, who didn't know a word of Eskimo. Their department had little respect for Eskimo culture and the government had no textbooks in the native people's language.

In contrast, the Eskimo people in Soviet Chukhotka on the other side of Bering Strait are taught in their own language when they start school. They also are given a higher education, after finishing high school, if they pass required tests. I learned this later, when I talked to two students from Chukhotka at a medical institute in Khabarovsk, in the Soviet East, while I was a correspondent in the USSR. These students were happy young Eskimo women. They came from cooperative fur farms, where their parents were prospering. They were looking forward to the time when they would return to Chukhotka to give free medical service to their neighbors and friends. I'm sorry that American Eskimos are not getting such advantages.

The school bell didn't ring next morning. The village was celebrating the return of twenty-eight seal hunters, who had been lost on the Bering Sea. The enormous ice floe on which they were hunting had broken away from the shore ice and drifted out to sea. The people hoped it had drifted to some island or to a distant spot on the coast. But after two weeks hope was turning to despair. The ice floes were cracking in spring. The lost men might go down like sailors on a sinking ship. The seal hunters' wives were feeling like coal miners' wives whose husbands are trapped underground after an explosion. And then—on my fourth morning in Cape Prince of Wales—the lost men tramped into the village. The current had carried them back to shore ice in time to save them.

The men had been walking all night. They were tired but otherwise looked well. Their cheeks weren't sunken from hunger. I was anxious to know how they survived. One of the men promised to tell me the story after he had a night's sleep. And next day I took the teacher's translation down on his typewriter as we talked in the schoolhouse.

The story ran to two thousand words. This was one of the most precious documents I ever possessed. Unfortunately it was lost in the following years, when I was living out of a suitcase as a bachelor. However, I wrote letters to my family about it, and the main details are etched in my memory.

I can see the narrator before me as I write. He was a middle-aged man with the tiny black mustache that many Eskimos grow, and he had a powerful physique. But I was most impressed with his extraordinary memory. He remembered every change of the winds and the currents at sea. He must have mentioned these changes twenty times at least. They might bore some readers if I repeated all of them, but they represented life or death to the men on the drifting ice floe.

The break with the shore ice took the hunters by surprise. A strong wind from the sea had been blowing the ice in all day and they felt safe. They devoted themselves to the hunt and were happy and successful. But the wind shifted suddenly. It became twice as strong as before. There was a loud, crackling sound. The ice floe was drifting out to sea and the hunters could do nothing to stop it.

An ice floe can't be paddled like an umiak, the narrator said with a smile. This floe was bigger than Cape Prince of Wales. It went where it wanted to go. At first it drifted westward. That gave the hunters hope. It looked as if the floe might stop at one of the two Diomede Islands, where the hunters had friends. These islands are in the middle of the Bering Strait, and one belongs to the United States and the other to Russia. But the Diomedians were one people, who often intermarried in spite of the difference in flags.

The ice flow drifted slowly. A fog settled down on the sea. The hunters couldn't tell where they were, although they were experienced men. Several days passed. The fog thinned a little. The dim shape of Little Diomede, the American island, rose out of the sea. If the Diomedians could see them, rescue was probable, my narrator said. The Diomedians would come with umiaks, dragging the boats over the ice to open water, then paddling until they reached the hunters' floe. But men couldn't be seen in a fog at ten miles, and the danger was becoming extreme.

The floe then turned toward the island, and hopes were rising in twenty-eight breasts until winds and currents shifted again. They drifted then to the southwest, still further from home. Long stretches of ice began breaking from the floe. The danger increased. The hunter who was telling me the story said that he was thinking of his wife and three children all the time. The youngest was a baby girl at the breast. He feared he would never see any of them again.

I told the narrator at this point that he looked very well. I could see that he hadn't been starving. The twenty-eight men had enough to eat most of the time, he replied. They cut up the seals they captured and devoured everything except the bones and the toughest sections of skin. They had no fires or cooking equipment, and ate the meat raw. When I looked at his perfect teeth, I understood how he could do this. His teeth had not been spoiled by white men's food.

The second week on the ice floe was almost over when an extra-heavy fog blotted out the seascape again. Winds and currents shifted back and forth, and the lost men drifted in the world of nowhere for two more days. Then the fog thinned and disclosed a sight that roused the hunting instincts of the twenty-eight men. A huge polar bear—perhaps weighing half a ton—was prowling on another ice floe hundreds of yards away. It was useless to shoot at him. The booty could not have been recovered and Eskimos never killed just for the sake of killing. As for the bear—he was too prudent to seek trouble with twenty-eight men and trotted off into the distance.

Then came a storm that almost brought death. It came from the west and lashed the floe with such fury that much ice split away. The storm was a friend, however, because it drove the floe eastward. The eastward drift continued, until shore ice was reached southeast of Cape Prince of Wales. The floe was now only a quarter as big as when the hunters first set foot upon it.

"I don't think we could have lasted another day, and we would have gone with it," my narrator said.

"We didn't bring back any seals, but we brought back our lives," the hunter added with a happy smile.

The seal hunt, like the whale hunt, was a cooperative venture. Had the men brought back any seals, the meat would have been divided among the twenty-eight hunters and the other people in the village.

The twenty-eight hunters were honored guests at a village dance the next day. Eskimo dances tell stories. This dance, which was really a ballet, told of a polar-bear hunt. The village dance floor occupied the entire space of a walrus-hide house that was perhaps thirty feet square. It was packed tight. Dancers, drummers and spectators were crowded together.

The bear was an athletic young Eskimo inside a polar-bear skin. He growled as he charged on all fours at the hunters. I could hardly hear his growling, however. The four drummers drowned out other sounds as they pounded the tight skins on their drums.

I've never seen a bear hunt, but this one looked like the real thing. It developed into a series of rushes and dodges. The bear would plunge at a hunter. The hunter would nimbly jump aside and hurl an imaginary spear at the furious beast. Sometimes half a dozen hunters were hurling their spears together. And sometimes a hunter would be sent sprawling by a blow from the bear's mighty paw. But the monarch of the ice floes was conquered at last and dragged away. And the talented young actor inside the skin was given much applause as he crawled out.

I met the young artist at a dinner in the teacher's igloo next day. He was a graduate of the village school. He told me that the dance described a bear hunt in his grandfather's day. But the white bears were still dangerous if one got in their way. They resented any intrusion on their ice floes.

Once a she-bear almost got him. He was standing by an ice hole with spear in hand as he waited for a seal to come for air. It was a very foggy day, and he did not see two white bear cubs parked nearby, nor the mother who was coming to them. But the mother saw him, or smelled him. And she was almost upon him when he saved himself by jabbing his spear in her face as he backed away.

Fog had hung like a curtain over the West since I arrived on the cape. I had not seen the sun setting for five days. Then suddenly the curtain lifted at eight or nine at night, as I was walking on the beach. The Bering Strait, with its rugged hummocks of ice and its twin Diomede Islands, lay spread out before me. And a gorgeous sunset—of crimson, purple and gold—flamed on the hills of Soviet Chukhotka, forty-six miles away.

This was my first view of the Socialist land. It stirred me profoundly. It symbolized for me the beauty of the Socialist world. I knew that Socialist power had not yet reached this most distant part of the Russian workers' domain. The Socialist revolution had taken place only five months before, and counterrevolutionary armies had severed Moscow from the Soviet Far East. But I was confident of the Socialist future. And I longed for the day when I would stand on Socialist soil for the first time.

Jesse and I got a heart-warming farewell next morning. A hundred or more school children and their teacher ran alongside our sled, calling out invitations to come again. They stayed by us until we were a mile from town. I often wish I were with them again.

I loved the children's families as well as the youngsters themselves. I never met more hospitable people. I visited a dozen or more igloos during that happy week on the cape. I shared the families' meals and was welcomed as a friend in a warm and unaffected way.

In several igloos I saw orphaned children who had been taken in by neighbors when their parents died. No child was left homeless by these socially-minded people.

I also admired the way whalers and sealers shared the results of their labors among themselves and other village people. I was fortunate in living in this Eskimo village while remnants of the era of primitive communism survived.

Mushing was more difficult on the return home. Soft spring snow lay deep on the trail. Our dogs sank in up to their bellies. It was necessary to pack the trail. This was hard work, and my companion and I took turns at trail-packing. We were wearing snowshoes about three and a half feet long. The front half was webbed like a gigantic tennis racket. The trail-packer mushed ahead of the sled and pressed the webbing down into the snow. This provided a firm road for the dogs' feet. The difficulty came in lifting each snowshoe out of the hole without catching it in the snow. We were very tired at the end of the first day.

Mushing was much easier on the third day, when the temperature dropped far below zero. The snow was again hard under the dogs' feet. Our trail-packing labors were ended. But on the fourth day the mercury went down to thirty-eight below and the wind was in our faces. My cheeks were frostbitten for the first time. The white scars of frostbite stayed on my face for several days.

36 · Asian brothers

I rushed to the beach one midsummer morning in 1918 in response to friend's call. "The Russian Eskimos are coming," he said. I arrived in time to see strange Eskimos pulling big umiaks out of the water. They were led by a broad, heavy man of sixty or sixty-five years. His neck was ringed with polar-bear claws. His chin had tattoo marks I had never seen before. And a haircut had left a round, naked circle on the top of his head.

Behind him were fifty or sixty men and women. They had been paddling their walrus-hide boats for a week or more. They had come two hundred miles, from the Chukhotka peninsula, the northeast corner of Asia, to trade in Nome.

Many of the Asians had visited Nome in earlier trade missions. They were welcomed as friends by the Nome Eskimos. The Asian and

Alaskan Eskimos were really one people. They had a similar Arctic culture. And they conversed in different dialects of the same language, though with some difficulty.

This Eskimo brotherhood was demonstrated when Nome's chief fur trader tried to buy Chukhotka furs at prices far below their value. The old Chukhotkan would hold up a precious silver-fox skin. The trader would reply by spreading out ten fingers, then closing his fist and spreading the fingers again. That meant he was offering $20.

The trader followed this gesture by flashing a double eagle—a $20 gold piece—in the rays of the morning sun. He had found this very effective before. But the Nome Eskimos told the old Chukhotkan man that $20 wasn't enough. When the old Chukhotkan shook his head, the trader raised more fingers. The second offer was turned down and the bargaining went on, until the Chukhotkans got much more than the Nome buyer wanted to pay.

The trading went on until all the furs and other Arctic treasures in the umiak flotilla were disposed of. Among them were several white bearskins and a choice collection of walrus ivory.

The Chukhotkans were paid in gold. They had no faith in paper money. The old man tested each double eagle, every eagle and all the $5 coins with the edges of his excellent teeth. He told the Nome Eskimos that a Russian trader once gave him lead rubles that had been gilded to resemble gold. But his teeth had detected the fraud before any furs were transferred.

Most of this gold money stayed in Nome. Local Eskimos took their Asian brothers and sisters on a shopping tour through the Nome stores. The umiaks were loaded with iron pots and pans, knives, whetstones, hammers, axes, razors, mirrors, shotguns, rifles, ammunition and a harpoon gun.

The old Chukhotkan spoke freely when I interviewed him, with the help of an interpreter. We met in the igloo of one of my Eskimo friends. I gave him some Winston-Salem tobacco, which he smoked in a homemade pipe that used a brass cartridge casing for a pipe bowl. He was very relaxed. The trading had been successful. He spoke warmly of his Nome friends. He had often visited Alaska, he said. The first times were in his youth, before white men's stores appeared on the northwestern coast. His people traded with the Eskimos at Cape Prince of Wales and other northern villages. They had no money. Their currency was tobacco they got from Russian traders.

What they wanted most then was wolverine fur. It was found on the

Alaska side, not in Chukhotka. Wolverine fur was used on the parkas' facial edges overlapping the mouth. It had a special merit. Breath never congealed upon it. This saved a musher from frostbite when congealed breath melted on his cheek and froze again.

The old man didn't talk long about Alaska. His mind was on his homeland. Chukhotka was the best of all places, he told me. It had plenty of whales, seals, bears, walrus, deer and foxes, And—best of all—there was no czar any more. Soviet power hadn't reached Chukhotka, but he knew about the revolution and said it was good. The czar's men were robbers. They had taken the hunters' best furs.

I was about to ask him what he wanted from the revolution, but our talk was interrupted. Half a dozen Chukhotka Eskimos crowded into the little igloo. The weather was threatening, they said. The umiaks were loaded. They wanted to start home with no delay.

I did not know then that the U.S. flag was being planted on Chukhotkan soil while the Chukhotkan Eskimos were visiting Nome. I got this strange story when my brother Walter returned to Nome. He had been absent a month on his annual summer trip to the Eskimo schools and reindeer herds at Point Barrow and other stations on Alaska's northern coast. Walter always made these trips on the *Bear,* the Coast Guard cutter that had been patrolling Arctic waters for a generation. But this year the captain had o. ier orders. Instead of staying in U.S. waters, he swung left after leaving Nome and continued westward until he anchored at Anadyr on Chukhotka's southern shore.

This was part of Soviet Asia. Walter was shocked and amazed. "This is Russian territory," he told the captain as the gangplank went down.

"It's American now," the captain replied.

The town of Anadyr, where the captain disembarked, was the home of many different peoples. The Chukchis, a reindeer-herding people, were the majority, but Yakuts, Eskimos, Russians and others lived among them. I had heard much about this Arctic community from my IWW friend Harry Osborne, the skipper of a tiny trading schooner.

The invaded region was potentially rich. Chukchi reindeer herds roamed the tundra. Important deposits of tin, lead, zinc, coal and gold lay under the surface. And the navy also prized Anadyr as a strategic base for controlling the Bering Sea.

The captain's takeover had a feeble start. The *Bear,* after all, was only a cutter. That was the smallest armed ship under the U.S. flag. It

was all the government had in Arctic waters, however. But the
arrogant skipper wasn't worried. He had the illusion that
Chukhotka's hunters, fishermen and reindeer herders would welcome
a takeover, to escape from the revolution.

Walter said the captain did his best to stage an impressive martial
show with his tiny forces. Clad in a dress uniform, with a sword at his
hip, he swaggered into Anadyr under a Stars and Stripes bigger than
himself, carried by a flagbearer beside him. Behind him was a small
file of uniformed men with rifles, who marched to the tune of a brass
band. And behind them, the *Bear's* gunner was standing by a small
artillery piece in the bow of the ship.

The Anadyr people seemed confused but not impressed, Walter
said. A thousand or more Chukchis, Yakuts, Eskimos and others were
watching the cutter captain's show. They stared in surprise as two
uniformed men dug a hole in the ground and the flagbearer planted
America's national banner in their soil. And the people were talking to
each other in half a dozen languages as the captain began speaking in a
harsh, bellowing voice.

The captain's preparations for the coup were wretched. He had no
interpreter, and Walter could see that hardly anyone knew what the
American was talking about. Several minutes passed before the
speaker woke up to this obvious fact. When he did, he bellowed for
someone who knew English to come forward. No one responded. One
of the cutter's officers repeated the request, and a young Chukchi
finally volunteered. The captain began questioning him, but the
Chukchi's English vocabulary was so limited that Walter had to guess
at what he was saying. He became the interpreter, however, after
accepting a $10 gold piece. And Walter was sure that the Chukchis got
only fragments of the captain's speech, while Yakuts, Eskimos and
others got nothing.

The captain was assuring the people that the United States was their
friend. He pointed to the Stars and Stripes as he said this. The people
of Anadyr and the rest of Chukhotka were now under U.S. protection,
he said. America would give them freedom and save them from the
"Russian reds," he declared.

The captain continued shouting against the Russian reds. But
Walter remembered little that he said. "I was too much interested in
the people to listen closely to that stupid piece of brass," he told me.
"The people were talking to each other. Some were laughing. They

didn't look as if they shared the captain's worries about Russian reds."

The captain blundered on blindly until he was tired. Then he took the first steps towards setting up a new government, with himself as its temporary head. He did this when he announced that he would sit as Anadyr's "judge." If anyone had any complaints against anyone else, let him come forward, he said.

The captain's courthouse was a small wooden church with the rounded Orthodox cupola on top. The captain led the way in and grabbed one of the few chairs for himself. The hundred or more Chukhotkans, who packed themselves in, had standing room only. No complainants came forward, however. Many people were leaving and the captain was showing his impatience when a young Chukchi approached the "judge." He complained that he had given his sweetheart a ring and some furs when she promised to marry him. Then she took another man instead. And he wanted the "great American judge" to get his gifts back.

This complaint brought grins and laughter from the Chukchis in the audience. They weren't taking the "great American captain" very seriously anymore. And the judge was angry. He had come to take over Chukhotka. Now he was stuck with a case for a small-claims court. And he didn't know what to do until one of his officers whispered in his ear. Then he announced that witnesses on both sides should come to his cabin in the *Bear* the next morning.

But no witnesses appeared. The young lady kept her presents. And two days later the *Bear* departed, taking the flag with her.

The attempted occupation of Chukhotka had come to nothing. "One can't do anything with ignorant people who have nothing," the captain told Walter. Next time, he said, he would meet first with the Chukchi leaders. "Some of them are rich traders and reindeer men," he said. "They will welcome our help against the Russian reds."

I had talked to the captain during a visit to the *Bear* in early summer. And the reader can judge him by his opinion of American seamen. I had remarked to him that the *Bear* had an outstanding history and looked like a fine, seaworthy vessel. "It must be a pleasure," I said, "to sail on such a beautiful ship."

"We're doing all right now," the captain replied. "I got a new crew this year. It's a crew of students. They do what I tell them. I like them much better than the old-fashioned seamen I had before. There were too many sea lawyers among them."

After the collapse of the Anadyr adventure, the *Bear* took Walter to Point Barrow, and to other Arctic stations. He found the schools and reindeer herds doing very well, he told me. I was very happy to see him again. We were close friends as well as brothers.

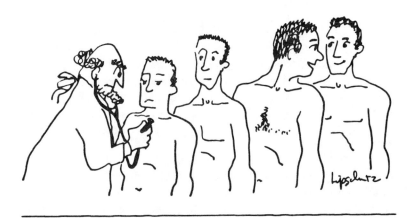

37 · *Army*

I sailed for Seattle late in August, 1918, after parting from Walter with regret. I did not dream then that I wouldn't see him again. Nor did I expect that his hopes for the Eskimo-owned reindeer industry would be blasted. I could not foresee that the courts and President Harding's administration, which would take office in 1921, would give control of the deer to Jofet Lindberg's reindeer syndicate.

Seattle was a booming shipyard city. I got work as a lathe operator in the machine shop of Skinner and Eddy's big yard. I was hired by the U.S. Employment Service, which controlled shipyard jobs, and was sent to the AFL Machinists Union. The wartime government of President Wilson was collaborating with the AFL in order to keep the IWW out of the yards. The Wobblies came in, nevertheless.

I enjoyed the company of my fellow workers. My foreman, a staunch old craft unionist, often talked about the long strike against the Bethlehem Steel Company in 1910. He had been an organizer for the Machinists Union during that 108-day struggle. I was a student in Bethlehem then. When I asked why the battle had been lost, he replied, "I blame Sam Gompers (the conservative president of the

AFL). We needed help from the entire labor movement and old Sam gave us nothing but words."

Some of my shopmates had enthusiastic memories of the *Shilka,* the first Soviet ship to visit the U.S.A. It had anchored in Seattle harbor on December 21, 1917, six weeks after the Russian workers' revolution. My shopmates marched in demonstrations that compelled the Seattle authorities to free the Soviet seamen, who were confined to their ship for several days. And my fellow workers heard the story of the revolution from the Russian sailors at big mass meetings after the crew was released.

My shopmates and I belonged to Hope Lodge 79 of the Machinists Union. This was the most militant organization in the city's metal trades unions. Many of its members also belonged to the IWW, whose leaders were in prison. The IWW wanted all power for the workers. Many non-Wobblies also looked forward to a working-class revolution. This outlook was reflected in strong resolutions that were passed at Hope Lodge meetings, telling President Wilson to release Bill Haywood, Eugene V. Debs and other political prisoners, and to grant diplomatic recognition to the embattled Russian republic. And it explained why hundreds of copies of the *Liberator,* a left-wing cultural magazine, which carried John Reed's articles on the revolution, were sold in the lobby of our union hall every month.

Thousands of other copies of the *Liberator* were sold on the skid road, where loggers and other workers congregated. John Reed became the most popular writer in this working-class city.

This revolutionary working-class atmosphere had an overwhelming effect upon me. I looked forward confidently to the time when workers would control the entire world.

I was also influenced by a group of young worker-intellectuals who discussed world affairs while the coffee went down. We met once a week at the home of Paul Bickel, a mathematics teacher in a Seattle high school, who lost his job when he joined the Seattle general strike several months later. Bickel, a good Marxist, often led our discussions.

My young friends were contributors to left-wing Socialist publications, though they were closer to the Wobblies than to the Socialist Party. Among them were Harvey O'Connor, a merchant seaman who had also worked in logging camps; Hays Jones, a logger and shipyard worker; Joe Pass, a poet and former Yukon River boatman, and his brother Morris, an artist.

I'm happy to say that the Seattle spirit stayed with my friends for life. Harvey O'Connor became a leader in the struggle for civil liberties against America's political police. He also wrote two valuable books on the oil monopoly, and a series of biographies that exposed the devious deals of the Mellon, Guggenheim and Astor families. Hays Jones, who joined the merchant marine, had a gift for satire that workers liked. He became a popular and effective waterfront union editor during the stormy struggles of the 1930s. Joe Pass became a brilliant publicist for progressive causes, and his brother Morris's cartoons enlivened progressive journals for years.

My draft number came out in the conscription lottery a few weeks after my ship landed. I had registered in Brooklyn in 1917 as a conscientious objector. But the example of the Russian troops, who left the front during the revolution, convinced me that rank-and-file soldiers had a decisive role to play in the struggle for peace at this time when the United States was about to invade Soviet Russia. So I knew what to do when I entered the army office in Seattle.

I was given a big envelope containing my Brooklyn draft records to carry to the army camp with me. As I received the envelope I sank it below the clerk's window and ran a finger under the flap before it gummed tight. Later I removed the card that registered my conscientious objections. And when I presented the envelope at Camp Lewis (now Fort Lewis), I was enrolled as an ordinary soldier.

I was put in a company of about two hundred men. We were quartered in a long wooden barracks made of boards hastily clapped together. Almost all my fellow conscripts were workers. Most were deeply tanned after years in lumbering, ranching, construction and other outdoor jobs. They were congenial companions, with many good stories from their job experiences and their free-time adventures.

One of my best friends was Jerry, a logger from the big-tree forests of Washington State, who had taken part in the victorious IWW strike for the eight-hour day in 1917. Other pals included Tom, a sheepherder from the Montana grasslands, who played all the popular airs on his harmonica; Eddie, a muleskinner from a big hydropower construction camp, and Jack, a horseshoer.

I wanted to learn all I could about soldiering, but all I got was endless drilling under the guidance of officers whom the men called "Ninety Day Wonders." They had acquired their commissions by spending just three months in an officers' training camp.

Our officers' middle-class backgrounds were evident in the lectures they gave us. These lectures came on the rainy days that soaked the drillfield two or three times a week in that wet fall of 1918. One officer referred several times to "my business." It turned out that he was the son of a rich butcher in Portland, Oregon. One day, during a talk on the bayonet, he told us that a soldier must enjoy "sticking his enemy and seeing his guts spill." And he continued: "It's like killing a hog in my slaughter house."

This didn't impress my companions. "I wonder how much sticking he did in his ninety days," remarked Tom at our bull session that night.

Nor were my comrades-in-arms impressed when another officer quoted President Wilson's assertion that this is a "war for democracy."The officer added, "We must all be ready to die for this land of freedom."

"It's not free for lumberjacks," Jerry said at night. "Many men I went on strike with are in prison."

No one disagreed with Jerry. I heard only three men in my company ever say a word in favor of the war.

President Wilson's military intervention against revolutionary Russia was just beginning. The first regiments came from the Pacific Northwest. And one day I was summoned for a special physical examination. Rumor was that we were going to Vladivostok to help Admiral Kolchak, the counterrevolutionary commander.

The scene in the medical examination room is fresh in my mind after sixty-five years. Twenty or more nude men were standing side by side. A bearded doctor with a stethoscope was moving from man to man quickly. At my left was a muscular youth of twenty-three or twenty-four years, whom I hadn't seen before. He looked very angry. And the doctor was only a few men away when the young man whispered in my ear, "I know which side my gun will be on when we get over there."

I did not reply. The doctor was too near. But I was not surprised. I had heard workers talking like this in Seattle.

I did not go to Siberia. A strange sickness, the Spanish influenza, intervened. The worst flu epidemic in U.S. history was sweeping the land. I was sent to an army hospital, where every bed was occupied by a sick or dying man. One doctor confessed to me, "We know nothing about this disease." The symptoms were so unusual, he explained. I suffered from violent hemorrhages from the lungs, and nurses afterward said they had expected me to die.

At last the fever went down. Then two letters from my mother were laid on my bed. They brought heartbreaking news. My two oldest brothers were dead. Ted, a draftee in an artillery battalion, was killed by the flu soon after reaching the combat lines in France. And Walter, whom I loved dearly, died in Nome with many other flu victims. Hundreds of Eskimos on the Bering Sea coast lost their lives at the same time.

My grief was mixed with anger at the greedy warmakers. I knew that Ted and Walter were war casualties. The so-called Spanish flu was a war disease. It was carried from land to land by the world's armies. And Ted was doubly a war victim. My mother was told in a letter from a man in Ted's company that Ted was convalescing from a milder attack when he was sent back to duty and fatally stricken.

The Spanish flu was very weakening. I collapsed with acute pains when the head nurse put me to work carrying meals to other patients after my temperature went down. I decided then to take a complete rest until I was stronger. I had the doctors' backing in this. They instructed me to stay by my bunk until they authorized my return to duty.

I was quartered in a barracks with other convalescents who had similar instructions. Our top sergeant, a former bartender, was a good fellow, but he told us that he had orders from the captain to make us work. I told my comrades what had happened to my brother when he had gone on duty too soon. We were fighting for our lives, I said. We dare not disobey orders. We must use special tactics in enforcing the doctors' instructions to rest.

We then agreed among ourselves to accept every order. But working was a different matter. We would be physically unable to work when we tried. So when the sergeant took us outside and told us to carry heavy chunks of cedar to the kitchen stove, we found we could not lift the wood. After other examples of this kind, the top kick came over to our side.

The climax came when our captain, a heavy, scowling man of fifty or more, inspected our quarters. "I came to see why these men are not working," he told the sergeant as we stood by our bunks saluting. Then his eye fell on me. "What's wrong with this big cripple?" he growled.

And the good sergeant replied, "This man can't work. He has a broken back."

That lie was sublime. The captain left with an angry growl and never bothered us again.

The German Kaiser abdicated a few days later, after a German naval revolt. Peace was signed on November 11, and I was discharged late in November, while Seattle and Tacoma workers were preparing for a big shipyard strike that would be accompanied by the first major general strike in the United States.

That story will begin the second volume of my memoirs.